Sounds *of the* Citizens

Sounds *of the* Citizens

Dancehall and Community in Jamaica

Anne M. Galvin

Vanderbilt University Press
Nashville

© 2014 by Vanderbilt University Press
Nashville, Tennessee 37235
All rights reserved
First printing 2014
First paperback printing 2020

Library of Congress Cataloging-in-Publication Data

Galvin, Anne M., 1971-
Sounds of the citizens : dancehall and community in Jamaica / Anne M. Galvin.
　pages cm
　Includes bibliographical references and index.
　ISBN 978-0-8265-1978-8 (hardback) —
　ISBN 978-0-8265-1979-5 (paper)—
　ISBN 978-0-8265-1980-1 (e-book)
　1. Dancehall (Music)—Jamaica—History and criticism.
　2. Dancehall (Music)—Social aspects—Jamaica. I. Title.
　ML3532.G35 2014
　781.646097292—dc23
　　　　　　　　　　　　　　　　　　　　　2013039759

For Ellen and Brendan Galvin, my parents

Contents

	Acknowledgments	ix
	Introduction	1
1.	"Money Move": The Sociality of Circulation, Violence, and Respect	25
2.	"Give thanks for that man deh fi di place": Patronage, Power, and Shifting Burdens of Care	47
3.	Dancehall Dilemmas: Sounds from the Disquieted Margins	76
4.	"Got to mek a living": Dancehall as Industry	111
5.	The Contradictions of Neoliberal Nation Building in Jamaica: Community Development through Dancehall	142
6.	The Long View	167
	Notes	177
	Bibliography	187
	Index	211

Acknowledgments

This project has been the result of the generosity of so many people that it is hard to know where to begin saying thank you. First I need to express my deep gratitude to the residents of the communities where I lived and worked, and to the employees of Wicked Times, who opened their lives, homes, and offices to me. I wish I could call you all out by name, but I am most certain that you know who you are anyway! Beyond this group, without which none of what followed would have been possible, I need to thank so many members of my shifting and expanding academic community, who provided encouragement and feedback from the very beginning. While I attended the New School for Social Research, Deborah Poole of the Graduate Faculty was a fabulous advisor, who pored over innumerable project proposals and early drafts with her keen eye for detail. Don Robotham, at the City University of New York, Graduate Center, grounded my research in a deep understanding of Jamaican culture and politics while also facilitating many personal introductions that proved invaluable to the completion of the research and, of course, which were always offered with an exceptional warmth and sense of humor. Gage Averill, then at New York University, allowed me, an unknown student from an alien university, to register with him for an independent study in ethnomusicology in the African diaspora that expanded my focus beyond the anthropological training I had received, and then he continued to serve as an advisor as I completed my fieldwork and wrote up my research. Steve Caton was encouraging and supportive of the direction my work was taking as an early proposal advisor and as an always positive and constructively critical voice, and Norman Stolzoff was kind in his willingness to accept a phone call from a neophyte graduate student seeking advice on conducting fieldwork on dancehall in Kingston. Donna Kerner, my undergraduate advisor at Wheaton College, has been a wonderful guide through the world of academic anthropology; I was fortunate to have received my earliest education in the discipline from such a warm person and thoughtful scholar. Jaime Bradstreet, anthropologist, sometime research assistant, and longtime friend, also provided both emotional and academic support to me as I worked at this project.

During my fieldwork in Jamaica, beyond the residents of Guy Town, Patricia Anderson of the University of the West Indies, graciously shared space in her home with me as I settled into the life of a researcher in Kingston. She was welcoming and encouraging and even took the time to remind me to take care of myself because of the stress I might be under. She also facilitated my affiliation with the university, which allowed me access to the excellent libraries and archives and the helpful staff. When it became clear I would need a research assistant to help with my fieldwork as I adjusted to Jamaican English and navigating unfamiliar spaces, she introduced me to two graduate students who would work with me during the first half of my stay. Patrick Peterkin, who I now consider a lifelong friend, is one of those people, and Richard Pasley is the other. Even beyond those great gifts, Pat's niece Camille Daley was the first person I met upon my arrival in Kingston. She picked me up at the airport and took me on a trip through the KFC drive-through before dropping me off at her aunt's house. Camille is also someone who was a wonderful interlocutor about Jamaican culture and someone who exposed me to the joys of "uptown" life, as someone who was spending most of her time below Halfway Tree. She also included me in her own research activities, inviting me to documentary film shoots and lectures throughout my stay. Clinton Hutton opened the doors of his office to me on several occasions to discuss my observations and is a great asset to the students at UWI. The late Barry Chevannes welcomed me to sit in on his lectures on Caribbean culture, a once-in-a-lifetime experience that seems even more significant now that he is gone. Ifetayo Fleary, my friend, a Canadian Exchange Student at UWI during the time of my study, was also a wonderful sounding board as we navigated our year in Kingston from very different perspectives, hers as a member of the diaspora and mine as a Euro-American newcomer. The time I spent with her and our dear friend Paul Johnson, gone much too soon because of an act of gun violence, was notably time well spent. Lygia Navarro, Beth Fladung, and Themis Chronopoulos are each important friends who joined me during various parts of my fieldwork, and who, in their own ways, shaped my experience as a researcher. For that I am thankful.

When I returned to New York, Lauren Leve helped me reorient myself as her teaching assistant and provided much good advice as I looked to the next phases of my research and of my career. She also introduced me to David Graeber, who sat with me in a Greenwich Village diner and discussed how I might develop my chapter on community economics. My cohort at the New School also provided continued encouragement through the writing process. Erin Koch, one of the best friends a person could ever hope to have, read more drafts than I care to count and fielded more panicked phone calls and text messages than I care to admit. Other interlocutors and friends from the New School who require my gratitude are Karolina Follis, Simanti Dasgupta, Lois Woestman, Laura Roush, and Sarah Orndorff. Robert Kostrzewa was also always an encouraging voice as I applied for research funding at the New School. It is, in part, because of him that I was awarded the dissertation fellowship that allowed me to embark on my field research. Just one step beyond my life at the New School, Caroline Yezer has been, in turn, both a wonderful intellectual and social coconspirator who always allows me to bend her ear.

In the final phase of the project, Barrett P. Brenton and my other colleagues at St. John's University provided motivation, support, and friendship. I also need to commend the Center for Teaching and Learning at St. John's and the Writing Center for creating faculty writing retreats that provided quiet space and productive company as I worked on revisions. St. John's University also awarded me a summer support of research grant that funded one of my follow-up trips to Kingston and granted me course reductions that facilitated my having the time to finish this book, the completion of which was also crucially aided by the wonderful, constructive comments of the two anonymous reviewers who provided feedback and by Eli Bortz who has been a terrific steward of this process.

I also need to thank the numerous friends who drew me out of my, at times narrow, academic world and into the real world when I needed it. In particular, Joe Keilch, an excellent DJ, and a better friend, enabled me to enjoy cheap and much-needed nights out at the Rub when I was living as the cliché broke graduate student. His friendship and encouragement have been a very important part of my life since the time we met back in 1992.

My parents, Ellen and Brendan Galvin, have been exceptionally patient and generous during this entire process. Beyond the typical support parents provide, they also paid close attention to the issues related to my project and frequently sent e-mail and newspaper clippings alerting me to popular coverage of my topic. Their sustenance and advice has helped me immeasurably as I completed this project and in life.

Thanks also to Bill, Diane, and Molly Galvin, who welcomed me to join them on my first trip to their favorite place. I must especially acknowledge the efforts of my uncle Bill Galvin, who accompanied me on my initial journey to Kingston so that I might discuss the possibilities of this project with faculty at UWI. I am so appreciative that he took that trip with me.

Lastly, I need to express gratitude to Harold Butler, my always-optimistic husband, who insists on showing me the bright side of every situation, and who popped his head into my office as I was writing this, handed me a cool glass of water, and asked, "What can I do to help?" He has patiently encouraged me through the times I have been away on extended research trips and during the times when I didn't know where my job search would take me, as well as when I needed to close the door to my office behind me in order to concentrate. He even humors my obsession with pit bull rescue. I have, indeed, been very, very lucky.

I am afraid that there must be omissions to these acknowledgments. If you feel you have been left out in error, please contact me directly so I can issue you a personal apology! While this project could not have come to completion without this broad community of support, any errors or omissions are decidedly my own.

Sounds
of the
Citizens

Introduction

During the summer of 2009, Martin, whom I had by then known for almost a decade, asked me to accompany him on some errands that took us down the narrow streets of downtown Kingston in his newly acquired passenger van. When I first met Martin back in 2001, in the Kingston garrison community I have named Guy Town, I was a graduate student and he was completing a postsecondary program in engineering.[1] Since that first meeting, he had traveled widely, apprenticing on merchant ships, and had finally found full-time employment after a series of heavily exploitative jobs. One of the worst jobs involved an employer that rented Martin the tools he needed to complete his assignments.

I was happy for Martin. His perseverance had begun to pay off. Since my last visit, two years prior, he had invested in the passenger van in which we traveled and a nice used Toyota sedan in order to run a taxi and sightseeing service and as a kind of savings account. He explained that the cars were investments that safely tied up his money, which could then be quickly liquidated if necessary. Martin lamented to me that younger men in his neighborhood now viewed him as someone who "had" and local thugs would periodically visit him for a payoff, though he insisted the shakedowns were not as bad in Guy Town as they were in other communities.[2] He complained that people now saw only the money he seemed to have. They had forgotten the years when Martin traveled up and down the road at all hours of the day and night, commuting between various jobs and school. They didn't know that during those years his woman had been investing in him, continuing to live with, and take money from, her baby father to help put Martin through school.[3] To Martin, many of the young men in the area looked upon him as lucky rather than understanding that it was hard work and planning that had allowed him to purchase his vehicles and put food on the table.[4] He described the intensive efforts he had made to reason with the youths that looked up to him because of his economic position, attempting to persuade them to resist the appeal of the gun.

By the time of my 2009 visit, things had finally calmed down in Guy Town once again, after an extended period of violence that had left many people dead, adults unable to commute to their jobs, and children unable to attend school. The violence was sparked by the murder of Guy Town's don. A resulting vacuum created the opportunity for bitter rivalry among some of the neighborhood's young men to flourish into violent contests over who was to fill the powerful role. This type of violent contest is particularly dangerous in such a small area where almost everyone is related either socially or by blood. In such an environment reprisals often take the form of violence against family members or friends, thereby anxiously entangling the whole community in dangerous webs of distrust. Once the new don had established himself, he foolishly attempted to unseat the much more powerful don from a neighboring area, extending the duration and reach of the conflict.

This was how another acquaintance, Hugh, ended up settling in the neighborhood where I later met up with him. His nephew had been a foot soldier for the more powerful don, who, it was alleged, did not provide his men with sufficient financial benefits. His nephew had sided with the group from Guy Town in their attempt to overthrow him. The nephew had a reputation for fearlessness, and his alliance with the Guy Town group posed a grave danger to anyone he and the group came up against. The nephew shot one of the neighboring don's men, which led to a manhunt for both the nephew and members of his family. As it turned out, one of his relatives was working at the don's brother's home at the time of the incident and was immediately executed. The family was forced to flee the area, resettling in another part of the city.

The violence that went on for more than a year was both devastating to area residents and a disappointment to advocates of urban renewal. Given all the attention Guy Town had received for its efforts at community development and reform, the inability of the program to move area men away from criminal pursuits showcased the complexities of community level politics and social dynamics that could not be addressed with remedial education and small-scale income-generating projects. It was Guy Town's notoriety as a success story that first motivated me to select it as a field site. The development programs and linkages with the Jamaican music industry were what initially landed me in the neighborhood back in the fall of 2001. However, what I ended up studying was the unraveling of these attempts at reform. This unraveling process during a hegemonic moment in the history of neoliberal globalization ended up being more revealing of the fissures in Jamaican society, the contradictions of neoliberal governance, and the complexities of ghetto life than a success story would have been.

During our travels, as Martin and I discussed the unraveling of the Guy Town initiatives, he turned to me and reflected on the outcome of the remedial education classes. He indicated that they must have had some kind of effect on the young men that attended them because, according to him, the "shottas" had at least "conducted the war more intelligently" this time. This sentiment echoes a well-established association, most recently articulated by Obika Gray, who points out that the Jamaican history of political party-based training and population armament, covertly implemented to manipulate voting blocks in garrison communities, ultimately educated populations to be exquisitely effective organized criminals (Gray 2004). For Martin, within the local context of Guy Town, which is also a product of these same party politics, the educational initiatives intended to provide young men with opportunities for a new, self-directed, life course, had unintentionally prepared them to be more intelligent warriors who, largely out of necessity, continued to engage in the seemingly endless cycle of conflict that has lingered within West Kingston for decades.

This book is, in part, an effort to capture the ironies and contradictions created by neoliberal globalization, as it exists in Kingston. The grounding of this analysis requires a working definition of neoliberal globalization, and I have found the work of James Ferguson to be extremely helpful for this purpose. He identifies a set of "new governmental rationalities" that emerged in the Thatcher-Reagan era as follows: "Neoliberalism in this account involved the deployment of new, market-based techniques of government within the terrain of the state itself. At the same time, new constructions of 'active' and 'responsible' citizens and communities are deployed to produce governmental results that do not depend on direct state intervention. The 'responsibilized citizen' comes to operate as a miniature firm, responding to incentives, rationally assessing risks, and prudently choosing from among different courses of action" (Ferguson 2009, 172). Ferguson's work focuses on the ways in which neoliberal tenets might be repurposed for progressive ends, and, in particular, he seeks to identify a specifically African brand of neoliberalism that leads to unique strategies for contending with unemployed urban populations that promote the responsibilizing elements of social policy, but without arguing for the wholesale dismantling of state-centered social supports (Ferguson 2009). By bringing together these real and ideal renditions of neoliberal governance and by reflecting on the principles these distinct versions share, Ferguson is able to identify how "'arts of government' developed within First World neoliberalism might take on a new life in other contexts, in the process opening up new political possibilities" (Ferguson 2009, 173).

Jamaican development and governance models established in poor urban communities, which, similar to those in Ferguson's study, contain a large population that is unlikely to ever partake in formal wage labor for reasons I will discuss further in later chapters, are heavily modeled on strategies espoused by "First World" neoliberalism. These strategies include an emphasis on the privatization of formerly state-sponsored initiatives, a focus on personal responsibility and entrepreneurship on the part of citizens, and the selective minimization of the state in the day-to-day affairs of Jamaican citizenry. However, I am arguing here that these basic tenets of neoliberal ideology take on a distinct meaning and present unique social outcomes when implemented within Kingston garrison communities.

Several elements shape the contours of Jamaican neoliberal practices and outcomes. First, Jamaica's status as a postcolony of England has heavily determined the country's position in global economic and racial hierarchies and shaped the internal politics of the country in its struggle to become a nation-state. Second, the long democratic socialist political history of the country still informs the values of citizens in significant ways that I explore further in Chapter 1. This period, emergent during the 1940s, prior to independence, formally spanned the majority of the 1970s. Traces of democratic socialist influence were maintained into the 1980s and onward, first under Michael Manley's direct leadership, and then under the influence of his legacy as a popular national figure after his death. Democratic socialist governance was characterized by efforts to increase Jamaica's economic independence, in part, by nationalizing industries that had been under foreign control. Additionally, the People's National Party created programs designed to promote the social ownership of businesses by workers in order to increase self-reliance. The party also pushed to incorporate formerly marginalized segments of the poor black population by selectively elevating their cultural practices as a valued part of Jamaican national culture (Stephens and Stephens 1986; A. Waters 1989). The selective promotion of black cultural practices during this period foreshadowed the aestheticization of difference, a key characteristic of 1980s-era liberal multiculturalism (Melamed 2011). Third, an entrenched, but dynamic, system of patronage has entailed Jamaican party politics and sustained poor populations since before the time of national independence (Stone 1985). Fourth, a lack of job growth has contributed to the development of distinct survival stratagem by urban poor populations in West Kingston. In relation to these communities' African counterparts, Ferguson refers to "urban improvisers" as an alternative to the term urban "unemployed" because he rightly identifies this as a population that is unlikely to benefit from any significant upward mobility into formal-sector employment (Ferguson 2009, 168). This change in classification might encourage a rethinking of policies intended to improve the lives of these groups who often eke out a living as part of a shadow economy, but are often misidentified in Jamaica as lazy or idle.

By examining the ways neoliberal practices have been employed and understood within Jamaica at the community level, it is possible to better understand many of the "inner contradictions" of neoliberalism as a global project, which broke apart during the global financial collapse of 2008 (see Robotham 2011). In its relocation to Jamaica, the precepts of neoliberal ideology and governance (self-sufficiency, entrepreneurialism, privatization, and flexibility) have taken on new meanings and created unanticipated outcomes in urban settings like Kingston.

In Guy Town, community development projects designed within the state's sanctioned logic of nation building resultant from Jamaica's colonial history and national economic and social pressures ultimately became an additional source of short-term supplementary benefits for participants once reinterpreted by the urban improvisers. Programs simultaneously encouraged contentious partnerships between the state and organized criminal networks that proved to be proficient at maintaining a tenuous sense of order, even if, in the end, such partnerships effectively undermined the nation-building aspects of the projects themselves.

Examination of these strategies as of a piece reveals a Jamaican state that in many ways appears to be working against itself in a reactive attempt to maintain order within a setting of limited economic resources and opportunity. The Comaroffs have aptly captured this unevenness of governance across Jamaica with their concept of the "postnational." They explain that, "spaces of relative privilege" are "linked to one another by slender, vulnerable corridors that stretch across zones of strife, uncertainty, and minimal governance" (J. Comaroff and J. L. Comaroff 2006, 9). I have argued elsewhere in favor of the term "neoliberal" as opposed to "postnational" in relation to Jamaica. As a former British colony, and then as a small, economically dependent postcolony, Jamaica has never truly enjoyed a period of national self-determination, even as the importance of the role of the state becomes increasingly clear within this era of intensive economic globalization (see Galvin 2012).

What follows is an anthropological study of the music industry's participation in community development efforts in a Kingston ghetto populated by working poor and unemployed residents (urban improvisers). This ethnography is based on sixteen months of field research conducted in Kingston, Jamaica, as well as through ongoing relationships with several community members via mobile phone and Facebook, and through transnational associates, over the period of 2001 to the present. The focus of this research is on the economic practices and associated grassroots development programs within a ghetto community affiliated with the People's National Party. When I began the research, I was particularly interested in gaining a better understanding of how patronage practices relate with the culture and economy of the dancehall music industry and operate as a strategy for nation building based on the empowerment of black populations through education and income-generating projects. In the end, the realities of Guy Town as a field site called me to expand my focus to include a central concern with organized crime as a mode of governance.

As Martin's quote at the beginning of this Introduction suggests, the programs I researched and participated in as an instructor were not successful in quelling community violence or fostering economic opportunity on a large scale. The problems of the Kingston garrison are embedded in too many macro-level issues that the grassroots programs were not able to address. A lack of economic growth and job opportunity within Jamaica as a whole fails to create the space necessary to accommodate the participation of the long-term unemployed. A lack of governance in the social and economic margins has promoted the development of long-standing, entrenched, informal systems of financial acquisition and social control, often linked to organized crime, that have been established to maintain poor communities given the meagerness of Jamaican state resources. This problem of governance in the margins has only been exacerbated by the Jamaican state's adoption of neoliberal policies. The small-scale community-level projects, in the end, may have helped a few residents connect with resources that would allow them to struggle their way into the workforce, as Martin had, but did not create the potential for any transformative change to occur within Guy Town as a whole that would allow community residents' participation in the rights of full citizenship or, on a cultural level, true membership in the creole nationalist imaginary.

The Jamaican dancehall music industry, one of the primary sources of patronage in Guy Town during the time I initiated this research, provides a unique setting for examining the specificities of nation building within the current context of neoliberal globalization. The music's content expresses points of contention in contemporary Jamaican culture from a working-class black perspective, including frictions over gender norms and sexuality, crime, violence, economic inequality, and political corruption. For this reason, the genre has become a critical trope in public debates over the proper substance of Jamaican national culture (Cooper 1993; Hope 2006a, 2006b, 2006c, 2010; Stanley Niaah 2010; Stolzoff 2000; Thomas 2004). In addition, the industry is a provocative field site where the complex interconnectedness of economy and culture, production and consumption, can be fruitfully studied because of its interstitial social position. The industry, as a producer of cultural commodities for local consumption and for export, must carefully negotiate local and international music industries and straddle "uptown" and "downtown" class cultures. It is a space where "market values influence cultural values expressed in Jamaican cultural commodities produced for 'glocal' consumption" (Saunders 2003, 96). The music industry also serves as an important conduit for disenfranchised populations to take part in the global economy both through the circulation of their artistic products and through the rare opportunities participation provides for those with few assets to gain access to foreign travel and work visas.

Participants in the music industry are largely products of poor urban communities that were steeped in the democratic socialist values prevalent within the Jamaican State, to a varying degree, from the 1940s up until 1989 when the dramatic ideological shift toward neoliberal capitalism occurred (Stephens and Stephens 1986). As such, many successful participants, given their disproportionate access to the global economy, have made efforts to give back, which include the sponsorship of community development programs. These programs, taking place in a period of political-economic transition, are public-private partnerships that can be looked at as part of a larger nation-building strategy utilized by the then, and now once again, ruling People's National Party. Using such programs, the party aimed to incorporate marginalized populations under circumstances of intense social conflict and limited national social welfare resources.

These forms of nation building are challenging for governing elites in former colonial societies such as Jamaica, where the legacy of Black Nationalist political visions runs up against the demands of neoliberal economic policies that clearly privilege the economies of North America and the European Community. As has happened in other parts of the "developing world," the political and economic adjustments brought on at the height of neoliberal restructuring remove the burden of care for citizens from the sphere of the state and place it instead on local communities and community-based organizations via public-private partnerships driven by volunteerism. In the case of Guy Town, the burden of care has been taken on by members of the dancehall music industry in conjunction with a variety of nongovernmental organizations and the Jamaica Social Investment Fund. As I will argue, this burden of care takes on a particular meaning and dynamic within the sociality of urban poor communities, where it fits into dynamics of reputation and respectability, which will be further elaborated throughout the book.

Jamaican social relations and cultural divisions are not new sites of academic inquiry, nor has the nation's island status ever allowed anthropologists to treat it as the functionalist organic whole, disconnected from global processes. The island's history as a British colony created as a site for wealth extraction and formed through the importation of enslaved Africans, indentured Europeans and Asians, and British planters and colonial administrators has had a marked impact on the formation of Jamaican society, the dynamics of which have been heavily debated and well studied. Attempts to understand contemporary social organization have worked within three primary, and well-critiqued, frameworks: creolization, pluralism, and the plantation society (Beckford 1971; Braithwaite 1971; Robotham 1980; M. G. Smith 1965; R. T. Smith 1967; Wilson 1973). Each of these models can be seen as an attempt to reconcile the Caribbean's colonial past with contemporary social and economic conditions that are marked by racial and class stratification. These theories attempt to identify the systems, processes, and forces that integrate formerly colonial societies where diverse and antagonistic populations were once unified only under the rigid organization of plantation slavery. These questions continue to be relevant to contemporary research even now that the explanatory power of grand narratives has been taken to task.

While the plantation society model has proven to be a durable framework for understanding stratification in Caribbean society, theorizations of reputation and respectability, initially defined to be class-based and gendered systems of social recognition, have been honed by contemporary ethnographers to take on new analytical utility (Wilson 1969, 1973). Wilson himself suggested some fluidity in the prestige system he sketched out in his ethnographic account of Providencia, but his emphasis on reputation as a potentially transformative "constellation of values" that did not "recognize absolute difference" and the use of respectability as a category of contrast to reputation minimized reputation's potential as a concept that captured the creative uses of systems of prestige among the populations he studied (see Wilson 1973, 227). From the publication of Wilson's *Crab Antics* (1973), Caribbean social scientists have built upon and critiqued his opposed concepts of "reputation," as masculine cultural resistance rooted in an "indigenous," socially derived, status system, and "respectability," which is associated with individualistically derived prestige and the regressive perpetuation of European value systems largely by Caribbean woman. New applications of Wilson's analytical framework add utility to reputation and respectability by treating them as a dynamic system of symbolic social codes that can be manipulated by actors in various social contexts. Reputation and respectability are revealed to be used differently by men and women as they navigate the gendered, racialized terrain of social class (See Austin 1984; Besson 1993). The categories are no longer rigidly associated with particular groups. Instead, contemporary researchers focus on how Caribbean subjects are able to select from a shifting symbolic repertoire consciously through the utilization of a distinct body of cultural knowledge. Once delinked from strict identity groupings, reputation and respectability are recognizable as tools utilized by men and women equally, and that are demonstrably better characterized as a set of strategies for gaining social capital within particular social contexts (Freeman 2000; Ulysse 2007).

Jamaica, which has been independent of England since 1962, continues to face internal conflicts that relate to issues of race, class, and culture as its leaders attempt to forge a national identity that both unifies the population and distinguishes the country favorably to its global audience at a moment in which global economic competitiveness is a critical imperative (P. J. Patterson 2000; N. Rose 1999). It is within this space that the state's role becomes crucial. As has been well established by political anthropologists, the state is not a unitary thing, but must be understood as a project (Alanso 1994; Coronil 1997; Ferguson and Gupta 2002; Gupta 1995). Those who form its structure must actively engineer an appealing vision of community for its citizenry and its world audience (including its potential investors) (Anderson 1991; Robotham 2000). In order to effectively govern, states must also make deliberate, strategic decisions regarding the economic future, even under circumstances in which options are limited by regulated deregulation and market penetration.[5] James Scott has argued that one of the traditional goals of states has been to make their populations "legible" to quantification and, through quantification, management. Such management strategies often fail, according to Scott, owing to a lack of practical knowledge (J. Scott 1998). Das and Poole, focusing on the concept of "the margins of the state," take the idea of the state's inability to manage populations a step further, suggesting that these unruly marginal spaces and populations actually constitute the state and its practices (Das and Poole 2004; Poole 2004).

I have argued (see Galvin 2012) that state governance takes on a particular texture in Jamaica. Neoliberal modes of statecraft resemble those of the British colonial era in that the limited reach of state-based governance in both colonial and contemporary Jamaica fostered a culture of "legal liminality" that has proven beneficial for governments struggling to expeditiously create social order with insufficient resources. Building on Bourdieu's interpretation of Weber, I suggest that European colonization initiated the Caribbean as a zone of legal demystification. The Atlantic World, as a frontier space, was a legally ambiguous universe in which "the official rule determine[d] practice only when there [was] more to be gained by obeying than by disobeying it" (Bourdieu 1990, 108). The recognition that an efficient outcome regularly overrides the rule of law has what Bourdieu refers to as "a salutary effect of demystification" (Bourdieu 1990, 108). Demystification creates space for acts that are simultaneously illegal *and* licit (see Roitman 2006) as expediency takes priority over legality. Poor populations in Jamaica, historically, have been acutely aware that legality is manipulable in economically and socially advantageous ways, as demonstrated first by the British colonial government itself and, now, by the contemporary Jamaican state, which utilizes illegal, but licit, partnerships in order to extend its own reach into tenuously governable marginal spaces. Infractions of law can be "officialized" in order to lend legitimacy to illicit acts by "regularizing the agent's situation, putting him in the right, in a sense beating the group at its own game by presenting his interests in the misrecognizable guise of the values recognized by the group" (Bourdieu 1990, 108).

In the contemporary moment, these governance strategies are fundamentally tied to neoliberal globalization. While many anthropologists have examined the changing cultural realities of transnationalism, highlighting the transformations brought about by compressions of time and space and the porous nature of national boundaries which now permit the flow of people, goods, and ideas because of new technologies in conjunction with the incapacitation of nation-states, others have insisted that the role of the nation-state has been transformed, rather than weakened by economic deregulation and new technologies (Appadurai 1996; Basch, Glick-Schiller, and Szanton Blanc 1994; Hannerz 1996). Philip McMichael has insightfully traced the shift from the development paradigm to the global paradigm, insisting that both need to be examined as deliberately constructed historical projects. He suggests that the former is marked by the goal of managing national welfare via nationally regulated economic growth, while the latter is based on the goal of debt servicing, which requires nations to strategically position themselves within the global economy (McMichael 1996). Rose, in slightly different terms, has referred to this process as the "marketizing" of "economic life" (N. Rose 1999, 142). Anderson and Witter bear out this analysis in their Jamaican case study of structural adjustment (Anderson and Witter 1994).

Theorists have done an admirable job of teasing apart globalization as a historical project, identifying the groups with vested interest in the maintenance of global economic policies that selectively deregulate national markets, create an international division of labor with formerly colonial countries serving as the working class of their former colonizers, and promote a global economic environment favorable to speculative investment practices that encourage economic risk taking (J. Comaroff and J. L. Comaroff 2001; Petras and Veltmeyer 2001). Invested parties, according to Petras and Veltmeyer, include "ascending states and their dominant economic enterprises," "their political and economic counterparts in the dominated countries," "high-level state functionaries," and "key elements of the dominant capitalist class," which include "bankers, financiers and importers and exporters of goods and services" (Petras and Veltmeyer 2001, 31–32). Meanwhile, as within the development paradigm, technology becomes a key resource (whether the industrial technology of development, or the information technology of the global age), which is controlled by the "ascending" countries as the dominant engineers of globalization (Cardoso 1972).

On an ideological level, it has been suggested that practices of racialization have also changed in relation to neoliberal globalization. Melamed tracks shifting "official anti-racisms" historically in order to understand how these discourses serve as "ideological modes for making inequalities generated by global capitalism appear necessary, natural, or fair" (Melamed 2011, xvi). In the neoliberal era, she argues, official anti-racisms change form from the muffling aestheticization of conflict, violence, and activism during the 1980s and 1990s, or what she terms "liberal multiculturalism," to the "neoliberal multiculturalism" of the 2000s. The project of aestheticization successfully limited possibilities for combating racism by representing the United States as normatively multicultural, in the period predominated by liberal multiculturalism. Neoliberal multiculturalism is different, in that it operates beyond the bounds of sovereign nation-states to naturalize the status of the beneficiaries of neoliberal globalization and to normalize the status of the excluded majority that exists on the losing end of the spectrum. What these strategies hold in common is the justification of a status quo that benefits the functioning of capitalism, where "race has continued to permeate capitalism's economic and social processes, organizing the hyperextraction of surplus value from racialized bodies and naturalizing a system of capital accumulation that grossly favors the global North over the global South" (Melamed 2011, 42). Within neoliberal multiculturalism, racialized winners are demarcated as being "multicultural, reasonable, law-abiding, and good global citizens," while populations that fail to benefit from the system are explained away as "monocultural, backward, weak, irrational—unfit for global citizenship" (Melamed 20011, 44). This racialization then justifies the suffering and vulnerability of those lacking adequate "neoliberal subjectivity." It explains their exclusion from full citizenship, their lack of access to material wealth, and other forms of power, as a natural outgrowth of cultural or other deficits that inhibit people's participation as global citizens, while simultaneously positing neoliberal globalization as a neutral market system that will provide economic benefit to a diversity of nations and that purportedly serves as a globally equalizing force (Melamed 2011, 36).

The Jamaican state is operating within this contemporary global system comprised of a hierarchy of nations that, not coincidentally, correspond to global racial hierarchies initiated during the colonial era and that have been bolstered by contemporary neoliberal multiculturalism (Basch, Glick-Schiller, and Szanton Blanc 1994; Melamed 2011; Robotham 1998). Within this context, Robotham has contended that, given a history of shared oppression, the Jamaican black bourgeoisie who largely make up the leadership of the ruling People's National Party could potentially institute policies of benefit to the nation's majority, the black poor in particular, in order to strengthen their own political power. In addition, he suggests that the ruling elites run the risk of jeopardizing foreign investment if their agendas appear too overtly Black Nationalist in character (Robotham 2000). More recently, Deborah Thomas has argued that the predominant creole nationalist project, efficiently symbolized by the national motto "Out of Many, One People," has been widely rejected by lower-class black

Jamaicans, who instead ascribe to what she refers to as "modern blackness." Modern blackness jockeys against creole multiracial ideologies that have failed to include poor black Jamaicans fully as citizens. Thomas characterizes modern blackness as not rooted in folk tradition "grounded in the past" as a source of national culture, but instead as "presentist" in orientation, embracing a modern transnational cosmopolitanism (Thomas 2004, 13). Heavily associated with dancehall culture, modern blackness, according to Thomas, has created a national discourse of moral panic because of its "coincidence" with state retraction and escalating crime and violence (Thomas 2004, 13). Intriguingly, participation in the dancehall industry also frequently provides subjects excluded from the benefits of neoliberal multiculturalism because of their class, racial, or cultural background opportunity to participate in global citizenship through alternative economies of performance, production, and circulation that draw them into the world market. Modern blackness is located within the logic of neoliberalism and shares an emphasis on globality, self-sufficiency, and entrepreneurship. Building on Thomas, I argue that what she has termed modern blackness might also be fruitfully examined as an interpretation of neoliberal globalization, as it has been filtered through the accumulated cultural, political, and economic expertise of Kingston's poor populations. This black, urban, working-class rendition of neoliberal ideology now permeates aspects of Jamaican culture as a whole, with Jamaican dancehall culture being one of the primary routes for its dissemination. I argue that these acts of interpretation on the part of poorer Jamaicans bestow new meanings on the flagstones of neoliberalism and change the social and economic purpose of the community development projects in the lives of area residents who must face the realities of grinding poverty that has only been exacerbated by economic austerity measures.

Neoliberal globalization has had a deep impact on the Jamaican economy. Import restrictions were loosened in compliance with the regulations of the International Monetary Fund. The IMF also encouraged widespread privatization of government-owned industries not accounting for the insufficiency of influence to draw necessary foreign investment for the maintenance of these private enterprises. The result has been what the Planning Institute of Jamaica described as "devastating consequences," which include a decline of living standards and the reduction of government spending on education, health, and social welfare programs (Planning Institute of Jamaica, 2000, 9). In order to ameliorate these effects, Patterson's People's National Party government encouraged public-private partnerships to provide support for impoverished communities that could not be fully serviced by social welfare programs. To this end the Jamaica Social Investment Fund was established as a temporary, governmentally and privately sponsored community development agency that partners with communities and private entities to improve infrastructure, education, and community health. The design of these programs reveals a vision that Patterson's government had for the country, both culturally and economically. However, the way these projects operated within their community contexts raises an additional set of issues regarding social tensions within the nation at a new political moment. The challenges of successful implementation of these nation-building development projects within heavily disenfranchised poor communities might be viewed as an instantiation of a reinterpreted neoliberal practice on the part of urban improvisers bumping up against the nation-building goals of the Jamaican state. This association creates short-term benefits to savvy participants but cannot ultimately transform overall social and economic conditions at the community level without a dramatic rethinking of the needs of the urban poor on the part of the Jamaican state. In particular, the dancehall sensibility that permeates Guy Town and served as a primary source of patronage and development funding contradicted the goals of the community-based projects in significant ways that will be enumerated in later chapters.

Discourses around the ostensible culture of violence in Jamaica are widely associated with urban poor populations, with particular emphasis on black males and dancehall culture, and have been constructed on a longer history of "epistemological violence" that pathologizes black families in ways that justify the continued existence of a racialized class-based inequality (Thomas 2011). Since the families of lower-class Jamaicans largely fail to conform to the normative nuclear, male-breadwinner-centered family model, the lynchpin of modern development theories linked to industrial models of economic production, this "deviance" was largely identified as the key barrier to economic stability for black families and national development in many postcolonial societies (Thomas 2011). In its current iteration, as noted by Roderick Ferguson, black males are pathologized for being "reproductive," but not "productive" (Thomas 2011, 66). The decline of industrial development in the current economic era suggests that the public scrutiny of the "failure" of black males may have grown obsolete; however the discourse continues to prevail and remains an efficacious instrument in the maintenance of class distinction (Thomas 2011). The durability of this stigma might be productively explained by the ways in which the narrative of the pathological black male continues to serve the purposes of neoliberal multiculturalism, which also utilizes the evocation of such deficiency as an explanation for inequality and the inaccessibility of global citizenship to such stigmatized figures.

By once again turning to James Ferguson's understanding of contemporary urban unemployment as a new normative state of urban improvisation, and taking seriously the economic reality that there may never be stable employment opportunity available for all able-bodied and qualified citizens (see Ferguson 2009), it is possible to also shift the discourse on contemporary Jamaican family forms away from the pathologizing comparison with European nuclear families (which are, themselves, rapidly transforming in the contemporary era). This shift in socioeconomic emphasis might also open up space for a further consideration of masculinity in relation to new configurations of work and family so that, over time, black males might grow to be socially valued beyond the constraints of the breadwinner role.

Within postcolonial settings like Jamaica, popular performing arts have been identified as a part of black people's search for autonomy within urban contexts over which they often have little control (Copland 1985). Here popular production is treated as part of the creation of culture, particularly in urban settings that have been, at times, cast as spaces of "social disintegration." National debates over the inclusion of "minority" culture represent struggles over what the national identity will be and who will be part of its definition (Moore 1997; Thomas 2004).[6] Averill has emphasized music's ability to evoke emotion in its participants, which makes it a useful political tool. In his research on Haitian popular music, he suggests that when national governments attempt to control music's production, it is because they recognize cultural production as a powerful activity for oppressed people (Averill 1997). Scott advocates that anxiety over popular culture can, in fact, serve as an indicator of postcolonial crisis (D. Scott 1999, 91). Sonjah Stanley Niaah contextualizes the unsettling power possessed by the Jamaican poor in her work on the performance geography of dancehall when she writes, "Whether on ship decks, in school rooms or shrubs, or on the streets, the enslaved and, later, the freed Africans or peasantry settling across the island of Jamaica, and especially in Kingston, occupied marginal lanes, river banks and gully (ravine) banks, not only for housing and subsistence, but for performance as well. Articulation of the self in these spaces was, and continues to be, potent, as their marginalization is at once their power" (Stanley Niaah 2010, 18). Hope affirms this relationship between dancehall and contested sociopolitical spaciality by introducing the term "dis/place" to describe the existential space of dancehall. The term is intended to capture a complex of meanings, including "this place from within which we are forced to re-create and claim our resources, identities, personhood, and self-esteem by any means" (Hope 2006b, 26). However, the marginality of dancehall's creators does not guarantee that dancehall's content is purely counterhegemonic. Though the composition and performance practice of dancehall music may at times serve as a metaphorical disruption of the status quo and an erogenous celebration of womanhood (see Cooper 1993), in significant ways, dancehall culture also supplements the declining disciplinary roles of the church and the state through policing gender norms and sexuality, with a particular emphasis on regulating women and condemning sexual practices associated with homosexuality (Saunders 2003). Simultaneously, it has been argued that women's performance in dancehall can serve as a form of liberation, as the dancehall provides space for women to assert their own desires and to express an empowering apathy to male sexual attention, while upending patriarchal norms of male dominance (Skelton 1995). Jamaican dancehall, central to ongoing debates about national culture, is clearly a potent form of expression because of its rootedness in the oppositional practices of the urban poor, thereby making the Guy Town initiatives particularly fascinating as a nation-building strategy as well as a site for the examination of lower-class Kingstonians' skillful urban improvisation in a neoliberal era.

In this book I argue that neoliberalism creates a distinctly Jamaican set of contradictions when it is filtered through and adapted by Jamaican society, particularly within poor urban communities. Here privatization of state benefits becomes private sponsorship that reinforces the connections between private industry and organized crime, while simultaneously solidifying the role of organized criminals as community-level providers and unacknowledged extensions of the state itself. Self-reliance, personal responsibility, and entrepreneurship ironically exist both as desirable, cultivable, traits within community development initiatives, as well as traits that morally justify illicit economic activity and contribute to an individual's success within the shadow economy. The line between entrepreneurship and criminality is carefully traveled using the social symbolics of reputation and respectability as tools for the careful manipulation of social identity and intention. Nation-building strategies enacted through community development projects, which, in the case I study, are funded by the dancehall music industry are undermined by this complex of contradictions. Programs are incorporated into an arsenal of short-term survival strategies that utilize project benefits as an added financial and social resource. However, program participants continue to be compelled to take part in illegal activities in order to survive economically and socially within the garrison environment. The end result of the implementation of the neoliberal project in Jamaica, and in Kingston in particular, reveals that economic globalization and neoliberal governance are not the panacea that international agencies like the World Bank and International Monetary Fund once claimed them to be. The constellation of values and practices created by the Jamaican adaptation of neoliberalism effectively *undermine* community development agendas in poor urban areas as well as Jamaican nation-building efforts as a whole.

In order to consider these issues ethnographically, I conducted formal interviews in the community and within the administrative and creative ranks of Wicked Times, a community-affiliated dancehall production company. I also collected data through participant observation at community organization meetings, remedial education programs, and celebrations, and during daily routines. At the dancehall production company, I observed recording and engineering sessions and the day-to-day operations of the business.

The member of Parliament welcomed my presence and graciously requested that his special assistant guide me through the area, introducing me to key community members, including members of the local power structure and the dancehall production company. I was also formally introduced to residents of "Guy Town" and "Perry Town" as an anthropologist conducting a research project in the community during a Youth Organization meeting in which I was also asked to participate in women's remedial education classes as a weekly instructor. Teaching turned out to be an advantageous decision for several reasons. In the weeks following the inauguration of the women's classes, the community opened to me in ways I was not expecting. Most community members had a relative or friend who attended my class. Beyond the usual respect afforded to teachers in general, community members expressed their appreciation for my commitment and concern, and I, in turn, felt good about contributing something within my capacity to people whose generosity toward a total stranger was, at times, astounding.

The teaching facilitated my "adoption" by a small group of women, one being the mother of a teenage girl who was my student. The adoption process began with their accompaniment on my journey home via taxi each evening after class. Given that the taxi man was local and would need to return to the area after dropping me off at my uptown student apartment, it was a prime opportunity for them to make a sojourn out of Guy Town. In the beginning I had an extremely difficult time understanding what they were saying in the rapid patois they spoke, and the boisterous laughter that emitted from the back of the cab often left me wondering if I was the butt of some hilarious joke. However, as a few weeks passed, my level of understanding grew, and I came to realize that everyone and everything was, indeed, the butt of a hilarious joke! It was only after I requested interviews with them, and we talked about their life experiences and became more familiar with each other, that the seriousness of their struggles emerged. Though the gravity of their circumstances was clearly visible through observation, the details of their lives would not be openly shared until I'd been well tested.

The testing took several forms, including some prodding aimed at determining if I could take a joke. Much of it revolved around the women's evaluation of my own sense of propriety and status, as revealed by the bawdiness of humor that was aimed at me. Having passed the humility section of the evaluation, I was granted further approval when it was determined that I enjoyed eating the "poor people food" that they began offering me from their own evening family meal. Finally, without my realizing it, they began encouraging me to participate in behaviors that were considered breaches of propriety. As someone unfamiliar with the ways of Jamaican street-side etiquette, I did not know that eating food while sitting out on the sidewalk was considered inappropriate, yet I was consistently brought a dish of whatever had been prepared that evening to consume in full view of the neighborhood. I was being deliberately schooled in bad manners.

Once I had met with the groups' approval, they began taking me with them on daily errands and family visits. While they were explicitly helping me with my research by exposing me to the multiple facets of their lives, it also seemed that my company added additional excitement to their routines given the novelty value the presence of a white middle-class American woman had within the circles they traveled.[7] With the help of these women and a few members of the community's Youth Organization, I was introduced to a wide variety of area residents, as well as outsiders, who had developed a concern for the welfare of the community. Through these introductions, an array of people granted me in-depth interviews and generally allowed me to hang around during their daily activities and take part in special occasions and events.

During this first thirteen-month-long research stint, I rented a small apartment in a complex near the university that housed numerous female students. The uptown option seemed the most logical given that I had been told not to attempt living in Guy Town because of safety concerns. I followed this excellent advice, which allowed me ample time to participate in the community without wearing out my welcome and also enabled access to the outstanding libraries and lectures available at the University of the West Indies. However, when I returned to Kingston for a month-long follow-up period six months after having completed the initial research, I was invited by a friend in Guy Town to stay in her home for the month. I took her up on her offer, and, while it was a valuable experience that deeply enriched the resulting ethnography, it was also an incredibly stressful period for me and for my hosts. I lived for the month as a resident of Guy Town would live, with the critical exceptions that I had access to credit and a bank account when food ran short, could leave at the end of the month or if trouble arose, and could travel more or less freely during my visit. In addition, I was explicitly being treated to the immense hospitality extended to visiting guests. However, my time there did expose me to the rhythm of daily schedules, including the events that would be considered disruptions or exceptions, and to the experience of living with overcrowding. During my stay my friend and her two children shared with me their small room, which contained one double and one twin bed. Another friend that lived across the street allowed me access to her private shower and toilet, a luxury for the wider population, who largely shared a public facility in the town square. However, as an American accustomed to a fully outfitted bathroom a few steps down the hallway, crossing the street with all my "essentials" for a cold morning shower and strategically rationing out trips to the bathroom during times when my friend's yard was not locked took a good deal of thought. Though I largely felt safe during my stay, there were times when I would be jolted out of sleep by some unfamiliar noise, at which time my mind would race through all manner of possible scenarios.

These experiences bring to light some issues that arise when conducting research in volatile places. I am lucky to have had the opportunity to stay in Guy Town for those four weeks. In the months that passed between that July and my third research stint, a year after the previous month-long trip, my residence in the community had become impossible. When I saw the state of the community only a year and a half after having concluded my initial research, I was depressed to witness the transformation that had occurred. It brought home to me that anthropology really must be understood as a "history of the present," given that whole ways of life can be radically altered with exceptional rapidity. Ethnography, like life itself, is conditional. In this case, the transformation in daily life was linked to the first phase of the aforementioned upheaval of the local power structure. There were forces attempting to oust those at the apex of the structure, and there was a sort of civil war occurring within a set of communities that were generally thought of as unified. The internal nature of the conflict intensified its deadliness because no one was clear who was involved and with which side of the conflict various residents had aligned themselves. There was a generalized feeling of suspicion and uncertainty that was operationalized in a radical change in community practice. People were no longer freely socializing in corner gatherings along the street side. Children were no longer playing in the communal town square. The street was no longer a strip of tar changed into a living space by overcrowding but had resumed its intended role as laid out by city planners. Transformed by the threat of violence, it was now a mere conduit from point A to point B. In the wake of this upheaval, community programs were suspended, curfews imposed, children kept home from school, and workers had to plan travel to and from their jobs carefully. Outsiders were viewed with heightened suspicion, and the relatively free travel between communities that was enjoyed by residents during my initial research period was curtailed. This lack of freedom had deeply restricted residents' ability to scrape together a living because channels of redistribution and social practices of giving were disrupted. Though the ethnographic moment I initially attempted to depict has passed, I am now able to provide a long view based on more than ten years of continual involvement (both direct and from a distance, as I have been incorporated into the New York node of Guy Town's transnational network).

With these comments by way of introduction, I will now lay out my chapter outline. Chapter 1 examines local moral economies of giving within Guy Town. I suggest that local mores around giving, based on conceptions of the sharing of blessings and a shared position of struggle rooted in the democratic socialist period, inform the private patronage practices that continue to flourish in downtown Kingston. I explore the ways giving practices intersect with normative conceptions of manhood, womanhood, reputation, and respectability, which also articulate with the appropriate use of violence within this context.

Chapter 2 examines the private patronage practices that have become a crucial part of life in Jamaican ghettoes where the state's resources have been limited through global neoliberal economic policies and where the burden of care for citizens is in the process of being transferred to individuals and community organizations. I suggest that the effects of these policies include the solidification of informal power structures based on the provision of goods and services, which are deeply rooted in the local moral economies examined in the previous chapter, a growing distrust of agents of the state as alien and inefficient within garrison communities, and a concomitant reliance on these informal power structures for the meting out of a "fair" and swift version of community justice.[8] These local structures are not entirely separable from the state. Although at times they operate outside the realm of legality, they nonetheless receive the tacit approval of state agents, who require them to maintain control over marginal populations whose presence threatens to interrupt public order and national development.

Chapter 3, "Dancehall Dilemmas: Sounds from the Disquieted Margins," addresses dancehall lyrics, participation in the genre, and public consumption of the music in Guy Town. Here I argue that dancehall music and ghetto communities, in a sense, are coconstitutive. The music is an expression of the ghetto, but the worldview and practices taking place within the ghetto are also reinforced through the lyrical content of the music, in the practice of creating the music, and through the ways the music is utilized and enjoyed both publicly and privately. The margins are examined as constitutive spaces because ghetto communities contain political populations central to the operations of the state and have created a form of expression, in dancehall, that has become central to the public discourse around what Jamaica, as a nation, is and should be. I suggest that while Jamaican dancehall and Jamaican ghetto communities may coconstruct and reinforce each other, they also interrupt the normative imaginary of what the Jamaican Nation is and shape the ways in which the Jamaican state must operate.

In Chapter 4 I explore the position of the dancehall industry, as an enterprise that exists at the intersection of wealthy uptown and working-class downtown Kingston, and also of Jamaica and the global economy via the multinational music industry. I do this by first examining the ways in which Wicked Times is a fundamentally local company, which grew out of downtown Kingston as well as Jamaica's own musical tradition.[9] I argue that this position requires versatility that allows the company to bridge the ghetto milieu, which fosters the creation of dancehall, and a business milieu that requires an understanding of professionalism both locally and abroad. I then examine the issue of marketing dancehall overseas, suggesting that the way this issue gets addressed by members of the company reflects the compromises and maneuvers necessitated by Jamaica's position within global economic and cultural hierarchies and the impact that position has on the company and its performers with regard to career-building strategies.

In Chapter 5, "The Contradictions of Neoliberal Nation Building in Jamaica: Community Development through Dancehall," I examine the grassroots community development programs instituted by Wicked Times in conjunction with nongovernmental organizations, the Jamaican Social Investment Fund and the University of the West Indies. I suggest that these projects, which include remedial education classes focused on imparting a "disciplined masculinity" on at-risk youth and the teaching of history rooted in Pan-Africanism as well as the implementation of small-scale income-generating enterprises, are one part of a People's National Party agenda of nation building based on the empowerment of black populations. However, I argue that since the neoliberal state has abandoned its caregiver role, which was a crucial component of the democratic socialist political moment, and this task has been taken on by the dancehall industry, these projects play out contradictorily. While programs advance the agenda of disciplining the unruly space of the ghetto, a place with a reputation for crime and violence, which jeopardizes tourism and foreign investment, the implementation of the projects through dancehall, a genre created by ghetto residents and rooted in their sociality, creates a contradiction. The at-risk youth are simultaneously being instructed in what I argue is a type of dual citizenship. They are taught to create a public image of model citizenry by exhibiting self-control, positive relationships with agents of the state, and an admirable ingenuity, while their community citizenship is also reinforced through the bolstering of loyalty to private power hierarchies rooted in illegal activities and a normative masculinity that incorporates the deployment of violence and the fathering of children with multiple women as its key status signifiers, thus undermining the crucial image of stability and compromising the legitimacy of the state.[10]

Finally, in "The Long View" I attempt to make sense of the changes that have occurred in Guy Town between the time of my initial research in 2001 and the present, a significantly tumultuous period consisting of economic collapse, violent conflict, and social upheaval across the globe. These changes and the outcomes of the projects I began studying more than a decade ago reveal class and cultural tensions within Jamaica as a nation. In this final chapter, I explore the implications of these tensions for urban poor populations as they adjust to the shifting terrain of a shaky global economy and a globalized conception of neoliberal governance. At the same time, their experiences are also couched within the struggles of the Jamaican state. They are in many ways navigating the insecurities of the present moment with an added element of uncertainty as the country of their citizenship continues to engage in the old postcolonial struggle to carve out a viable economic and political space for itself as a sovereign nation in a global era characterized by eroding sovereignty and marketization.

CHAPTER 1

"Money Move"

The Sociality of Circulation, Violence, and Respect

> *Now tek out some money for all your bredren . . .*
> *Make a move, make a move*
> *Make a conscious move*
> —Barrington Levy, "Money Move"

Giving and generosity in Jamaican ghetto communities are markers of reputation and respectability where other cultural markers, including the use of Standard English, European marriage patterns, and success through education, have been largely unattainable or deliberately rejected.[1] These socialized values shaped by gender roles and access to employment are fundamental characteristics of ghetto culture, and, I would add, necessary ones, under circumstances in which the majority of the population is not regularly employed and in which the pool of state resources for the provision of necessary basic services has dried up.[2] However, these crucial practices are rooted in a prior political moment. Before the neoliberal turn of the late 1980s, which dramatically reduced the social welfare resources available to community residents, there was an extensive period of democratic socialist policy on the part of the Jamaican state as envisioned and executed by the People's National Party under the leadership of Michael Manley.

This strategy, explicitly pursued by the party as of 1974, was not without its detractors, both within the People's National Party itself and on the part of the opposing Jamaica Labour Party. The Cold War was in full swing, and, given the dependent nature of the Jamaican economy, a communist label could have had a significant impact on foreign investment. Although Jamaica was openly an adherent of the Non-Aligned Movement, the country's warm relations with Cuba and democratic socialist domestic policies stirred up fears among the capitalist class and created hesitation among international investors and lending agencies.

Even given the controversial nature of the democratic socialist path, the People's National Party was able to cultivate a base of mass support through a party ideology that successfully incorporated previously marginalized segments of the population into the Jamaican nation, leading to heightened political engagement and electoral involvement. For the first time, impoverished black populations were made to feel like full citizens through the party embracing, and at times advancing, aspects of their culture and their class interests in a heavily elitist society (Stephens and Stephens 1986).

Normative giving practices, extant throughout Jamaica, are part of a moral economy deeply impacted by Christian values and decades of democratic socialist policies marked by a state-led, mixed economy and state-sponsored efforts to encourage egalitarianism and social inclusion. These giving practices, prevalent in the daily lives of ghetto residents, must be considered in order to understand the patronage practices of members of the new black middle class. They shape local understandings of giving and receiving and, therefore, the social relations that are produced through acts of giving and receiving. Additionally, the practice of giving and sharing is imbricated with community-rooted social distinctions based on the evaluation of community members' conduct toward others as a measure of social status.

Such modes of social distinction, once characterized as exclusive to a masculine behavioral repertoire, were first identified with the label reputation within Caribbean anthropology (see Wilson 1973). However, the categories of reputation and respectability, insightfully introduced by Wilson in the 1970s in order to explain distinctly Caribbean understandings of social status within poor communities, have greater analytical utility when understood not as disparate status categories but as part of an arsenal of personal strategies utilized by Caribbean subjects in order to attain social mobility through the creation of social capital. Rather than being the property of particular gender groups or economic classes, reputation and respectability can be more fruitfully seen as interpersonal strategies employed based on deep cultural knowledge and selected from a wide range of possible approaches in order to gain the greatest benefit within a specific social context (see also Ulysse 2007; Freeman 2000). With this revised understanding, reputation and respectability are demonstrated to be porous rather than distinct status types that are the exclusive domain of highly specified social identities. Here, respectability, which often references values of propriety originated by the British and that has been heavily associated with Christianity and traditional European marriage patterns, is used alongside reputation as necessitated by the social setting of the interaction and the specific parties involved. A person's reputation will, in part, be shaped by his or her willingness to give to others in a socially appropriate fashion. Members of the new black middle class, as patrons, were socialized within these moral economies of redistribution and continue to take part in them even now that the democratic socialist model has given way to a neoliberal free-market capitalist one.

Moral values around the mutuality of people's needs have remained intact, and the need for wealth redistribution is at its height at a moment in which the state has sought to turn individuals into "entrepreneurs of themselves" and citizens into potential "allies of economic success" (N. Rose 1999, 142, 162). Along these lines, according to the *Social Sector Strategy Report on Jamaica* drafted for the Inter-American Development Bank, social protection programs "are now viewed as active mechanisms that can assist the poor in investing in their own productivity" (Inter-American Development Bank 2001, 18). One of the limitations of this strategy, which relies on skills training and the cultivation of citizens into human capital, is that there are simply not enough jobs for the portion of the population that already possesses adequate training. Though the supply of trained and credentialed labor has steadily grown, limited national economic growth has created a situation in which there has been no simultaneous increase in the demand for skilled labor (Inter-American Development Bank 2001). Within this context of limited economic possibility and a heavy domestic debt burden, poor populations are caught in a deadly bind. While the state is drastically reducing the social safety net for its citizens in the interest of austerity, privatization, and the instilling of self-sufficiency, there is only limited access to employment opportunities that would allow people to actually become self-sufficient.

By 1998, the 62 percent share of the gross domestic product dedicated to debt servicing was drastically greater than the reduced amount of 18 percent made available for social-sector spending (Inter-American Development Bank 2001, 19). According to the same report, even though 90 percent of the funds dedicated to social services were targeted for education and health initiatives, the most well-funded nutritional program, the

Food Stamp Program, assisted only 15 percent of the poorest quintile of the population, and those who did receive benefits were relieved of only 1 percent of their total food expenditure (Inter-American Development Bank 2001, 19–22). Is it any wonder that informal redistributive practices continue to exist in this new political moment? This period of economic transition and uncertainty, as I will demonstrate, is marked by a sense of betrayal among the urban poor at the retraction of the state from their care. Contradictorily, in this period of transition, the population's redistributive actions can be simultaneously recast in the terms of neoliberalism as private initiative supplanting the care once provided by the state.

Downtown Kingston

A collection of newspaper articles published in the late nineteenth century is a valuable resource for understanding the long-standing condition of downtown Kingston (Moore and Johnson 2000).[3] In one article, originally published in 1892, fifty-eight years after emancipation, and titled "A Disgrace to the City," an area in the vicinity of Guy Town is described as follows:

> The water tables along the centre of the streets besides being a perpetual eyesore, become blocked with dirt of every description and the water, which should run down freely, is in consequence stagnated and most offensive. On a dark night it is almost impossible to proceed any distance without repeatedly stepping into some sort of these pools and progress is as difficult as it is dangerous. When the rains are on, the road is a quagmire with mud almost to the knees.
>
> One would imagine that as a means of locomotion are so inconceivably bad, precautions would be taken by the City Fathers to provide plenty of light to make some amends for their neglect. This, however, is far from being the case. The village boasts two lamps, both on the Spanish Town Road, the rest of the district being in complete darkness. Is it any wonder that Smith's Village bears a bad name for evil deeds? To a great extent, the members of the Council are responsible for the outrages which are constantly being committed in the neighborhood as by their want of attention and carelessness they practically place a premium upon crime. Everything is favourable for those who have any inclination to break the laws. The streets are to a great extent lonely and deserted at night, and even where more thickly

populated, the people are so thoroughly accustomed and inured to deeds of violence, that they take comparatively little note of what is going on; on nights when there is no moon the darkness can almost be felt and as the police are about as numerous as the gas lamps there is absolutely no protection. (Moore and Johnson 2000, 13–14)

After emancipation, migration from rural areas to Kingston was heavy, based on a lack of available cultivable land in the country and the attraction of high wages that were purportedly available in the city. This population growth was not matched by heightened city planning efforts until the early twentieth century (C. Clarke 1975). Robotham has identified settlement in Kingston as heavily class based, with inhabitants dividing up the spaces of the city by populating distinct areas according to their membership in particular economic strata (Robotham 2003). By the late nineteenth century the wider area in which Guy Town is now situated had become a major settlement, and by the 1920s the area was comprised of "densely populated tenements" (C. Clarke 1975, 34). According to Colin Clarke, in the 1940s "the vast majority of the accommodation in Kingston and in St. Andrew consisted of only one room, and more than half the population of the city lived in minute, single room dwellings with less than 150 square feet, and averaging 2.5 occupants" (C. Clarke 1975, 60). These conditions resemble the overcrowded environment that currently persists in Guy Town, where population pressure is coupled with poverty. While I am not able to offer a complete account of the development of the city of Kingston to the present, the ethnographic account that follows is situated within this setting.

Everyday Forms of Exchange

In Guy Town it is not uncommon to hear a passing neighbor say, "Beg you a twenty dollar?" asking for a coin in order to buy a soda or small snack.[4] In most cases the giver provides the money assuming that the next time they "beg a twenty dollar" some equivalent person will, in turn, give it to them. Variations on these types of transactions take place on a regular basis and create a system that aids the poorest members of society in meeting basic survival needs through passing small quantities of money from one person to the next.[5]

People who don't take part in the sharing of resources often enough earn poor reputations for being "mean" (miserly). Meanness is often discussed in local gossip, which is not taken lightly.[6] In one instance I witnessed, a middle-aged woman who sat on a scrap of carpeting on a Guy Town street corner asked her friend for a little money to buy some flour. Her friend replied that she didn't have any. The woman covertly turned to me and under her breath whispered, "She never have nothing yet." Vocalized with a tone of critical disbelief, the speaker indicated the improbability of someone lacking resources to the extent that they are never able to help out when asked. In another instance, a local woman socializing on the same corner accused another, on an adjacent corner, of meanness. The accused's friend came to her defense with, "She not mean! When she have, she give." This interaction demonstrated the severity of being labeled mean, which required a friend to offer up a defense because of the accusation's damaging effect upon the person's personal reputation as a community member. The exchange also laid out the rules for attaining an upstanding social status in the community. When it comes to sharing, when you have, you give.[7]

Because of widespread exclusion from mainstream production through regular wage employment, giving has become one way the community reproduces itself.[8] Though there are residents of Guy Town that take part in formal employment and can, therefore, be considered producers, and there are patrons affiliated with the community who are also producers (some quite literally, record producers), a large portion of the community's residents are able to survive because of the redistribution of resources over time, which is a fundamental aspect of life among the Jamaican poor. Whether these resources come from remittances made by friends and relatives "aforeign," by residents who have relative to the rest of the community, or through relations with locally recognized patrons like merchants and don figures, there is a dependence on the redistribution of resources.[9]

Open-ended exchanges like these are not conducted tit for tat and are rooted in the assumption of a "timeless human commitment" that suggests relations will continue into the future (Graeber 2001, 225); that is, the transactions I described above are open-ended, based on the supposition that obligations and the mutuality created by these obligations will continue to exist. Additionally, these economic relations of mutuality are embedded within the ongoing social relations that create one's reputation. Open-ended transactions can be contrasted with ones that are expected to eventually dissolve into autonomy and thereby require expenditures to be recouped immediately and in kind. This is a basic, but illuminating, distinction. It has been suggested that closed exchanges are predicated on an idea of individuality; obligations are to be kept to a minimum in order to maintain autonomy (Graeber 2001). From a Jamaican perspective, these are the sorts of exchanges that Euro-Americans are noted for.[10] One day during my fieldwork, a woman from Guy Town attempted to explain the practical difference that I am indicating here to another community member. She told her neighbor that if a person aforeign borrows a tin of condensed milk from their neighbor, they are expected to also return a tin of condensed milk as soon as they can afford one. This scenario was seen as an absurdity within the cultural milieu of the ghetto, where a person would usually give the tin of condensed milk without any expectation of ever seeing it again, thereby, consciously or unconsciously, helping to create an open-ended system of exchange. The exchange systems I observed in Guy Town are based on social tendencies in which individuals are less concerned with autonomy than with understanding and responding to each other's needs (Graeber 2001; Mauss 1990 [1950]). By understanding the needs of others, community members can maintain reputations that confer social status on participants for their contextually appropriate manner of social interaction. This system is an important feature of Guy Town and other poor communities, in part because much of the population is not engaged in regular wage labor. The unemployed often contribute informal favors to wage-earning neighbors, like trips to the market downtown or the provision of childcare, as a way of accessing the monetized economy and accruing social capital. In this setting, capitalistic individualism has not uniformly won the day. Christian and socialist values of mutuality remain pervasive and aid in sustaining marginalized communities.

I am not suggesting, however, that Guy Town is some sort of egalitarian utopia. While there are open-ended exchange practices that regularly take place in the community, there are also points at which this system breaks down, as well as limits to people's willingness to give what is theirs.[11] This breakdown is widely described using the Jamaican adage that speaks of poor people as "crabs in a barrel," with each pulling the other to the bottom in a competitive effort to reach the top. This adage can also be linked to values around reputation and respectability, where breaches of mutuality through either meanness or excessive greediness—sometimes characterized using the epithet vampire, as in one who feeds off of others—are equal targets of social condemnation. Clearly, the socially accepted range of daily exchange practices in Guy Town is not purely self-maximizing but, as demonstrated by residents, contains elements of both socially incorporative and economically transactional behaviors (Barth 1966; Paine 1976).

Economic exchange in this context must be linked to local understandings of reputation and respect and the means for attaining positive social status and social capital. Exchanges, as acts of generosity, generate respect and a positive reputation, suggesting that modes of exchange that are incorporative may simultaneously be self-maximizing in ways that are not purely economic. The dynamic relationship between acts of exchange and the attainment of reputation and respect in Guy Town undermines the utility of analytically separating economic practices from other aspects of the social (Douglas and Isherwood 1979; Mauss 1990 [1950]). Within local systems of exchange, the contribution of a fourteen-ounce tin of condensed milk may not be given with the expectation of a fourteen-ounce tin of condensed milk in return. Instead, acts of giving are practiced in order to accrue interpersonal respect on an individual basis and a positive reputation within the wider community based on recurrent appropriate responses to others' needs. This type of social status is valuable in that it creates a source of power through the ties it creates with other community members who may then be called on when needed or who may come to a person's aid as an expression of loyalty.

The relationship between generosity and reputation and respect became clearer to me on the day that Mita, a well-respected "big woman," in her late forties at the time, gossiped with me about her younger cousin who was consistently complaining about other people's stinginess.[12] She blamed the problem on her cousin's meanness, which Mita then contrasted with her own generosity. She stated that if someone asked her for some money, but she did not have any, she'd "search up" her whole house for something in order to help. According to Mita, this effort guaranteed that when she found herself in need, resources would always be made available to her. She followed up by saying, "Anne, you cyan' mean with people," implying that her cousin was not behaving respectably or "living loving." Interestingly, when interviewed, Mita's cousin told me that she believed people in Guy Town were basically selfish with each other. However, in explaining her position, she also described herself as the kind of person that would give away her last pound of flour. In a formal interview I asked her for sensitive information regarding how she got money together.

> Mita's Cousin: It hard to say right here now because mi not working at this moment and mi have one and two friend weh more time me a check them and mi tell them what's wrong with the situation and

them will give you a likkle thing, but mi don't really check them on a regular basis because you don't really want nobody get tired of you. But as a fact now, work hard to get and you have good friend weh you can really go talk to fi get something from.

Anne: Are your friends that help you out from the area, or from outside the area?

Mita's Cousin: Some of them are in the area, but most of my friends that help me out, is like, most of them are deh aforeign. Like [Dads] now, him is in the area. So I don't really ask nobody more than him. Yeah but more time where mi get my help from is foreign like a friend them and my son grandfather. Him will send a likkle change for him.

Anne: How about on a day-to-day basis if you need a little food money or something? Are there people you would go to for that?

Mita's Cousin: No, that is the same person, but have to know how to budget the money and how to buy the food fi it serve. But at first, [. . .] I used to do a likkle hustling for mi-self, but my father take sick, so I can't go out on the road again to do that. If I get something to do at home, that would be much better.

Anne: So do you think in general that people in the community are sharing with each other or selfish?

Mita's Cousin: On the whole you have some people round here selfish. You and them are friend today and tomorrow you na no friend. You and them will reason now about something and you feel seh you trust them, but a nah trust you trust them because them gone tell somebody. So, you don't know fi trust nobody. Them nah share nowadays. It depend 'ca somebody can hungry and I wan go to them ask them if them have anything and pull them a two pound of flour and can give them pound and them go fix something. But is not everybody are like that.

Her response also indicates the importance of gossip in the area, which was a primary source of social tension and conflict, a mode of social control, and a means for disseminating social information that was particularly critical during periods of violence. She describes the instability of friendships, where confidences are at times spread around the community, and says that a person never really knows whom to trust. The appropriate deployment of gossip is a source of power in such a close social setting, and one that is intimately tied to issues of interpersonal respect.

Respect is a socially significant category in Jamaican ghetto communities.[13] One example of its social significance is the regular use of the word in daily conversation as both a noun and a verb. "Respect" also serves as a salutation at the conclusion of interactions.[14] The word "rate" or "ratings" is also widely used to stand in for the word respect. Rate is a verb meaning to respect someone. A person can "give ratings" to another person. This phrase, shortened simply to ratings, is also frequently used as a salutation. Both terms relate to a community member's reputation in that respect and ratings are earned from others through continually appropriate social interactions. This usage of respect would be significantly different from the etic anthropological classification of respectability as an individual identity, rather than a socially derived status. The terms of admiration, or conversely, derision, as in "mi nah rate her," can be heard peppering streetside conversations across Guy Town and throughout Jamaica more broadly wherever patois is the preferred mode of communication.

Respect can be looked at as a valuable, much like wealth. The power of wealth is in its potential. Having money stashed away makes the possessor powerful because of the potential it creates for future action (Graeber 2001). An accumulation of positive reputation via respect and ratings also enables future action by its possessor. Applying this explanation to the patronage system helps to clarify the type of power patrons possess. It is power derived from both wealth and reputation reciprocally. Wealth, properly utilized, can facilitate the accumulation of respect and respect can also be mobilized for the acquisition of further wealth. In addition, as I will demonstrate later in this chapter, the power of violence is also in its potential. Violence is often the third variable in Guy Town's power equation because it can also be leveraged for both wealth and reputation.

On the Corner

Ghettoes in Kingston vary depending on their location and history, but generally speaking, social life in these communities is centered on the corner. Corners serve as geographical markers in downtown communities and are often identified using the name of a prominent person or crew that occupies the space. Daily use by community members carves up local space, creating alternative maps that exist on top of the names and cartographies imposed by city planners.

The corner is like an outdoor living room, typically only several feet from people's homes. This extra space is crucial under overcrowded conditions in which, at times, entire families live in one room. The level of overcrowding in Guy Town creates circumstances in which residents share a forced intimacy where people walk through the streets as if they are inside their own homes. A morning trip to the bathroom often means a bleary-eyed trek through the streets, toothbrush in hand, to the shared men and women's facilities in Guy Town Square. This intense intimacy, with all its inconvenience, is a celebrated element of ghetto life, which area residents frequently contrasted with Kingston's middle-class areas where inhabitants are perceived to be lonely, isolated, and locked away in their single-family homes.

Corners are generally populated by the same people, who congregate based on gender and networks of friends and family each evening when the housework has been finished and the sun has grown less intense. Acts of redistribution occur frequently between ghetto residents, who use these corners as primary sites for socializing. Redistribution practices range from the giving of spare change and extra food, and from communal cooking (called "running a boat"), to the giving of more substantial sums during emergencies or out of familial obligation.

Practices and expectations in reference to giving are shaped by access to employment as well as gender roles. Community members who are known to be regularly employed are considered people who have. These people may establish regular arrangements with other community members where they contribute a small amount of money toward household expenses or they may simply provide support when asked. As Mita's commentary suggests, even those without resources can be respected if they give appropriately within their means. These small acts of giving create extended support networks through a sense of mutuality and accrue community recognition that contributes to a positive reputation, which, as I will demonstrate, amount to an enhanced sense of both economic and personal security in an environment wrought with scarcity and violence.

"Haves" and "Have-Nots"

There was a barber that ran a shop in Guy Town, who at the time of my initial research was in his early thirties. He had begun taking some social work courses at the university and currently holds a professional post in a local community development agency. Given his access to the monetized economy, he was considered someone who has. When I interviewed him about the responsibilities this status comes with, he told me, "There are more people than some who come regularly for what you call 'help' from me, but it varies sometimes. Sometimes old people that I know very well come, sometimes young people whose mothers don't play a significant enough role. Sometimes I chip in, but not regularly." After a brief thoughtful pause, he went on to say, "Well . . . regularly enough, regularly enough. I think it is a part of the culture, part of the socialization. People ask you for things. It's really a part of our social well-being to give or to ask or to expect." He explained that whether the favor gets returned depends on the position of the person doing the asking. If a person is in too desperate a situation compared to the giver, the giver will usually not expect a return. He attributed these practices to the highly social nature of ghetto communities, which stems from overcrowded conditions, and also to the fact that age groups within the community grow up together and establish long-term relationships.[15]

I also spoke with Alesha, a woman from the community who, while not regularly employed, still does what she can for other people. She was in her midthirties when I first met her and had worked in the Free Trade Zone sewing underwear for a United States–based company before quitting because of what she characterized as an oppressive level of discipline. At the time of our conversation, she was an unemployed mother of three who scraped together odd jobs like taking in laundry and babysitting to make ends meet. Since that time she has migrated to the United States on a temporary work visa, taking short-term jobs in ski lodge cafeterias, hotels, and nursing homes all across the country in order to send money home to her now teenaged children back in Kingston. She told me:

> Sometimes people you don't know will beg you to give them and I will give them same way because they say blessings come from above. So you just give. You don't look to get what you give back from them still, but sometimes out of the clear blue they just give you something and you wonder how you got it back. 'Nuff time I give because sometimes I go to town [the hectic shopping area where poor Kingstonians buy food and clothing] and see people who say them get pick [they've been pick pocketed] and don't have bus fare and I have the livity to buy this and buy that and I give them a fifty dollars or I give them a hundred dollars. People sit down and cry because they don't even have bus fare, so you just give them and then you're short with your thing, you know, you're short because there was something you were going to buy with it, but it just work in back.

Alesha is not considered someone who has by community standards and, in contrast with the barber, is not an established giver within Guy Town. However, she still recognizes times when it is important for her to take part in sharing because she feels that sometimes she has been given things for no reason and should be appreciative of that by showing compassion to others. These examples are indicative of local understandings of giving, in that mutual obligation is often explained through religious conceptions of the sharing of blessings and through understandings of a shared position of struggle that stretches redistributive practices beyond the established networks to include strangers in need.[16]

Romance and Finance

In addition to employment status, gender roles also play a part in giving. Though nuclear families are not commonplace in Jamaican ghettos, there is still an ideal of the male as provider. Flirtations between men and women often involve the man offering to buy things for a woman he likes, and once a longer-term relationship has been established, even when the woman has her own income, it is still expected that the man will contribute part of his finances to the woman's household to pay for food and bills.[17]

Martin, in his late twenties when I met him, was regularly, but temporarily, employed. He described the financial obligations men have for women when I asked him who depended on him. He first listed his mother, who had just recently passed away, his disabled brother, his girlfriend, and "to a lesser extent" her two children. I followed up on this question by asking if it is expected that when a man enters into a relationship with a woman he will provide something for her. Martin responded almost incredulously, "Yeah, man! It's the Jamaican culture; well, in downtown, the ghetto culture, and I think it's for most of Jamaica anyway, once you enter into a relationship at least certain expense for the house is automatically yours. Bills, food, stuff like that are automatically yours and you are also, um, what should I say now, it's also mandatory for you to give your woman money when you get paid that is for her sake." When I asked him if there is a rule of thumb about how much a man is supposed to give, he explained:

> No, just if you feel like giving her half of your pay this week then, if she give you something what sweet you that much, and you want give her all of it, it's fine! [laughing] But it depends on her needs at the time

too. She might come to you and say bwoy, this week I would like to have this for myself. Or suppose you always put down a certain amount of money in the house and she might say, well we are running short on this or we need this for the house. For example, the time is very hot and she say "bwoy, the only fan we do have is breaking down too regular. We need another fan." You know, this week you might have to put down a little bit extra inside the household. But, men generally do. When we have we provide for the house and provide for the women. That's a general culture that's here. It almost embedded in our psyche that man are supposed to take care of our women and child.

He concluded, "It's not like she fi go earn her own and you earn your own and you do what you have to do and she do what she have to do. It's not like that. Even most time if the woman is working the man still gives her money. It's the culture."

At that time, I collected similar information on this issue from the perspective of women in the community. While discussing employment with two women, one a nail technician in her twenties and the other a bartender in her thirties, the conversation shifted fluidly from work to gender relations when I asked if their occupations provided sufficient income for them. When I interviewed Blossom and Debbie, I asked them if their incomes were sufficient for them to get by. Debbie responded vehemently, "No! Of course, you know you have to have a spouse." When I asked her how a spouse might help, she told me laughingly, "Supports you financially, among other things . . . if you know what I mean!" Blossom agreed with Debbie, and I then asked them about a woman's role in romantic relationships. Blossom replied, "Just like any relationship, you know you have a man and a woman and you perform duties maybe cook, wash, whatever, just stuff like how you take care of your family." However, when I asked the women if they would be more likely to do the cooking and other domestic tasks than their spouse, Debbie responded, "Not necessarily, you know, but sometimes there's swapping, you know. You work for me, I give you sex, and you give me money." After Debbie had finished her point, Blossom added:

> I think it's a male thing to support a female. If you really say she's my female. It's not really that he's bound or it's a must for him to support you. [. . .] I'm not saying that it's not like a female can't give a male like to go shopping or something, or if she see something she can't pick

it up for him. It's just a vice versa because if you love something you take care of it. So you have a male, you've been together for a couple of months, and three months probation, six months relationship . . . You know if you work, you know seh him still ago' chip in now and again. And some say, "here is your food money, or here is your money to spend on yourself." If you have a child, a little thing. Some males, not all. I think men, not boys, think like that.

Blossom's distinction that men as opposed to boys support women financially is an indication of the linkage between financial responsibility and masculine reputation and respectability. In order for a Jamaican male to be considered a man, he must provide for his family. In the next section of the interview, this "Jamaican cultural tradition" gets subtly contrasted with local perceptions of North American gender and economic relations. Debbie suggested that it is customary and a part of Jamaican culture for a man to take care of a woman. She continued:

Not like maybe in some custom and culture where some men ask the ladies, "You have to give half." Here in Jamaica, a real man, or, a good man, as Jamaican, he would turn to take care of all of the bills and don't ask his lady to chip in. That is in Jamaican culture. That is what we grow up with, you see? And that is what most woman expect from a man in Jamaica. Yeah, and sometimes it's bad and sometimes it's good.

When I inquired about how this expectation might sometimes be good and other times be bad, Blossom said:

To be dependent on a man can be bad. That mean like whatever time he might leave you, you can't really find food. So it's good to be independent then as a female in Jamaica because the only thing mi say you can depend on—Sure of God, can't sure of man. Friend remind me, girlfriend, you can live very good and say bwoy, you deh dere wid me for ten years and dem remind me there are people deh in relationships for fifteen to twenty years and break up! At the end of the day it still a come out to rely on yourself as a female!

In the first part of her response, Blossom emphasizes the severe consequences of overdependence on men. If a woman depends on a man and he decides to leave, she may not be able to gather enough resources together to feed herself, or those who depend on her. During the next part of our conversation, she uses Debbie's relationship with her boyfriend, a soldier and the owner of the bar Debbie maintained, in order to explain a more gender-balanced economic relationship.

> [Debbie] might have her bar, her boyfriend might give her money, but it's not all the time man will have it to give her. Maybe a day will come when he nah have it and can say, bwoy, "[Debbie] mi a ask you fi lend me a money" or "give me a lunch money, now!" or "give me a bus fare, now!" Right, so it's vice versa, it depend on the situation and the relationship you is in. Right? It depends. To me it depends, because it's not easy to live in Jamaica. Financially it's so expensive. Plus, if you have kids going to school—very expensive. School fees, books, uniforms and you have to have lunch money. Back home, them have food to eat. If them have to have transportation fees, money, lunch money, bus fare, all of that inna it. It good to when you can work and your one and fi him own make two. So if a day come when him nah have it, you can say, "alright, mi save this for rainy day so can chip in." But I know it's not every man mind them woman. You have some man who may buy them food, "buy me a clothes," but them nah give them money. And some when they have something say, "Alright baby, see your money here, see your food here, buy this for the house, and this is yours to keep."

Debbie supported Blossom's point, adding, "So it's just who you get pack up wid. You just have to be grateful for certain things. Not all men, not all men, support their females. Most like, most ladies that are dependent, when the man leave the whole world crumble." To this, Blossom echoed, "The whole world crumble down!" Debbie then summed up the moral of their story saying,

> It is wise for woman of this century to get themselves employed or learn a trade or something. That, you know, it pays for any woman, anywhere in the world, to be independent. Yeah! You never know when one day it end there. You never know. I guess it's just by nature, some people grow up to love and some people just wicked. They just want to move on and they'll tell you it's "greener pastures" and they're gone to graze!

The conversation provides a window into the complexity of gender relations in Jamaican ghettos. The balance between female independence and dependence on men is a delicate one that is further destabilized by the pressure put on men to "perform" their masculinity by being involved with more than one woman (Chevannes 2001).

Ultimately, this interview foreshadowed Debbie's own experience. Her romantic partner had been with her for nearly fifteen years but also maintained a primary household that included another woman and several of their children. Debbie became pregnant with his daughter after years of trying to conceive, but rather than solidifying their relationship, as the birth of a child frequently does, after the birth of their child they ended up estranged. Their strained relationship placed Debbie and their daughter in an economically vulnerable position because her lover was also her employer. Money, for a man, is one of the tools required for this sort of sexual freedom. By the same token, women, at times, use their romantic relationships with men as a strategy for accessing money. The conversation also suggests the fragility of these relationships. The idea of "greener pastures" and men going "to graze" is a regular part of the discourse around masculinity in which the precarious position of women gets highlighted.

A woman from Guy Town expressed to me the practical utility of having a man back in 2002 as I waited in the community square for the regular Tuesday night Youth Organization meeting to begin. While I sat on one of the benches that line the perimeter of Guy Town Square, a paved public area and popular space for socializing located directly across from the concrete community Youth Organization clubhouse, a group of curious children gathered around me. One little girl climbed onto my lap and sat there while I talked with Julian, a man who introduced me to the girl's mother, Lisa, a woman in her midtwenties. Julian was flirtatiously telling Lisa that she needed to find a man for herself, and she responded by telling him that there was no such thing. Julian then told her that she just needed to find the right man, who would be stable and respectful. Lisa continued to say that she didn't believe it made sense to have a man around if you have a job because, when you aren't working, a man can help you with your finances, but when you think you have a man they are usually "out a road" (out with other women). Later, after Lisa had taken her daughter up the street, Julian explained to me that people might view a woman who has sex with a man for money as a "skettel" (whore). He emphasized that, in reality, they are only looking out for their children's future, not their own future, expressing that the children are often put first in sexual decision making.

The issue of the line between prostitution and male financial support of their lovers was one that people were understandably sensitive about when trying to explain local gender relations to me.[18] Krystal, who has a particularly bawdy and frank sense of humor, expressed this tension to me one day by joking with me within earshot of her lover. In a loud voice, in the middle of the street in front of her house, she bellowed, "Hey Anne, he just bought $130 worth of pussy!" At the time $130 was about the equivalent of $2.50 in the United States, so the statement was intended as a way of shaming him with the idea that the quantity of pussy that would be equivalent to the pitiful amount of money he'd given her would be miniscule. She continued with the gag, saying, "But I didn't give him any because I don't sell it." To which the man joked that he was "paying down" (making a down payment for something he would receive in the future). The obvious tension within this explanation of their romantic relationship lies in the fact that differing, gendered, local conceptions of reputation are in play. A male won't be respected as a man if he does not support his lover, and $130 is not sufficient support. However, a female will not be respected as a woman if she is viewed as a prostitute and will also not be seen as respectable if she appears to "give 'it' away for free." A woman must get something beyond physical satisfaction from her sexual relationships with men or she will be considered foolish at best, and loose at worst. This is yet another example of the ways in which local exchange practices are tied to gendered strategies for gaining and maintaining reputation and respect.

Violence, Reputation, and Respect

The perils of lacking a positive reputation were illustrated to me on two occasions that both involved women and interpersonal violence. In one instance, a nineteen-year-old woman from the community had a physical altercation with Marla, another teenager, also from the community. It had been made clear to me that the nineteen-year-old, called Mattress, was not well regarded within Guy Town.[19] Her nickname, to begin with, was a title of disrespect, where most other young women in Guy Town would be nicknamed Princess, Diamond, or Finey. She was often the subject of gossip and ridicule among people out on the street. Once, when I was interviewing her, she explained to me that she had a baby that died shortly after birth. An eleven-year-old boy who was listening piped in that she had "eaten it"—a clearly disrespectful statement that no one challenged. When the altercation broke out between Mattress and Marla, I was talking to Flava, a man from the adjacent community, who was not a regular visitor to Guy Town. We watched the conflict escalate in the middle of the street until Marla produced a rock and struck Mattress on the forehead. The fight ended with Mattress bleeding from a superficial head wound, the clear loser, and Marla marching toward home, angrily triumphant. Flava shook his head and explained to me that Mattress, given her name and the fact that none of the "big men" had gone for their machete to stop the fight, must not be respected within the area. He went on to tell me that it was good that the woman who tended to her after the fight was there to "take her under her wing" because that woman had a "broad chest," an indication of personal strength and pride. Mattress, because of her poor reputation in the eyes of the community, did not possess enough social capital to guarantee protection by other community members, who often ridiculed her and rarely related with her companionably. It often seemed as though her poor reputation would somehow rub off on others by association. It was only owing to the attending woman's reputation as a big woman with a broad chest that there was no risk of being degraded by association with Mattress, and, in fact, the act of kindness toward the outcast young woman only served to reinforce the big woman's reputation for being generous, caring, and in control.

An associate relayed the second example of the risk involved in lacking the respect of neighbors to me after I had returned to New York from my first summer research trip. Mita gossiped over the phone with me about Angela, a woman in her midthirties, who has two children and lived, at that time, with her baby father. Angela could frequently be heard screaming at her baby father, children, or no one in particular, from within the confines of her yard. Neighbors often speculated that she must be possessed because of her irrational ranting. One of my neighborhood associates once told me that she wanted to "push a stone in her mouth" because she yelled and screamed so much.[20] Upon my return to New York, I was speaking on the phone with Mita. She asked me if I remembered the possessed woman and went on to tell me that she had been beaten to the point of hospitalization by a group of men who she had publicly accused of being "batty" men.[21] Mita continued, somewhat laughingly, telling me "not a soul would help her." This type of public spectacle would generally draw a sizeable crowd to the scene, and, as Mita indicated, if she had had a positive reputation as a member of the community, one of her friends would have intervened on her behalf. These two events illustrate the social capital, including influence and greater personal safety, that accompanies positive reputation, and the vulnerability created by lack of participation in sociable acts that accrue respect within the community.

These events also illustrate the prevalence of interpersonal violence in Guy Town. Violence is almost always on the table as a possible method of conflict resolution. A person's capacity to utilize violence is a component of his or her personal power and reputation. However, in order to accrue respect, a person must understand when violence is appropriate and how to successfully commit a violent act. Failure to respond appropriately or to fight effectively is a source of embarrassment and usually catalyzes shaming practices enacted through community gossip.

The point about appropriate violence was driven home for me one day when there was rampant gossip circulating throughout Guy Town about a twenty-six-year-old social pariah. He had lived in the United States from the age of ten but had been deported several months prior after allegedly being imprisoned on a domestic violence charge. His deportation had landed him in the middle of Guy Town through family connections, but he was widely viewed as a suspicious stranger by residents and was notable for his clear Brooklyn accent. The scuttlebutt was that he had drawn a gun on a respected elder community member during an interpersonal conflict. The conflict was ended when a group of neighbors intervened. Word spread quickly that the deportee, as he was known in Guy Town, had inappropriately introduced a gun into the dispute. Later, additional gossip circulated that another area youth was talking about killing him and making it look like "the JLP" had done it. The justification for this murderous plan was that the deportee consistently disrespected the wrong people.[22]

On one of my follow-up trips, I, once again, encountered this young man, who was now often if not always seen carrying a Bible. Given his inability to generate respect and gain a positive reputation, it appeared that he had become Christian with a capital C, a rare choice for a man of his age. Joining the church provided him with new forms of protection in that, as a respectable Christian, he was able to join a community of support that provided an alternative to the male sociality of Guy Town, though the church community certainly also overlapped with the Guy Town community. Additionally, being a Christian enabled the young man to circumvent the expectations of ghetto masculinity, which he had not been successful in performing, because he could claim new behavioral constraints prescribed by his religious affiliation. Wilson, in his analysis of reputation and respectability, points to the unique position of Seventh Day Adventists, who he describes as "forswearing" the social requirements of reputation because their religious beliefs condemn many of the behaviors required to accrue reputation, including drinking, gambling, and premarital sex (Wilson 1973, 185). In his estimation, the Adventists' rejection of reputation amounts to an inability to achieve respect, which ultimately leads them to become "respect*able* before their time" (emphasis mine) (Wilson 1973, 185). However, the example of the Brooklyn deportee demonstrates that even respectability acquired through religious affiliation can be utilized as a social strategy within an environment that is extremely dangerous for young men.

Most of the interpersonal violence I witnessed in Guy Town occurred between women or young boys. The explanation that Flava gave for this pattern was that violence between men is more likely to escalate to the level of fatality and so is resorted to less often and, also, that conflict between men is often resolved over a drink at the rum bar.

Conclusion

Generosity, violence, and respect, in the context of this Jamaican ghetto community, which is characterized by widespread formal unemployment, are all resources critical to survival. This is not to say that all community residents take part in the three equally. Each variable is utilized differently by different community members based on their age, gender, employment status, and personal beliefs. The three elements, as resources, are also crucial to understanding local patronage practice because they constitute, in part, the patron's social power.

The retraction of the Jamaican state has intensified the need for, and retooled the meaning of, moral economies of wealth redistribution, contributing to the intensification of local patronage practices and informal power structures. Under neoliberal logic, these practices have also been reimagined as enactments of self-reliance and privatized social support. Choices with regard to sharing and the use of violence are integrally linked to personal strategies for acquiring respect and reputation within specific social contexts where wealth redistribution, the performance of normative masculinity, and the deployment of violence must be evaluated and used appropriately in order to maximize social capital. It is my contention that the private patronage relationships and informal power structures that have also grown out of this value system ultimately undermine the legitimacy of the state and its actors in the eyes of ghetto residents by providing them with economic support and personal protections that the state has failed to provide. Local recognition of the lack of concern for the vulnerability of ghetto residents on the part of the state coupled with the intimacy and efficiency of patron figures has ultimately served to solidify community loyalties to those who most effectively provide care. The need for such community patrons and the power they wield both informally and within the formulation of the state has only intensified, as I will demonstrate in the next chapter.

CHAPTER 2

"Give thanks for that man deh fi di place"

Patronage, Power, and Shifting Burdens of Care

The Patronage Landscape

Patronage, in Guy Town, is a multilayered system that includes different sorts of patrons who provide different kinds of resources. As background to the more detailed discussion of the patronage of Dads, the record producer, I will briefly highlight the activities of other patrons in Guy Town and the wider area. The first is a local entrepreneur who runs a retail shop and serves as a patron providing other types of resources and services to members of the community. The second is a political patronage arrangement, which involves the People's National Party and its agents as well as agents of the local ghetto power structure. Political patronage in relation to the formation of garrison communities in Jamaica has been heavily analyzed by political and social scientists (Chevannes 1992; Figueroa 1994; Stone 1985). From the 1970s onward, it has become a regular part of the national discourse around the problems of crime and violence in Kingston, as well as the popular discourse among the working class, expressed through popular music, regarding the hypocrisy of the Jamaican political system. However, the loyalty of party supporters has much deeper roots than those created solely through patronage. Contemporary party support is integrally tied to the formation of the two parties during the 1930s and the racial and class affiliations that developed from their respective trade union and anticolonial orientations (Phillips 1988; Post 1978). It must also be noted that the support given the People's National Party by poor black populations, like those residing in Guy Town and Perry Town, was also fostered by the strides toward social and political inclusion made by Michael Manley during the democratic socialist period (Stephens and Stephens 1986). Therefore, the political patronage activities that I am describing here are only one small aspect of a broader political process. The two accounts, which are illustrative of economic and social arrangements that exist throughout Jamaica, will provide comparative material with which to examine the unique patronage of the dancehall record producer in Guy Town.

A Local Entrepreneur

When you open the metal gate to Mr. Lee's shop, a dusty courtyard containing neatly stacked plastic beer crates and a self-serve glass cooler full of soda, beer, and rum cream greet you. Groups of young men linger near the wall of the shop talking soccer, and people pass in and out of the yard making small piecemeal purchases—one diaper, a Cup O'Noodles, two beers, a cigarette, prepaid cellular phone cards—purchases that reveal the minute-to-minute economy of the community. A dark, narrow, iron-gated area has been built onto the side of the stucco building. This enclosure contains a wooden counter with a cash box where business is transacted. Mr. Lee, a mixed Chinese and Irish Jamaican, sits behind the counter serving customers and collecting money. Mr. Lee, by his own account, has been part of Perry Town for more than fifty years. His parents owned and operated the local shop before he took it over twelve years prior to my arrival in 2001. Though he didn't want me to record our conversation, he willingly talked with my assistant and me about his experience as a businessman and patron while I took notes and he cashiered.[1] He told me that twelve years ago the shop, then run by his father, was robbed, and in the process his father was pistol-whipped and later died in the hospital of a brain hemorrhage. The thieves, who were notorious gunmen according to Mr. Lee, were caught by the police and extrajudicially executed. Mr. Lee then noted that this was a period of political instability in the area, and the JLP and PNP were competing over territory. I expressed amazement that Mr. Lee had chosen to remain in the area after this incident, but it was explained to me that his role in the community provides him with a measure of protection. As Flava, the man who introduced me to Mr. Lee, stated, if anyone tried to rob Mr. Lee, they would be killed. He told us that now during times of instability the shop remained open and that he would lock the outer gate and conduct business through it rather than the one he is usually enclosed behind inside the yard. He also told me that he keeps only three or four employees, on an informal basis. These employees are all relatives because, Mr. Lee said, outsiders might try to figure out how the business operates in order to rob him.

I asked him if he thought that the shop staying open during times of instability made people in the community more loyal to him, and he said he thought it did. He then continued, on this theme of loyalty, to describe the annual Valentine's Day dance that he throws, providing liquor and other favors. I did not know at the time, but later realized that the ability to keep a successful dance indicates a level of power and respect. He provides something to the community in the form of a night of entertainment, where he hires sound systems to play music and provides beer and liquor for purchase, and community members express their appreciation to him by attending the event and buying his refreshments.[2]

I then asked Mr. Lee if the men hanging around in the yard were a regular crowd, and he told me no, that they were, in fact, waiting to do business with him. Toward the end of the visit, two of these men, tall and lanky with long dread locks, interrupted, saying they wanted to ask Mr. Lee a favor. He excused himself and invited the men to sit on the bench where my assistant and I had been. We moved with Flava into the yard, where the discussion of the area's champion soccer team continued. As Mr. Lee later told us, the two men had wanted him to lend them some money for airfare to go to England. He told them that times were tight and money was not flowing, so he couldn't afford that kind of outlay at the moment. He explained to me that part of his business was lending people money in exchange for valuables, such as a piece of jewelry, in what sounded like a pawn brokerage arrangement. In observing his transactions during the period of the interview, it also became clear that his shop extended credit to people who could not immediately pay for their purchases. The credit was noted in a notebook kept by the cash box. Flava indicated later that Mr. Lee would also cash paychecks for people, many of whom lack bank accounts.

Mr. Lee's participation in patronage through the provision of services that create some level of financial flexibility through alternative business practices enables him to maintain a positive reputation and a position of importance within the local economy and heightened levels of respect within the community. This arrangement enhances his ability to do business in the ghetto because he has developed a strong reputation, which generates customer loyalty and local protection from theft and violence.

Political Patronage and Donsmanship

Historically, intercommunity violence and selectively distributed financial incentives have been strategically utilized by political patrons to maintain party power by consolidating voter loyalty. Discussion of these blatant manipulations of voting populations has become central to public discourses around government corruption, in part because of the uncontrolled side effects of these practices, even though long-standing party loyalties have deeper historical roots, which pre-date the predominance of garrison politics (Post 1978). Through the distribution systems produced and maintained by the two major parties, the People's National Party and Jamaica Labour Party, semiautonomous organized crime networks were inadvertently created. While being demonstrably effective in quelling community crime and violence, political patronage has consolidated the wealth and power of "area leaders" and their associates, which, at times, results in violent power struggles impacting large areas of downtown Kingston.

Political patronage involves both the area affiliated political party, in this case the People's National Party, represented by the member of Parliament, party employees who act on the MP's behalf, and area leaders or "dons." Dons once served as brokers between political parties and local communities, but many now enjoy relative autonomy from the party system through engagement in "legitimate" business enterprises and participation in organized crime networks that traffic drugs and firearms between Latin America and the United States.[3]

The 1970s are a landmark decade in which political violence took hold. In the early 1960s, after independence, the two primary political parties, the People's National Party and the Jamaica Labour Party, attempted to strengthen their power in poor communities using strategies akin to gerrymandering. Here, rather than redistricting constituencies, parties constructed housing schemes that were then selectively populated with party supporters. Evidence suggests that the use of housing as a tool in national politics began as early as the late 1930s and early 1940s (Robotham 2003). Party loyalty was also bolstered through the provision of scarce benefits to these inner-city communities in exchange for votes. Residents were supplied with weapons and training so that they could route out and defend themselves from nonsupporters, demonstrating that the social value of these populations was defined by their service to power rather than by a commitment to their dignity as persons or to their rights as citizens. These areas, classified "garrisons" by Carl Stone, a noted Jamaican political scientist, grew to take on lives of their own during the 1980s, featuring local organized crime networks headed by leaders called dons or area leaders that now provide residents with protection and resources (Stone 1985). Whereas the political parties at one time employed these dons, the growth of the drug trade enabled them to strike out on their own. The growth of the drug trade also contributed to an influx of illegal arms that now plague the country and contribute to the high murder rate that is largely concentrated in poor communities (Harriott 2000).

The residue of political patronage arrangements taints Jamaican electoral politics into the present. While the heightened murder rates associated with election periods peaked in the 1980s, each election is anticipated with careful planning and speculation over the possibility of violence, theft of ballot boxes, and other methods of ballot-box tampering, as well as manipulation of voting lists and voter identification (A. Waters 1989).

Election Time

In Guy Town there are scars on the crowded landscape that serve as reminders of past political violence. One such reminder is a vast expanse of "bush" that has been cleared of all architecture. Looking out over this field of overgrown scrubland from Guy Town, the viewer's eye is suddenly halted by a pastel-painted, multistoried housing development on the other side. The development stands in a Jamaica Labour Party garrison. Residents of these two communities can peer at each other across the verdant, vine-covered boundary, which seems serene, nearly pastoral, until the reasons for its notoriety are revealed. At one time this expanse was a site of contention for the two political parties, and members of each community tried to claim it for their constituency. The shells of firebombed dwellings still stand as a reminder of the families that were killed or driven out of their homes in the effort to purge the community of residents suspected of loyalty to the JLP. Since the ground clearing, gunmen from the rival areas have used the bush as camouflage, enabling them to creep across community borders that they wouldn't be able to transgress openly. It has also served as a dumping ground for victims of political rivalry and other types of violent crime. During periods of intercommunity conflict, residents dwelling on this border relocate, pushing further toward the center of Guy Town as a means of escape from the inherent danger of residing in such an exposed location. This pressure intensifies the overcrowding in more sheltered areas of the community during periods of tribal war.[4]

Guy Town is located within a larger PNP constituency, whose voting patterns remain consistent with those of a garrison. According to the Citizens Action for Free and Fair Elections report on the 1997 Jamaican general election, more than 100 percent of the constituency's residents voted for the People's National Party candidate for member of Parliament, indicating a uniform lack of dissent formally if not in daily practice, (Citizens Action for Free and Fair Elections 1998). This statistic indicates that all registered voters voted for the PNP candidate and that tampering occurred, which inflated voting numbers to a rate greater than the number of citizens legally entitled to vote in the constituency.

The year I conducted my research, 2002, was an election year. Although I feared that election violence, in addition to creating casualties and disrupting lives, would prohibit my entering the community, the period was relatively peaceful. Even though those present could hear a marked increase in the sound of gun shots coming from neighboring communities at war, and a stray bullet had flown into Guy Town Square, nicking the colorfully painted mural depicting the faces of Wicked Times's stable of performers, internally things remained cautiously calm.

There was, however, a clear change in the feeling of the area for the two months leading up to the determined election date, October 16. At the end of August, Mita commented to me that she wished I didn't have to be around for the upcoming election because sometimes "it's not nice." However, she assured me that we were all safe within the community because "the men bleach" and come to some agreements and that it's out on the main roads that there's a problem.[5]

The first change I noticed, along with the preponderance of residents wearing the color orange, the color associated with the PNP, and the pro-PNP graffiti scrawled on the normally pristine cinderblock walls, was the tight monitoring of people's comings and goings. Cars entering the community were closely scrutinized, particularly if they were unfamiliar.

The second change I noticed was the increased number of vehicles carrying visitors to the corner that housed a group of men known to serve as community "security." One evening as Alesha and I sat watching the cars driving in and pulling out, she commented that they were full of "pure gunmen." About two weeks before the elections were to be held, Alesha explained to me that one section of the PNP constituency that contained Guy Town was warring with a neighboring JLP area. She told me that Guy

Town, while not directly involved, "backs up" the embattled section since they are all PNP supporters. She said that early on in the week Guy Town had been "pure tall up tall up and short up short up" and that a bullet had hit the Wicked Times mural in Guy Town Square.[6] She then proceeded to describe, in great detail, a new gun that had arrived in the community; a gun fitted with a spotting scope. Communities with particularly impressive weaponry become noted for that. Krystal and Alesha discussed one gun owned by another community that was well known in the downtown area and had been nicknamed "bammers." Bammers was said to be so large that it had to be transported in a wheelbarrow. They also mentioned that certain prized firearms would be leant between communities fighting for the same party. Krystal then piped in to tell me that women in conflicting areas often contribute to the war by standing opposite each other dancing, yelling, and throwing rocks and panties.[7]

During the months following the announcement of the upcoming election, the presence of People's National Party representatives in the community increased. Most notably, significant infrastructural improvements were made, including fresh paving of the crumbling asphalt streets adjacent to locations associated with prominent community members, including the corner associated with the area leader and the community Youth Organization, which is identified with the record producer–patron. The appearance of these improvements was no mystery to community members, who somewhat cynically indicated that the projects were yet another sign that election time had come.

Supplementing the infrastructural improvements, PNP representatives had also arrived to distribute work to constituents.[8] As Alesha relayed the story to Martin, a PNP representative had arrived with $250,000 and identified an area of vacant land that needed to be cleared. The representative had given a local shopkeeper the money to distribute to residents for the ground clearing. Alesha explained to me that this was basically a way of paying people to vote because, since workers would have money and would have "food run," they wouldn't be able to complain that the PNP had never done anything for them.[9] As it turned out, the shopkeeper kept the money for himself, purchasing new stock, appliances, and a gun, a result that was irritating to the listeners and induced Martin to comment that he never expects anything of the PNP's "scarce benefits and spoils" anyway.

In addition to PNP representatives, the member of Parliament was also more frequently visible. About two weeks prior to election day, the MP arrived in the area with a group that included his special assistant, his bodyguard, and a few other people. Their arrival was met with excitement within the community as it interrupted daily routines and contributed a new distraction. Residents gathered in the street around the MP and observed his activities. The aim of the visit was to evaluate the condition of the gully that carried run off wastewater out of the community. Gullies are known to fall into disrepair, becoming refuse repositories that develop into health hazards.

The MP, his assistant, and his bodyguard all recognized me from a previous tour of the constituency and visit to their ministry. Their recognition of me inspired some telling jokes among the women whose corner I regularly inhabited. Krystal laughed about the MP knowing me and requested that I ask him to fix my friend's house, as her father's roof had been leaking. Then Alesha commented that of everyone that lives in Guy Town, the MP recognized only me. She followed that up by saying that she wasn't going to vote for him because she'd asked him for some money and he hadn't provided her with any. Their comments revealed their feelings of alienation from the MP and from party politics in general, as well as a broader perception of their lack of value in the eyes of the state. Community residents' appraisals of the MP also reflect local standards of reputation and mutuality, which the MP had failed to meet from the perspective of those who had asked something of him. When I told them that the MP had said that I looked comfortable in the community, Krystal replied, "Yeah, because he's afraid to come down here. He doesn't come down without all of his bodyguards." Alesha followed this up by saying that the MP thought community residents might "eat" me. Though residents would often comment that they would not vote for the incumbent MP, I never heard anyone say they would vote for the JLP candidate. This gap highlights the nature of garrison politics and party loyalty. The uniform voting pattern really does not indicate uniform consent for the particular candidate but instead indicates a deep party loyalty related to people's racial and class affiliations, personal identities, and sense of belonging in the community, in addition to fear of repercussions for dissent.

The issue of personal and party loyalty was again brought to my attention during a community Youth Organization meeting, which was sparsely attended by four or five members. Flava had come to meet me in Guy Town prior to the meeting and was invited to join in, even though he was a resident of Perry Town. The area he resides in is thought to be more solidly affiliated with and supported by the MP than Guy Town, and Flava is known to actively support the MP. A few club members took the opportunity to discuss problems they found with the MP since Flava was there as both a sounding board and a "devil's advocate."

The loyalty issues were particularly well articulated in this context since Wicked Times's CEO, whose patronage activities support Guy Town, had announced that he would be entering politics for the first time, running for People's National Party MP in another ghetto community. Guy Town residents made their support for Dads clear by wearing his campaign T-shirts and marching more than a mile to appoint him on nomination day, even though his candidacy would not have direct political implications on their community. Tensions came out when Mary, a club member in her fifties, suggested that she wanted to transfer her vote to the producer's potential constituency rather than voting for the local MP. She and other club members agreed that they would not vote. Flava tried to clarify Mary's position, saying that she wanted to transfer her vote to support the person she received benefits from. One young man intervened, insisting that they could not let the JLP candidate for prime minister be elected and that while the choices of MP weren't great, having Edward Seaga serve as prime minister again would be worse. Mary then continued with her argument, explaining that it was impossible for certain people to see the MP one on one. She gave the example that if the MP received one letter from Guy Town and one letter from Perry Town, the one from Guy Town would be thrown away, dramatizing by throwing the leaf of paper in her hand to the floor of the clubhouse. It was a widely held belief that the MP felt less responsibility for Guy Town because of Dads's presence. Flava then suggested that if people felt that way they should "vote Labourite." The vice president of the Youth Organization, a man in his early thirties, who worked as an administrator at the local high school, became indignant, saying, "Never do that! I'm born PNP!"

"Calling the Shots"

My first introduction to the area leader was at the government ministry where I was spending the day with the member of Parliament's special assistant during the first days of my research.[10] The area leader was a hefty man in his late thirties wearing a netted marina undershirt with a loose-fitting, button-down, short-sleeve shirt over it, and his neck was decorated with gold chains. He was at the ministry to attend a meeting with the member of Parliament and a few other prominent businesspeople. As he entered the special assistant's office, the reaction of the other people in the room made clear that he was a figure who required deference.

The area leader approached the special assistant with a complaint. The member of Parliament had acquired a number of wheelchairs to distribute in his constituency, which had been given out one per person to residents who needed them. The area leader complained that he had received only one wheelchair, the same as the other residents. Luckily, the special assistant had kept extra wheelchairs aside in the office and was able to supply him with a few additional ones to give out as he chose. This was my first clue that the area leader was, indeed, someone who needed to be "managed" by the member of Parliament in order for things to run smoothly in the constituency. Their relationship was one of negotiation, not one in which the state's authority was clearly differentiated from the area leader's authority and had marked supremacy over the powerful residents of marginal communities, areas that often prove problematic to and definitive of the operations of the state (Das and Poole 2004). In addition, the area leader's presence and power within the government office building, the officially sanctioned domain of the member of Parliament, quite literally demonstrated how that which is considered marginal in terms of space as well as social power can also be mobile and central.

Martin once explained the role of the area leader to me during an interview about the community power structure. His articulate description freely spoken in the privacy of my uptown apartment highlighted the ambiguous relationship between official state and private community power structures. When I asked him who has power in the area, he described two primary forces. The first are the dons, who he called the "local representatives" for governing the community. The second are the politicians, who he described as "people of the outer city or out of the community." According to Martin, the rules of the community and guidelines for community justice are created by the don or area leader, and "whenever certain rules are broken, now we see that instead of being taken to the police station whereby justice through the normal means is . . . wayward, takes a long time. With the inner-city justice system . . . people might say it's fair, but surely though it's swift. It's swift and decisive." He continued, explaining that the trials initiated by the don and his cronies occur immediately, and sentencing ranges from a strapping to being locked up in a fowl coop with the chickens still inside. He then indicated with laughter in his voice that in some instances the chickens are housed at the top of the coop with the prisoner at the bottom, and he told me, "You know what comes down, and we are not talking rain! Right?" He explained that most communities similar to Guy Town and Perry Town have their own little prisons where people might be kept for a couple of days and fed crackers, bread, and water. In extreme instances, he admitted that people might be shot and killed if the don finds it warranted. Despite the efficiency of this local justice system, Martin indicated that the system also had its problems, including the fact that the don and his cronies might choose to punish people for crimes that they themselves are also committing. He raised the example of men who are beaten for having "relationships" with teenage girls, while the don and his cronies are doing the same thing. Such situations create a gray area that demonstrates to the community that power and affiliation have their privileges. The intricacies of the power dynamics within garrison communities like Guy Town became profoundly clear when Martin went on to say:

> But then again, you find the people feeling powerless to change that because [. . .] they don't have the power. They have support of the member of Parliament, but they don't have the financial backative and they don't have the power of guns that these dons have. So therefore they succumb and they continue to will over their power not to the police, but to the dons and their cronies. So whenever there is a flare-up of violence in the area, the dons are the ones who comes around and, say for example, [Perry Town] and [their JLP rival] might inna, the don might come around and tell everybody, "you know se, bwoy, everything is alright, we are going to stay up all night." We call it bleaching. "So we are going to bleach tonight . . ." and whatever. So that might happen so the people dem feel comfortable and them trust because those are the people they see on a daily basis. No matter what they do, those are the people who they see on a daily basis. Because I might, for example, rape a young woman and I was shot in my foot [leg]. But yet still, I will be after coming out of the hospital and still on the corner with the don shaking his hand and [. . .] talking with him. So I don't know if it's out of fear or out of respect that after somebody is disciplined by [. . .] the don and his cronies, they still show them that they have 'nuff respect and they still talk with them even though they . . . you know, have been dealt a bad blow.

Here, it can be seen that the community justice system has many of the same features of the state justice system in that there are set punishments for particular infractions of community law. Martin refers to community members' participation in this system as a "willing over" of their power to the don rather than to the police because the don's justice system is more efficient than the state's system. Community members also regularly see direct benefits from the don's power structure, whereas the benefits of the state power structure appear more intermittent as well as distant from the daily lives of residents.

The acceptance of these alternative power structures coheres with the neoliberal tenet that local settings should be the primary sites for the care and regulation of populations. From the perspective of citizens, however, these arrangements are often read as a betrayal on the part of the state, which cannot be depended on for the provision of basic services or the administration of incorruptible justice. In the context of the inner city, the don becomes a figure who is trusted and depended on for immediate results and support, whereas the state, its representatives, and its bureaucratic processes are largely seen as inefficient, outside the community, and as sources of suspicion.

Returning to the interview, Martin went on to describe the rules of the community justice system and how this system relates with state-sanctioned justice through the police force, once again emphasizing that it is a conscious decision among community members to cede the administration of justice to the local hierarchy rather than state-backed personnel. When I asked Martin how people know what the rules are, he replied:

> Well, they are basically rules of life. [. . .] I know that I mustn't go into your house and steal your stuff, but yet still there are people who do it. Now with that system, with just the police station, that would have been rampant, but with the system of the don and his cronies being around, I mean you can leave your door open! The only person who is going to do that is probably the cronies of the don and if it can proven that [. . .] the crony was the one who did that, he too will be disciplined. So, in a way, it's more effective than the justice system and it has its other side where, as I told you before, they are doing wrong and they are beating someone who is doing the same thing. Like inna Jamaica we say "thief a beat thief." You understand? [laughing] It's effective in a sense and in a different setting gives one person too much power over a group of people. But in most cases the people voluntarily give away that power. Not unconsciously they give away that power to the dons and not to the police. So whenever police comes around they will hide the don and their cronies, they block, they might

keep weapons for them and stuff, basically because they see them as protecting them.

He went on to explain how the don figure wins the trust, approval, and respect of community members so that he may successfully operate within the area. This relationship is multifaceted and based on the don's fulfillment of basic financial needs, in addition to residents' willing over of their trust and care based on expectations of fairness and familiarity. Since the dons have financial clout, Martin indicated, they are able to help community residents meet their day-to-day needs, including assisting children to attend school by providing uniforms and sponsoring back-to-school treats, where supplies like backpacks and notebooks are distributed. Loyalty is additionally bolstered when dons use their influence to empower those with the least social capital. For example, an elderly woman might need to get to the hospital, but not have the money to pay for the trip. After being refused by several local drivers, she might approach the don for assistance. In this scenario, Martin suggested that the don might instruct a taxi driver to carry the woman to the hospital without any argument. "So you cannot tell that woman that he is a bad man, though he will execute somebody just like that." To Martin, dons are not purely negative or positive forces in the community, but can be both helpful and harmful.

We then discussed the relationship between local power hierarchies and state structures, which are necessarily interwoven given the origin of local justice systems in party politics and the "problematic" nature of inner-city communities to the operations of the state. Garrison residents simultaneously submit to the don's control, which might be seen, at particular moments, as an ambiguous adjunct to state control. Given that tourism and foreign investment are crucial to the Jamaican economy, the appearance of safety and stability is a key component of national development. The apparent chaos in the form of crime, violence, and idle bodies that purportedly emanates from ghetto communities creates an impediment to images of the island both as a vacation paradise and as a hospitable business environment, while simultaneously reinforcing the neoliberal multicultural ideology that some people are simply unfit for global citizenship.

Martin described the changing relationship between area leaders and their affiliated political parties, which is based on a shift in access to resources. He indicated that dons interact with state officials when there's a need for work in the community, but that this was now a less frequent occurrence since "dons have become more independent because of the influx of drugs and gun trade now in Jamaica." Martin suggested that given this change in access to resources, the dons were now more likely to deal with MPs and other officials when election time draws near in order to profit from assisting with voter turnout. When considering election periods, he indicated that the dons were more likely to work with MPs "when the MP need votes, but before that the dons would negotiate with them, make sure that various works takes place within the community, road works, constructions and stuff like that so as to make sure that the don is benefiting from such an event, right?" Income generated through international trade in firearms and drugs, according to Martin, has created a situation that has provided dons with additional tools for brokering power relations with politicians. Dons can now provide goods and services to their communities without access to state resources. Members of Parliament are now forced into more subtle negotiations with local power structures during election periods because the resources they used to dangle in front of their constituents in exchange for cooperation have plummeted in value. Martin explained that government contracts and access to privileged information, in addition to the previously mentioned provision of public works, are all key bargaining chips.

> A couple of weeks ago, you might notice that with our minister of government [. . .] there are men who are on payrolls who don't go to work, but they are paid from [government projects]! So these are some of the things that takes place with the dons and MPs. They make sure that people, like the don and his cronies, are taken care of in terms of jobs and stuff. Well, not jobs. [laughing] I wouldn't say jobs, because they are not working, but a salary is provided for them. So these are the service they provide. The main service is to ensure that the MP wins his seat and then his payback is to make sure that the don and his cronies or the community benefit in various ways, providing jobs, make sure that whenever there are things cropping up, whenever there is going to be a raid, the MP might call the don or make sure there is some pipeline through which the don can hear that well, "a raid is going to happen so you know you just a clean up the area." "Lock all the machine [firearms] them" and thing like that. So there are instances like that where a don might get a call from a high police official who say, "Yo, lock the machine them, a raid a go happen at such and such a time." Probably now they have clamped down on it a little bit. I've seen where snap raids just take place and the don don't really have a clue

what was going on. Um, but those are some of the linkages that have been set up within the area. You know, contracts are provided for the dons, especially those who are educated.

He followed up, denoting that not many of the dons are educated and they mostly have "street sense." With this "street knowledge" and "orientation," they cannot be easily tricked, but "in order to read and write, they are not as proficient as that." The less educated dons might receive stipends and salaries from their affiliated MP, whereas the more educated might set up businesses and receive government contracts. He continued, "These contracts might extend outside of the community itself. You know so, they too benefit in a number of ways, make sure the MP wins his seat and the MP makes sure that they're taken care of financially."

Martin then described the changing role of MPs during periods of tribal war. He specified that the more blatant provision of weaponry by government officials has been publicly recognized and is no longer tolerated, and also intimated that dons' independent access to firearms has created the need for more subtle forms of illicit parliamentary support. Whenever there is intercommunity war, "the MP makes sure there is enough money to feed the warriors," he told me laughingly and then added that it is also important for the MP to "make sure ammunition is around." Martin then sketched out Jamaica's long history of MPs providing weaponry to garrison communities going back to the 1970s. These arrangements are difficult to disrupt, and he described a time when "MPs took guns and handed them out in person. [. . .] Now because the dons have their own little connections the most they might ask is for a funding [. . .] and they get what they want to get." He told me that by the late 1990s and early 2000s, the dons had become more independent of the politicians, and the dons now "call the shots and command the community without the support of the MP." Prior to this time, the don was dependent on the MP because the MP provided the don's "salary," so the don had to be careful about what he did and what he said to the MP in order to maintain his livelihood. Now that dons can acquire resources from other places like New York, England, and rural Jamaica through the drug trade, they are more independent. According to Martin, "they can call the shots. If the MP did make decisions he doesn't like he can say, 'Go to hell. I'm doing this.' Right?" He then qualified his assertion that dons enjoy newly unchecked power, advising me that the MP still has the ultimate recourse in turning back to the state's justice system when control over a constituency has been completely lost. Martin's statement reveals the manipulability of the official justice system by those with state sanctioned power, further bolstering the perspective that state justice is viewed as alien and unpredictable by ghetto residents.

> But he has to be careful, in a way, because the MP still has the backative of the justice system and they can manipulate that justice system in a way which has been done over and over again. When a don might pass his place, the MP might just decide to get rid of him through the justice system. Make him a wanted man and then soon him have to be up and down running and then he's cornered and killed by the police. Right, so that was the case in an earlier time, but now they are more independent, they can call the shots, they can import the guns themselves, they can have the ammunition by themselves now, they can command certain things by themselves. Most of them have established various businesses, as fronts to hide their various operation whether be it gun running or drug running, but most of them are involved in stuff like that.

When I asked if the situation in the community is better or worse now that the shift from strict political patronage to patronage facilitated through the drug and gun trade has taken place, Martin replied that he thought it was better in a way because the benefits to the community are more consistent. He also mentioned that "the various gang wars or the various tribal wars that has happened in the past are not now happening because you are not finding that people are fighting for a JLP or a PNP anymore. It's more about guns and drugs." What this means to area residents is that they can now talk to people from politically rival communities in a way that they could not during the more politically divided period. He said, "In the 1980s and stuff you couldn't wear green, you couldn't wear red [orange], go certain places, you would have been killed. You can go there and talk about your 'P' and talk about your 'J' and you are tolerated as long as you do not interfere with their drug running and their gun running, you are okay." During this part of the conversation, Martin expressed a belief that the shift away from political patronage to patronage based on the illegal activities of dons may have had a positive result within downtown communities because the flow of resources to poor people is less dependent on elevation cycles. Further, the violence that had been party-based tribal war in the past, which divided populations on the basis of residential location and the political affiliations of these locations, is now, instead, the result of competition over the drug and gun trades. The new inducements to violence involve the interruption of illegal activities and, for that reason, violence is less arbitrary because it targets the people directly participating in criminal networks. However, it is evident that the activities of the dons are still intimately tied to political parties, even if it is in a less determinate way.

The Member of Parliament

An interview with the member of Parliament for the wider Guy Town area revealed the interdependent nature of the state and unofficial power structures, how the MP views his responsibilities for the maintenance of order within this environment, and how the dons are implicated in the process.

When I asked the member of Parliament what his role was in maintaining order in his potentially volatile constituency, he indicated that rather than attempting to dismantle the local justice system, he utilizes it to his benefit. This is a controversial position, which has left him open to public criticism in the past, particularly after he attended the funeral service of the previous area leader. He explained that his role was "multifaceted" and that the member of Parliament has traditionally heavily influenced the area. The MPs for the area were commonly government ministers or "in the leading ranks of the party," and for that reason, he asserted, the MP's views and opinions are "closer to law." He claimed that he operated at somewhat of a disadvantage because there are "certain activities" that he doesn't condone, "but at the same time, if there are persons who have influence, the critical task is to move them towards using their influence positively." He described community-based methods of problem solving as "very primitive" and then explained that his office seeks to use the hierarchical structure within the community when violent interactions occur. In order to mediate conflict the MP indicated that, in his experience, "the first community you visit must be the one which has been attacked. If you visit the one which attacks first, then when you go to the one that has been attacked, it will be disastrous." Having made that error in the past, he is now briefed prior to visiting the area that has been attacked, at times, he remarked, "with good cause." At these meetings, he asks area residents to identify their leaders or who "speaks for" them. The next step is to visit the rival community and repeat the same process. He then approaches people that are recognized throughout the constituency, but who are not involved in the conflict, to join him in a third meeting with the two conflicting areas, where they make an agreement that "what was, was." However, these truces are often fleeting, and there are frequent internal disagreements with regard to who should be identified as leaders. He instructs community members that, "if there is a problem, your job is to go to your leader and the leader's job is to go to the person up above for the next stage. If you can settle it, settle it, and, if you can't, you come to one of the constituency leaders." He went on to tell me that by looking at the crime rates, it appears that this system of mediation has worked but did add that "it's tedious and it is a lot of stupidity and backwardness. All the ingredients which created the problem in the first place come out and you have to listen to it and you can't be dismissive because they then think you are taking sides and so." In the end, he said, those three meetings might take nine hours, "but you really hope that it will hold for a time."

Though violence is often isolated within particular poor communities, and for that reason has little effect on the rest of the city, intercommunity conflicts are not easily quelled, even with police intervention, and have required the MP to design particular dispute resolution techniques that conform to the established power structures of the conflicting communities. Here the MP also highlights the need for elected representatives of the state to maintain the appearance of neutrality. He confirms Martin's assertion that certain problems can and must be left for community residents to resolve on their own, both because the police are not an acceptable resource within the ghetto context and because some conflicts, while they may involve violence or criminality, are too small to require the MP's intervention.

When I went on to ask the MP about the dismantling of local power structures, his response also confirmed Martin's assertion about the interrelations of MPs and area leaders. He reiterated that, even as an agent of the state, he recognizes the efficacy of community justice and is reluctant to suggest to community residents that they can rely on the police for protection. His comment reveals the slippage between the state and the private, in that by suggesting the area leader's "review and intervention" is legitimate because of its efficiency, he demonstrates the ways in which these local power structures are, in actuality, state sanctioned, if not entirely controllable by the state (J. Comaroff and J. L. Comaroff 2006; Galvin 2011, 2012; Roitman 2006).[11] He is one of the few members of Parliament who willingly acknowledge this "public secret," though the "nuts and bolts" aspect of the MP's relationship to the local power structure remains relatively opaque. What does become clear through his account is that the power relations between the MP and area leader must be carefully negotiated. Given that area leaders are more intimately familiar with community members, and thereby often command pivotal influence over community activities, they can be crucial allies for an MP or impediments to plan implementation. With regard to the question posed about dismantling the don system, he told me that it didn't need to be dismantled when it could, instead, be utilized if the don "buys into" what the MP is doing. However, he claimed that his position was weakened because he refused to condone violence in any form. He explained,

> It weakens when you have dictated this process and then somebody violates it with violence because you can't tell them that the police will take care of it, because you know it's not true. But if you can, I know of specific instances where the police have a problem and they send it to the area leader because they know his review and intervention is much more swift than the formal justice system. No, it is not necessarily a bad thing. The bad thing is that if he is also corrupt or involved in illegal activities. That is a bad thing.

Given Martin's description of the system of punishments put in place within the local justice system, the MP's statements affirm that the state is also ceding some of its power to the dons because the punishments meted out to offenders, which include imprisonment, physical punishment, and even execution, issued outside the state legal system by private citizens would necessarily be classified illegal activities under Jamaican law. Representatives of the state are clearly aware of these systems and rely on them, to an extent, in situations where police involvement has proven ineffectual.

The public representation of the interconnected networks of government patronage and organized crime is a shell game of sorts. There always appears to be an evidentiary gap, which prohibits a clear assertion of wrongdoing from being established. In part, this is due to the nature of the system itself, which involves some of the most prominent businesspeople and politicians in the country, who are skilled at maintaining resource networks and keeping particular facts out of public sight. The character of this shell game became more apparent when I asked the MP about the difference between an area leader and a don and he replied, "I don't know." He then said,

> The definitions are always very strange to me. I seldom use them. I know what I know personally. In my constituency I know, but the fact is that any criminal or wanted person will receive no protection from me. The difficulty arises when people speak loosely about someone involved in criminal activity but no charges have been placed. I have seen that and, as you know, I will take immediate control because I refuse to back off. Because the fact is that there is someone in my constituency who was called a don by a major newspaper and who sued them and won a very big liable suit. The fact is that it is a very loose term, which is applied but I don't know what it means. If you tell me what it means, or what you mean by it, then I'll respond.

I clarified my question, indicating that my curiosity had been ignited by a sense that the term "area leader" is often used euphemistically. He responded, "Oh, it can be!" and then explained that area leader is a political term because the PNP structure includes area leaders, who are a "different thing" than a don. He told me that there are people in his constituency who "have had not so innocent pasts," and "one of the hypocritical things which we pursue is that the formal system utilizes such persons." He gave the example of a leader in his constituency with very close links to the police force, "and they are at the highest level, not illicit arrangement, but because they know in certain areas his intelligence network is superior to theirs, they often appeal to him. [. . .] At the same time they would never defend him if there were an accusation." Again, the area leader's intelligence network is acknowledged to be more effective than the state's and for the sake of maintaining control is utilized by the state as a supplement to the intelligence of the constabulary. The MP, refreshingly, admits to the hypocrisy of utilizing civilian intelligence networks that are not entirely divorced from criminality in order to solve crimes but does not go so far as to say that this relationship between the police and the area leader corrupts the pursuit of justice. There is a delicate balance that must be maintained here, where state agents now require the assistance of these community hierarchies, often based around organized criminal activities, but must not publicly condone lawlessness, which has been identified as a significant barrier to national development and transparent governance.

Recently this delicate balance was upset within the JLP government, when it was revealed that former prime minister Bruce Golding had furtively hired legal representation for the area leader of his Tivoli Gardens constituency in order to block his extradition to the United States on weapons and drug-smuggling charges. The exposure of what had been a publically recognized "secret" alliance between the JLP and organized criminal networks in Tivoli Gardens cracked open the social and political fissures in Jamaican society, resulting in civil unrest and police violence in Tivoli Gardens as residents sought to defend their leader from extradition, accusations by Jamaica's elite that Golding's decisions were illustrative of the corruption of Jamaican governance "from below," and ultimately, Golding's resignation in 2011.

Despite the public furor the revelation of these relationships aroused, as indicated by both Martin and the MP, lawlessness has become a critical tool for maintaining poor communities. Local patronage systems redistribute wealth, create a level of trust and respect, and, in a sense, contribute an admittedly delicate local order to spaces labeled unruly by the state.

The Fragility of "Informal Politics"

Though the interviews with the member of Parliament and many community residents indicated that the don system facilitated stability and security within garrison communities, the precarious nature of this stability soon became apparent. A series of events within Guy Town that began in April 2001, prior to my research period, and which continue into the present, demonstrates that changes in the power structure that might be desired by community members are largely attainable only through violent conflict rather than verbal negotiation. This violent conflict can disrupt and threaten the lives of all residents regardless of their relationship to the power structure.

In April 2001, the area leader for wider Perry Town was murdered by a group of men dressed in police uniforms, which led the member of Parliament to publicly hope the violent acts would not destroy nearly a decade of peace within the constituency. The peace was not shattered by this violent episode, and instead, the current area leader took over community governance.

However, in March 2003, an unsuccessful attempt was made on the current area leader's life. He was hospitalized in critical condition after being shot in a drive-by while playing dominoes on his corner. He managed to maintain control of the community even while hospitalized, though the incident created inter- and intracommunity tensions because of suspicions over the identities of the agents of the attack as well as the motives for the attack.[12]

An uneasy peace was maintained until April 2004, when disagreement from within the area leader's ranks came to a head over the construction of a multimillion-dollar public housing project within his territory. Conflict arose because the area leader was to be in charge of distributing the jobs related to the construction project to community residents, many of whom believed that the assignment of work would be biased toward particular community members. The result of this dissatisfaction was the splitting of the area leader's posse, some of whom joined up with former rival gangs, in order to remove the leader from power. These reconfigured rival gangs then clashed within the community, intimidating residents into leaving their homes with the use of scare tactics and firearms, also resulting in several fatalities as well as public school closings, curfews, and heavy police presence in the area. The member of Parliament convened community meetings intended to quell the situation. Up to the present, even after several attempts to overthrow the area leader within a decade's time, he has refused to give up his position. At one point, graffiti appeared within the community threatening that if the area leader were overthrown, the member of Parliament would also lose power.

Additionally, unusual incidents have taken place within the area, which indicate some residents' challenge to the rules of local authority. In order to counteract these actions, which might suggest a lapse in the local power structure, community justice has been purposefully instituted to make examples of those who have chosen to test the system. The primary example of this test and reassertion of power was the robbery of a bread truck in Guy Town. Under community law, robbery within the confines of the area is unacceptable. According to the local newspaper, the two men who performed the robbery were asked by the community dons to return the stolen money. Showing insolence to the local power structure, they refused and were summarily executed by agents of the community hierarchy, in a reassertion of control over law and order.

Political patronage arrangements, which have now morphed into patronage through organized crime, do provide a level of stability in poor communities even if the stability is maintained by illicit means and with the tacit approval of the state. However, the stability is a fragile one that requires ethical compromises on the part of agents of the state, who must turn a blind eye to infractions of Jamaican law in order to utilize local power structures for their own means. This form of patronage requires the same ingredients necessary for the acquisition of respect for ordinary community members and entrepreneurial patrons like Mr. Lee, as well as the patronage of members of black bourgeoisie, as I will demonstrate in the next section of this chapter. These ingredients include resources that can be utilized to appropriately respond to community member's needs: loyalty of community members, which can be used to accrue further wealth and protection, and the ability to correctly and effectively employ violence according to local community law.

The Record Producer as Patron

When I interviewed Delmar, we were sitting inside his regular spot, an old one-story building that, having lost its façade, now consisted only of three walls, a roof, and linoleum-tiled floor. A self-described "corner youth," Delmar was in his early twenties at our first meeting. I noticed his light "red" complexion and neatly cane-rowed hair, as he spoke about working odd construction jobs when they were available.[13] During our conversation, I asked him who he saw as having an influence on the community, and he responded, "One man alone in di place, man! One big man inna di place, man! You know who he is?" With my affirmative reply, Delmar added, "Right! Nobody else, that's [Dads]! You know that? Yeah, man, the likkle ghetto youth dem wish was he, you know? Yeah man, we love him like how Jesus Christ love the likkle children still, yeah man. Give thanks for that man deh fi di place still, you know?" His answer echoed other responses I had received to the same question, though depending on the proximity of the interviewee's residence to Guy Town Square, the center of Dads's operations in the community, reactions varied to include other significant figures, including the member of Parliament, the area leader, and church personnel.

Dads was in his midthirties when I began my fieldwork. He has dark skin and close-cut hair and typically wore blue jeans, a loose-fitting shirt, and basketball sneakers. At the time of our first interview, I noticed two gold teeth with decorative designs cut into them gleaming in his mouth when he spoke. As we sat in his air-conditioned office he told me that he had moved out of Guy Town in 1996, five years prior, but that he had been in Guy Town on a daily basis since then and still considers it his home, only utilizing his uptown residence in an upper-middle-class neighborhood as a place to sleep.

Dads's socialization within Guy Town endows him with deep ties to the area and an acute awareness of the subtleties of community life, as well as the practical challenges currently faced by Guy Town's residents. Dads's patronage is vital for residents of Guy Town. When asked why he directs so many resources toward the community, he echoed the sentiments of the other community residents I asked about sharing practices. Even though Dads's ownership of a prominent music production company places him on the fringe of the new Jamaican black bourgeoisie (Dads is respect*ed*, but not respect*able* in a manner that would allow him to attain social status under the normativity of the traditional Jamaican elite), and even though he and his family have relocated to a wealthy uptown neighborhood, his reply indicates that participation in community patronage is based on the same key ethics: empathy for those who must struggle for survival and the need to share "blessings" with others. He responded, "being a product of [Guy Town] [. . .] fortunately the light shined on me, so I think as long as I have the resources that I can put back something into the community, then I have to go that route." Though Dads poses his giving behavior as both a product of his socialization and in the familiar terms of "giving back to the community," others indicated to me that this generosity was also required of Dads so that he could continue participating in the life of Guy Town. This position is similar to Mr. Lee's in that his patronage role provides him with respect and protection from robbery and violence because of the reputation he has achieved. However, it was also frequently reiterated to me, particularly at times when people felt Dads was not doing enough, that Guy Town needs Dads in a way that Dads does not need Guy Town.

Maintaining "Order"

Socializing with the women who inhabit the corner adjacent to the community Youth Organization clubhouse and Guy Town Square became a valuable resource for developing an understanding of Dads's rights and responsibilities within Guy Town.[14] Though it was difficult to ascertain what Dads's disciplinary role in the area was, there were indications that he had some command over community activities, given that the reputation of the area was intimately linked with his own reputation and also to his attempts to attain respectability.[15]

This was demonstrated to me one afternoon when I arrived in Guy Town and it was clear that something out of the ordinary had occurred. A police jeep and two police cars were parked by a shop across from the

Skills Center. The police were obviously conducting an investigation, and a crowd of people had gathered to watch. On that particular day, Krystal, Alesha, and I were going to visit Krystal's father at Kingston Public Hospital, where he'd been admitted for some medical testing. I got into the taxi that was going to carry us to the hospital with one of the area's regular drivers and asked him what was going on. He told me that the police had busted a stolen-car ring that had been operating out of Guy Town. Krystal then told me that someone must have leaked information to the police, but Martin later indicated that someone driving one of the stolen cars had hit another car and that was when police suspicion was aroused. In no time the local television stations, CVM and TVJ, arrived on the scene to record news footage. A crowd of community members remained steadily throughout the afternoon until eventually they moved to Guy Town Square, where Dads had installed a television, to watch the story on the evening news.

Mita mentioned that Dads was going to be "vexed" because "things like this aren't supposed to be happening here." Krystal and Mita kept discussing how his phone must have been ringing off the hook, reflecting the fact that residents of Kingston and beyond associate his name with the rejuvenation of the community. Krystal later commented that if Dads stopped coming to Guy Town the area would "fall on its face."

I observed a further example of Dads's control over and responsibility for goings-on in the community one evening while Krystal sat on her corner with a crowd of children around her. She was lecturing a little girl, telling her that her speech did not "fit her size," and that she is a "school pickney dealing with grown people things." She asked her if her mother knew where she was and also asked where she lived. Krystal assured the girl that she wouldn't tell her mother but said that news travels fast and the children were "carrying her name out a road," so maybe the news would get back to her mother anyway.

After the girl left, Krystal explained to me that when the local children caught view of the girl, they chattered, "There's the one what get fucked yesterday." The girl came up and said she was looking for two men over on that side of the community. Krystal overheard the children's conversation and decided to intervene. The girl was only eleven years old, and the rumor was that an older boy in his early teens had given the girl $5,000 for sex. The girl claimed that this wasn't true. The next version of the story was that she had wanted to spend time with three boys, not have sex with them, but have them as friends. She had gone to an abandoned house with them, where the three of them had sex with her, gave her $150, and then took it back, leaving her with $30. This type of incident, in which a group of boys allegedly have consensual sex with, or rape, a girl is considered by some working-class Jamaicans to be an adolescent rite of passage for boys. In patois it is referred to as "running a battery."

Running a battery is one instance among many in which violence, in this case, specifically, sexual violence, has been normalized within poor communities. In her work on domestic violence ordinances in the Caribbean, with particular reference to the Bahamas, M. Jacqui Alexander has suggested that when normalized acts of sexual violence are "denaturalized" through public, mass-based interventions, it "challenge[s] inherited definitions of manliness, which had historically been based on ownership—sometimes an owner of property—but more often as owner and guardian of womanhood" (M. J. Alexander 2005, 32). Many of the tensions within contemporary gender relations pivot on this precise point as normative definitions of masculinity, which often position women as some form of sexual property (through paternal safeguarding or sexual ownership), scrape up against social practices that demonstrate female independence, personal autonomy, and sexual desire in ways that produce complex contradictions. These contradictions create space for the idea that an eleven-year-old girl might be characterized as choosing to invite sexual violence, especially given that, in order to be considered raised properly, little girls in Jamaica are generally socialized to stay contained within the safe domesticity of their home.[16] In the case of running a battery it is evident that manliness is actually determined by the sexual subjugation of adolescent or preadolescent girls by groups of boys, who bear witness to one another's experience.

When Krystal's friend Junie came by, she asked if the boys had raped the girl, and Krystal indicated that it hadn't been rape because the girl had "wanted it." Krystal then told Junie that when Dads caught wind of what the three boys had done, they would be beaten, and that someone needed to talk to him about getting the "sex house" torn down to stop the type of incidents that go on there.[17]

As is true of the other two patrons described in this chapter, it appears that Dads's patronage position allows him to command violence indirectly. In Mr. Lee's case, it is community loyalty and people's willingness to protect him through the use of violence that allows him to continue conducting business within the area. The area leader, however, delegates the use of violence to foot soldiers that enact violence on his behalf. No one I interviewed or talked to informally ever linked Dads to violent acts; however, the examples I mentioned above show that he has some recourse when community activities go awry, even if only to ask three boys' parents to physically punish them for their unacceptable behavior.

Dads Arrives: Day-to-Day Patronage Activities in Guy Town

It is well known that Dads arrives in the community relatively late at night. The sight of his red SUV, which is usually packed with young men from his record company carrying bags of fast food, and the smaller SUV driven by his recently acquired bodyguard, sends a ripple through the area. Word of mouth makes all community residents aware that Dads has arrived, and a steady stream of young men, part of his own intelligence network, rapidly gather around him to report local goings-on and benefit both socially and financially from Dads's prestige and generosity. Once the group of men has had their chance to talk, other community members, including women, begin to approach, usually with a story and a request for "a thing" from Dads. These requests may include money for sick baby mothers who need to go to the doctor, for children who need help with school fees, or for other personal situations. Dads handles them on a case-by-case basis, and at times people are turned away with a sternly barked, "I don't want to hear about that!" Dads's use of his corner as a location for socializing, gathering information, and redistributing wealth reflects the moral economy of residents who engage in daily social acts of small-scale economic circulation as elaborated in Chapter 1.

During the school year, Dads's visits include the appointment of a trusted young man from the regular group who is put in charge of the distribution of lunch money. All the children in the community are asked to line up in the street, where they receive fifty or one hundred Jamaican dollars to help carry them through the week. During this part of the visit, word of mouth once again spreads through the community, and even children who are already in their beds are brought out to collect the funds. Lack of lunch money or proper shoes often prohibits children from attending school regularly. Krystal told me that Dads gives out the money so that no child can use the excuse that they couldn't attend school during that week because they couldn't afford to buy lunch.

When asked about his own schooling, Dads told me about the financial challenges that induced him to leave at grade 9 and eventually led him to participate in the music industry. He attended primary school and was preparing to take the Common Entrance Exam, which might have provided access to government assistance for additional schooling. However, since he didn't have shoes to wear to school, he dropped out during the same time period in which the exam was being held. He stopped attending school in the ninth grade even though he was the prefect and the vice-chairperson for the student council. After dropping out he began attending training classes in electronics, where he met some youths that had a sound system while he was learning a trade.

In a familiar story, a lack of family resources created a situation in which he could not continue attending school, despite his own interest and active participation in school activities. "Training" is often used as a safety net for children raised in poverty, who often cannot progress in school. The obstacles to poor children's educational attainment consist of a variety of challenges that might include any combination of the following: hunger; a lack of adequate supplies, including uniforms and shoes; the inability to cover annual fees; a lack of emotional support and discipline; a lack of consistent utilities and adequate study space; inability to travel to school because of periods of violence; or the need to contribute to the household financially. Training is available through many outlets in Kingston, including private enterprises, as in Dads's electronics training, but also through government-sponsored programs and community and church organizations.

Training is usually geared toward the acquisition of a marketable skill, such as construction and furniture building for men, and sewing or catering for women. In Dads's case, his training in electronics placed him in the company of sound system operators who eventually took him on.[18] Through the sound system, he was introduced to the Jamaican music industry, which would eventually facilitate his aspirations to become a member of the black bourgeoisie and to participate in the day-to-day, as well as longer-term, development-oriented patronage activities in Guy Town.

Conclusion

Patronage practices in communities like Guy Town are rooted in moral economies of giving outlined in the Introduction that provide criteria with which to evaluate social standing through reputation, respect, and respectability. By successfully leveraging social status, patrons and ordinary community members alike are able to initiate relations of loyalty and mutuality that provide both personal protections from violence as well as access to financial and social resources. Historically, Jamaican political parties utilized patronage relations within this context of ongoing scarcity in order to influence voting patterns. With the growth of the drug trade and concomitant influx of illegal financial gains, the criminal networks that were cultivated by party patronage arrangements became patrons in their own right. Additionally, the perceived failure of government representatives, including MPs, to fulfill the requirements of reputation through sharing resources with constituents, alongside widespread austerity measures that have disproportionately affected poor communities, has created a struggle for community allegiance. The Jamaican government is now seen as alien and intrusive within urban ghetto communities, whereas the patronage practices of local community members including shopkeepers, record producers, and organized criminals have taken shape with a deep understanding of local values involving participants' appropriate response to the needs of others and the avoidance of meanness, in the cultivation of loyalty. Here, informal community-based systems of justice and economic redistribution connected to these community-level patrons have in significant ways usurped the activities of the state in caring for its citizens. As state retraction led to greater disenfranchisement of poor urban communities, the state's illegal but licit partnership with systems of community justice and wealth redistribution intensified as a crucial extension of state governance. Such alliances efficiently created a tenuous stability in areas that could no longer be effectively administered through traditional means because of the state's lack of financial resources and the shift to a neoliberal style of governance.

In the next chapter, I examine the role of Jamaican dancehall music, also a product of Kingston ghetto communities and their elaborate systems of patronage, in order to apprehend the social norms regarding class, gender, and social status expressed by performers and consumers; the special role of street parties within community systems of status attainment; and the controversial positioning of the popular style within Jamaican debates concerning the definition of national culture.

CHAPTER 3

Dancehall Dilemmas

Sounds from the Disquieted Margins

Jamaican dancehall music exists at the interstices of race, class, nation, and postcolony. It is a popular yet controversial genre in Jamaica and abroad, which has been the subject of heated public debate owing to its ambiguous position. The music has been widely criticized for promoting promiscuity, disrespect toward women, homophobia, and criminality, traits that are often ascribed to Kingston's black working class.[1] Dancehall is known for its bawdy, sexual lyrics, which can be considered misogynistic; its violent content, which at times glorifies the gangster persona; and its reference to drug use, in particular marijuana. It is also associated with flamboyant and revealing clothing and suggestive dancing.

The stereotype of the dancehall performer is a youth from the ghetto who values gold jewelry and material possessions and who carries a gun. He lives irresponsibly, having casual sex and not caring for the children he fathers. Women in dancehall are stereotyped to be promiscuous ghetto gals who have many children from different fathers and who would rather spend any money they have on the latest fashions rather than on school fees, books, and nourishing food for their children. Both of these stereotypes are derived from popular assumptions about Kingston's urban poor, who are often considered a problematic population that contributes to urban crime and therefore creates obstacles to national development, but who are nonetheless a large and crucial population culturally and politically.[2] At the same time, dancehall's international popularity and impact have made it an object of pride for many Jamaicans as well. For this reason, it has become a critical trope in the public debate over what Jamaica, as a nation, is and should be.

Carolyn Cooper, in her groundbreaking analysis of dancehall music and culture, has referred to the practice of DJ-ing as an act of "verbal maroonage"—expression freed from the middle-class, normative gaze (Cooper 1993, 136). In particular, she is concerned with deconstructing the dichotomous pairing of "slackness" and "culture" in relation to dancehall music, with culture having the double meaning of both "high culture" as determined by elite populations and as "roots and culture music," which is promoted nationally as a positive artistic contribution on behalf of Jamaica as a nation. Simultaneously, slackness, the term for pornographically sexual lyrics or depictions of violence in music, is condemned or, in Cooper's words, "feminized" and "censured" like "undomesticated female sexuality" (Cooper 1993, 161). She suggests that slackness is threatening because it serves as a "metaphorical revolt against law and order; an undermining of consensual standards of decency" (Cooper 1993, 141). However, she is also quick to point out that the use of sexual innuendo has a long and celebrated history within Jamaican popular culture, and that dancehall is a logical outgrowth of long-standing Jamaican folk cultures of orality (Cooper 1993).

As an urban-based form of expression, dancehall is rejected by segments of the population as being too rough or "butu," while others laud it as a genuine form of creative expression emanating from the oppressed but resilient urban black working class. These antagonistic stances align with Cooper's dichotomy, a set of oppositions that hearken back to the influence of British colonization and the struggles to define a "legitimate" national culture that followed. She characterizes the division as "one manifestation of a fundamental antagonism in Jamaican society between up-town and down-town, between high culture and low, between literacy and oracy" (Cooper 1993, 171).

Though dancehall may constitute symbolic revolt against law and order, it is important to understand that dancehall is entertainment, not a political movement.[3] It lacks a unified message. Much of dancehall's content is contradictory, at times raising opposition to injustices and at others tapping into commonly held sets of beliefs that reinforce traditional configurations of power. Because of these contradictions, it is a valuable site for examining cultural struggles among the Jamaican citizenry and debates over Jamaican national identity. These debates are frequently encountered within national politics and are regularly discussed by all strata of the Jamaican public. In addition, the space of the ghetto and dancehall as a space of expression are coconstitutive. Dancehall as a product of a masculinist, black working-class worldview rooted in ghetto communities buttresses the gender roles and mores found in these places.

So, while the form of the message and the lifestyle celebrated in dancehall music might metaphorically revolt against middle-class value systems, it is important to also consider the ways in which dancehall reproduces normative values, particularly in relation to sexuality. This reproduction of normativity via popular culture fills the social space that the church and the state used to fill in the provision of moral leadership up until the time that the state's social welfare programs were retracted and the church's conservatism toward the poor created a void (Saunders 2003, 106). Saunders highlights dancehall's tendency to "reinscribe the same conservative ideologies espoused by both the church and state," particularly in relation to the maintenance of heteronormativity and patriarchal masculine identity (Saunders 2003, 106).

Jamaican dancehall music emerged in Kingston during the 1980s and is characterized by singers and DJs (comparable to hip-hop emcees or rappers in the United States) who perform live over prerecorded rhythms or instrumental b-sides of singles, called "versions," in dancehalls during what were called "rub-a-dub" sessions. The DJ style was developed in the late 1970s with performers such as U-Roy and Brigadier Jerry but took hold in the form of dancehall music in the 1980s with acts such as Yellow Man and Josey Wales (Barrow and Dalton 1997).[4]

Rhythm styles have changed over time. The early days of dancehall were characterized by rhythm tracks, or versions, composed of instrumentals performed by a recording studio's in-house session musicians, Studio One being an early favorite. The current standard favors digital rhythms created on computers and studio mixers; these rhythms are built by studio engineers, not played by musicians on particular instruments. Vocalists now record directly over rhythms in a studio more often than they improvise over a b-side in front of a party audience. These recorded songs are then sold to sound systems or discos to play out at "juggling" sessions and "sound clashes."[5] They have been sold formally in music stores and via web download as well as through underground channels in the form of vinyl 45s and LPs, cassettes, and now more frequently, duplicated compact discs and flash drives.[6]

In order to make dancehall music, multiple performers record a variety of songs over the same rhythm, creating original works by varying the style and content of the vocals.[7] Dancehall selectors, who would be called disk jockeys in the United States, then play a string of songs recorded over the same rhythm sequentially. As suggested by the name dancehall, the genre is intended for dancing and emphasizes reverberating bass tones, which listeners can experience physically pulsating through their bodies when it is played at a loud volume. "Dancehall" as an appellation for this particular genre is somewhat deceptive in that a "dance hall" gives the impression of a designated, stable space, even though the dancehall genre is not constituted by any particular space, but instead by the ability to turn undesignated space into a dancehall "place" through performance, participation, and the reach of the sound as it carries across a wider geography (Hope 2006b; Stanley Niaah 2010). Therefore, rather than being a space, dancehall is better characterized as music and culture constituted by ritualized activity (see Stanley Niaah 2010) that includes a combination of musical style, subcultural style, and participation by consumers, sound systems, musical performers, dancers, and vendors.

Most rhythms now have particular dance steps associated with them and recently popular styles include songs voiced over particular rhythms that incorporate the name of the dance in their lyrics, encouraging audiences to learn and perform them. There are also recognized dancers who originate the new styles and often perform the steps at dancehall stage shows and in music videos, and who make guest appearances at street dances. Most notably, a dancer named Labba Labba was popular in the 1980s, and more recently, the now deceased John Bogle and John Hype defined the new dances. Elephant Man, an extremely popular dancehall DJ, is known to have solidified the pairing of songs with new dances. His song "Log On," which includes the lyrics "log on and step pon chi-chi man," both coins the "log on" dance step and expresses derision toward homosexual men. This is entertainment with a culturally embedded public message.

Dancehall, as a form, grew out of urban working-class communities, and while the genre expresses attitudes derived from this culture, it is not coterminous with black working-class culture, which itself is not a unitary thing; an important consideration given that the urban working class is often treated as a homogenous and problematic lot.[8] The class's persistent existence and its poverty serve as a reminder of the nation's rootedness in slavery and colonial relations, which established structural inequalities from the country's inception, as well as the failures of the independent Jamaican state to provide for its citizens. Meanwhile, the contemporary urban poor have also been assimilated into the discourse of neoliberal multiculturalism, which naturalizes their poverty and vulnerability as side effects of a cultural deficit that limits their ability to participate in the benefits of global citizenship (Melamed 2011). This population's existence simultaneously calls into question the core set of national values developed as an outgrowth of British colonization and codified during independence, including the creole nationalist value of unity in diversity and the social ideal of meritocracy. The views expressed in Jamaican dancehall emphasize these contradictions, reinforce mores, and also highlight tensions between stated values regarding gender, sexuality, race, class, crime and violence, ideas about success, and how they are experienced in daily life.

Jamaican dancehall creates a shocking visibility for populations some sectors of Jamaican society would consider better left unseen and also creates a "noisy" platform for poorer people to verbalize their struggles and criticisms of Jamaican society and the government. In order to better understand this visibility we must return to a discussion of social space because of the nomadic nature of dancehall practice, which allows for the utilization and redefinition of public spaces that were planned for other uses. These spaces include blocked streets, crossroads in particular, and shopping mall parking lots, in addition to the more foreseeable spaces of nightclubs, bars, and designated outdoor party areas. Hope argues that the space of dancehall performance and expression "operates as a site of revolution and transformation, effectively creating its own symbols and ideologies and negating, shifting, removing and replacing those functioning in the traditional social spaces" (Hope 2006b, 25). Stanley Niaah convincingly links this use of space to a longer history of marginalization in the Black Atlantic by examining the spaces inhabited by enslaved Africans, including slave ships, in relation to the spaces of contemporary ghettos. By making these associations, she is able to emphasize that the need for celebration went uniformly unrecognized in the development of these dehumanizing spaces whether by lack of concern for the population's psychological well-being or because of the pressures of rapid population relocation and overcrowding. By connecting the practice of limbo dance on slave ships with contemporary dancehall festivities through the concept of "spatial imagination" where "the plantation dances and urban dancehall events evoke memories of celebratory events held within spatially restricted, heavily policed, and marginal settings," Stanley Niaah is able to demonstrate the ways in which acts of celebration are also acts of rebellion for populations socially defined by their marginality and suffering (Stanley Niaah 2010, 35).

Many accounts of dancehall position its practices as particularly subversive to the hegemony of the Jamaican elite with their orientation toward "British values," however, these studies often ultimately reveal dancehall to be a mixed bag, at times expressing libratory, even radical, stances, while at other times reinforcing dominant ideologies (Cooper 1993; Hope 2006a, 2006b, 2006c, 2010; Stewart 2002; Stolzoff 2000). Further, to say that dancehall expresses a variety of black working-class values is not to say that black working-class values are necessarily politically radical or geared toward universal liberation (Averill 1997; Hall 1996; Saunders 2003; Thomas 2004; C. Waterman 1990). The expression of these values does, however, complicate attempts to construct a Jamaican nation that embraces its own diversity while simultaneously managing an internal culture war based on stark class-based inequalities.

Jamaican National Identity and Dancehall

The impact that the familiar, yet distinctly Jamaican, configuration of relations with Europe, North America, and Africa, including African diasporic connections, has had on the contours of the nation has contributed to a sort of identity crisis, which is regularly described with the following lament—Jamaicans are continually looking to the outside world rather than inside their own country for what Jamaica should be. Jamaicans, as postcolonial subjects, are continually involved in a struggle over the definition of their culture as something distinct from British culture, African culture, and, given their position within relations of neoliberal globalization, American culture. This struggle takes place on multiple registers, and Robotham has described it within the arena of national politics as a tight rope. Here, cultural assertions of "blackness" or "Africanity" by a growing black elite, politically affiliated with the People's National Party, might become detrimental in a setting where local economic elites do not fit that description. In addition, racial and cultural assertiveness may also inhibit crucial investments from white elites who are dominant within the cultural and economic world order (Robotham 2000).

A well-publicized incident raised these internal cultural conflicts to the center of public debate. Prime Minister P. J. Patterson, a member of the black bourgeoisie and the head of the People's National Party, who often used his blackness as a tool for signposting his connection to the Jamaican people, made a risky attempt to relate to the "average Jamaican" while addressing a large crowd at the National Arena in 2003. In the speech, he touted his political record and his improvements to the country by stating, "More man have gal than anything else." Having "gal" is a common refrain in the dancehall, where it serves as a marker of virility and also of prosperity because it takes funds to maintain a gal. "Gal tunes" thereby place male access to women in the symbolic service of masculine identity construction for poorer populations (though, arguably, the use of women as a status marker for masculinity is a value that reaches across the patriarchal social stratigraphy). In this case, the prime minister's attempt to appropriate gal as a symbol backfired because of the stark class divisions in Jamaican society, corroborated by the attention the statement received in one of the major national newspapers, the *Daily Gleaner* (September 23, 2003; November 1, 2003). Though his speech was repeatedly misquoted, the criticisms circled around the same set of issues. Patterson was accused of degrading the national discourse by elevating male irresponsibility, promiscuity, and disrespect for women by referring to them as if they were property, as a cheap method of gaining respect, which was ultimately insulting to Jamaican men *and* women. This is a characteristic conundrum faced by politicians in Jamaica as they attempt to position themselves politically. They require the votes of the poorer black majority, but must also gain the favor of the country's powerful and cosmopolitan upper class (the global citizens), who need assurance that their interests and values are being promoted as national interests and values.

In the Commentary section of the *Gleaner*, Peter Espeut, a sociologist and regular contributor, explains the logic of Patterson's statement as follows:

> The basis for the statement that "more man have gal than ever before," the Prime Minister reasoned, is that "more man have car" and "more man have land" and "more man have cellular phone"; and therefore "more man have gal" because that is what women want: men with land and car and cellular phones. And so more "man" should have respect for him.
>
> The character of the "gal" painted here is the gold-digger, the "vampire," the "bloodsucker," not motivated by love or a caring relationship, but by what she can get—material things. She is looking for a "boops," not an intimate, tender, love relationship. And so more gal should have respect for him too because they are getting what they want.
>
> This is the sector that the Prime Minister is pandering to, and the sector he is quarrelling with because they have little respect for him, despite all he has done for them. (Gleaner November 1, 2003)

This commentary indexes the set of issues around gender in ghetto communities that I discussed in Chapter 1. Patterson's use of the word gal described a particular kind of woman who would come from the population Espeut accuses him of pandering to. Since Patterson's statement was addressed to the nation, but in an attempt to gain recognition from the black working class, it was taken as an offense toward the "respectable" women of Jamaica and also as an offense to the types of romantic relationships in which "decent" Jamaicans would engage.

In the "Letter of the Day," written by a female attorney, the prime minister's statement is directly linked to the unsavory ascendance of "modern dance hall [sic] culture." Here, dancehall not only spreads the derogatory patois term gal throughout Jamaican society, tainting communities comfortable communicating in Standard English, and making its use acceptable, but also promotes "crude" and "brazen" womanizing behavior. While she admits that infidelity is pervasive, she also argues dancehall enthusiasts would defend such behavior because they view openness as "more honest" than the sneaking around that goes on in other sectors. She clearly is not suggesting that infidelity is acceptable behavior but gives a nod to a more "decent" and discrete handling of it.

> The Editor, Sir:
> The reference by Prime Minister P. J. Patterson to man having more "gal" than before as a marker of the success of his, PJ's, tenure and his subsequent apology to women are both predictable. Ever since the dance hall culture took over, the term "gal" which was previously used in an uncomplimentary way became generalized and (it seemed) accepted or indulged by both men and women.
>
> As to the phenomenon of one man having "nuff woman" this is of long standing and widespread. The difference today is that people are more brazen or some would say less hypocritical about it. The promoters of modern dance hall culture would say that at least they are more honest about it even if you do not like their "in your face" and crude style.

The writer then goes on to link Patterson's word choice via dancehall to connotative terms of respect derived from downtown political culture, which, to her, is characterized by criminality and corruption, by introducing the word don. In doing this, she simultaneously differentiates herself and other discerning people from "the masses" who would blindly follow uneducated entertainers and criminals in order to negotiate their own senses of morality.

> Poor PJ! In his attempt to melt in with the popular culture he has offended those who have no strength for the popular icons and established dons. He is an easy target. His apology is appropriate and necessary but in my view falls short.
>
> He should also have apologized to the men who make it their first priority to support and take care of their children rather than to flash their cash to run down women, and even to the poor men who are made to feel inferior, by men as well as women, because they have neither the will nor the way to engage on that front. (Gleaner September 27, 2003)

The uproar that followed Patterson's use of gal and the criticisms lodged in the *Gleaner* demonstrate the ways in which dancehall has been made central to an ongoing culture war that is based on class differences with racial and cultural connotations and implications for the unequal access to the rights of citizenship among the urban poor.

The controversy also grows out of a deep crisis of masculinity that exists in Jamaica and in other nations across the globe where populations of men no longer have access to labor through which to fulfill provider roles (Chevannes 2001; J. Comaroff and J. L. Comaroff 2001; Harrison 1997). Patterson, in expressing "more man have gal," in patois, not Standard English, was elevating the wrong kind of masculinity to the public eye in support of his leadership of the nation. This is a masculinity rooted in reputation rather than respectability, which is seen as a more appropriate style for public figures to promote in their official discourse, even while the value of a masculinity that is both productive and reproductive is simultaneously shared across the class divide in Jamaica (see Saunders 2003). Though Patterson may have been professing his political and economic strategies as ones that create employment opportunities, giving men the resources to attract women, the masculinity that his statement references is one that is thought to value getting rich quick through illegal means and which views women as gals through the downtown via dancehall male lens.

Dancehall Music and Downtown Kingston

Dancehall is a form of expression and entertainment rooted in Kingston ghettos. It is consumed publicly in downtown communities where particular corners will operate their own small-scale sound systems by hauling large speakers on to the street and broadcasting their private music collections for the enjoyment of the entire neighborhood. In other instances local businesses such as rum bars or retail shops will play music for their patrons, some hosting regularly scheduled music nights. In any case, the sound of dancehall's booming bass and rhythmic elocution pervade daily life in downtown Kingston, contributing a cadence to daily chores and a backdrop to evening corner gatherings, at times inspiring spontaneous street-side dancing, and at others inspiring the ire of neighbors engaged in quiet conversation or seeking rest.

Most dancehall performers and producers are, or were at one time, ghetto youth. Dancehall is perceived by many youth with few employment options to be a way out of poverty. Blake, an up-and-coming DJ in his midtwenties, who moved to Guy Town from the country as a teenager to pursue his career, describes the ways in which youth will participate in dancehall music at an informal level and how that has created the dancehall tradition. "You always see the youth dem on the street a beat them chest and a DJ and a gwaan and crowd surround them and a gwaan with the most excitement, seen?" He told me that the best of "our music" comes from ghetto people, with great musicians and artists originating in ghettos. He went on to describe the struggles great artist endured, shifting the conversation onto his own career path: "And them can tell you seh it never easy for them. Everybody come up through it rough. So . . . we na expect nuttin' easy right now and mi been past dem stage a long time so. . . . You know mi have a foot and a half inna di business right now so. You know, deh pon the little last leg, you know, a fi jump de hurgle [hurdle]." There are many examples of dancehall performers who worked their way up from similar humble beginnings who serve as models of success with their nice homes, cars, and expensive clothing. Successful performers often sustain ties with the communities from which they come as a way of preserving their reputation and respectability, conserving their ghetto authenticity within the dancehall genre by maintaining the economic relationships expected of those who have resources, as I described in Chapter 1, and, from an outsider's perspective, giving back to the community that raised them in ways that might create opportunity. Ties are maintained because of family and friendship bonds, to preserve links with both legal and underground business networks, in order to maintain credibility, and to provide assistance to those they left behind.

When I asked Loverman, a dancehall DJ who has had a successful and lucrative career and who has scored international hits in the United States,

Canada, and Europe in a duo with a well-known singer at Wicked Times, if he has worked on any particular community projects in the ghetto in which he was raised, he told me he did, but he was not focused on any one particular community. He said, "I try to share my love all over. You know what I'm saying? But I still go back, you know. I still pass through, I still mek everybody know I'm still '[Loverman] from de block.' 'I used to got a little now I got a lot.' [laughing.]"[9] As the song Loverman quotes suggests, it is important to him to show his community that he is still the person they knew when he was a "little ghetto youth" even though he moved away and now has money and fame.

Many of the dancehall artists I interviewed expressed their connection to the communities from which they came in similar terms to those with which people explained the sharing practices I discussed in Chapter 1. They indicated a sense of gratitude to both God and supportive friends and neighbors for their success. According to Blake:

> But music a di whole a me still, a na no part. A no just me brain alone it inna. It inna me hand, you know, me vein, everywhere. Anything me a do a just music and people rate me for dat. Seen? A na how me look cause, you done know, everybody have bad times, seen? And you know, you can't just through a man look certain way you na deal wid him. No. So a just dat me love dem for. Dem respect me and me give dem dem respect, so. . . . You know, when the good time come and everything smooth and nice, you done know, [laughing] you know who fi deal with. You see what me a say? Because you can't strength who na strengthen you. I don't believe in that. So, I haffi big dem up and love dem, you know?

Often, the DJ career path was described, as Blake describes it, not as a choice, but as something that is innately part of a good performer. The music erupts from the DJ, who has been blessed with the skills by God. It is described as if the songs grow out of the artist's body or bloodstream, almost against the DJ's own will.

Star status seems even more attainable because the youths aspiring to it know performers who have made it in the music business. According to Frass, an administrative employee at Wicked Times, who grew up in Guy Town and has aspirations to perform, "[Frass] is from [Guy Town] still, you see it? Growing up in [Guy Town] you around the music, you're around [Wicked Times] cause that's where it's from. You see it? So you get influenced by even the topper top people dem. You seen?" Guy Town's special links to the music industry through Wicked Times provide local youth with opportunities to relate with "the topper top people dem" meaning, in this case, highly influential performers and producers. However, most downtown communities have comparable connections to dancehall or can, at least, boast being home to a few successful recording artists. The influence of the industry is widespread and deeply embedded in downtown communities to the degree that practicing DJ skills has become a standard component of male adolescence.

Although dancehall as career path is often regarded as an easy way out of the discipline of the educational system and regular wage employment, to become a successful dancehall performer requires dedication and hard work and does not necessarily exclude the completion of education, an argument that is one among many in the public debate surrounding dancehall. It is part and parcel with the perspective that dancehall is detrimental to Jamaican culture and to the youth, in particular, who are seduced by easy money. This perspective neglects the reality of discrimination that ghetto youth face in entering the work force and cements inclinations to depict ghetto youth as deviant participants in their own exclusion.

Potential employers can easily identify ghetto residents, if not by the addresses they provide on their job applications, then by the accent that marks their speech. Stories of job seekers being turned away from places of business once they reveal their address are widely circulated through downtown communities to the extent that people sometimes choose to provide false addresses on applications to avert immediate rejection. In addition, the employment opportunities available to people who may have skills training, but not an extensive traditional education, and who often come from home environments in which unemployment has been the standard, are largely menial. These forms of employment are often especially exploitative and disciplined, attributes that would make these jobs unattractive, stressful, and even humiliating. This is in contrast to employment in the music industry, which is characterized by a working environment largely maintained by people who respect, or at least understand, what it means to be from downtown Kingston.[10]

According to many of the dancehall performers I interviewed, it is music that kept them out of trouble. Mr. Mention, one of the top Jamaican DJs, told me it was access to music and encouragement from his ghetto community that led him away from crime and encouraged him to take responsibility. While explaining that by the time a ghetto youth reaches fifteen, he has to start preparing for adult life, Mr. Mention told me, "You have woman, you are sixteen, your woman pregnant, you don't know weh you a go deal wit. You na have no job, you na mek no money. You see it? So, you eventually go pon de wrong side at times." That is where community comes in, "the people now dem come together and dem try fi straighten up your life. You know? And a say 'my youth . . .' dem try to keep you inna di trend weh dem know you at as a musician. Dem just call you dat. You know? Just to remind you." In this quote, Mr. Mention raises key issues surrounding what it is to be a young man in the ghetto. Male ghetto youth are often pointed to as a problematic category within the Jamaican nation. They commit the majority of crimes, including violent crimes, in the country. In a sense, dancehall is an expression of a deep seated social and economic problem, which is frequently understood only through the cold calculation of the crime statistic.

According to the *Economic and Social Survey of Jamaica*, in 2001, most major crimes were committed by men between the ages of sixteen and thirty-five (Planning Institute of Jamaica 2002). In the period between 1974 and 1993, there was a 30 percent increase in violent crime with young, urban, unemployed or self-employed males also representing the largest percentage of victims (Harriott 2001). This increase in violent crime correlates with a trend in which the labor force participation of men dropped in the period between 1985 and 1993 from 84 percent to 74.6 percent (Harriott 2001). According to the Jamaican criminologist Anthony Harriott, the increase in violent crime and decline of male labor force participation need to be examined in the context of the growth of the drug trade and organized crime that I previously referred to in relation to the "don system" (Harriott 2001). The unemployment rate hovered around 15 percent as of 2001 (well *before* the global economic collapse), and according to the 2000 *Human Development Report*, 23.62 percent of people under twenty-five years of age, and 20.68 percent of males in Jamaica are living in poverty (Planning Institute of Jamaica 2000, 2002). Under these circumstances, young men are often unable to provide for their families. As discussed in Chapter 1, the provider role is an accepted gender norm in Jamaican society, and this failure of normative masculinity results in feelings of humiliation and inadequacy.

Among many poor Jamaicans, alternative markers of masculinity, ones that are attainable without participation in regular, mainstream employment, have been adopted. These markers include the fathering of children; being involved with more than one woman at a time; access to the power of physical violence, which may include gun ownership, and adherence to codes of reputation and respect where perceived wrongs do not go unpunished; prejudice against homosexuals; and participation in income-generating criminal activities. To quote the late Jamaican anthropologist Barry Chevannes, "But generally speaking, the construction of male identity has as a principal building block the ideal of control over economic resources. We can therefore imagine the crisis of identity suffered by a man who is failing in the imperative 'make life,' but who must relate to women. The turn to illegal activities must be understood in this context" (Chevannes 1999, 28).[11] It is in large part these values of a marginalized masculinity that are expressed within the medium of dancehall.

Returning to where this chapter began, traditionally, the terms slackness and culture have been applied to dancehall, by both academics and enthusiasts, as a means of subdividing the genre. "Slackness" is a patois term generally used to describe situations in which people are not attending to their duties adequately, but it can also describe the sexually explicit content and violent lyrics of dancehall. "Culture," by contrast, includes lyrics that are designed to teach a positive message and generally uplift the listener, whether by pointing out the corruption of the political system, indicating what it means to "live loving," or by demonstrating what a nurturing relationship looks like. Jamaican dancehall, as music of praise and condemnation, is always edifying, regardless of its intended message. The lyrics are a source of amusement, which utilize clever wordplay to create fantasy narratives of power involving wealth, invincibility, violence, and sexuality. Such content refracts the realities of suffering stemming from a lack of opportunity and control over the future as well as the fragility of life in an environment where the prevalence of normalized violence leads many young men to report that they'll be grateful if they manage to survive their twenties.

Gendered discourses in dancehall, including its frequently homophobic, explicit, and misogynist content, are "part of a cultural dialogue of gendered identity that draws on the historical and cultural legacies of Jamaica," rooted in postcolonial forms of patriarchy that reflect "values underpinning the traditional male ideal," where "personal, social and economic relationships that enable men to have power over women and the services they provide" are "produced" and "reproduced" (Hope 2006b, 36–37). The specter of the traditional male ideal casts a particularly long shadow across ghetto communities, where economic exclusion from the trappings of normative masculinity has created space for an alternative ghetto-based masculinity characterized by control over and access to women (Prime Minister Patterson's gals) as well as the fetishization of guns as a manifestation of masculine power. Within the dancehall culture, women, sex, and violence have become potent symbols on which a masculinity of marginalization gets constructed.

Dancehall reinforces mores around sociality, violence, sex, and gender norms.[12] However, the positions expressed in dancehall should not be considered uncontested. There has been a recent resurgence in the popularity of "conscious" music, and there are listeners who flatly reject the value of slackness in favor of the conscious alternatives, which emphasize knowledge of black history, equality, self-care, and mutual respect, as well as the condemnation of both locally and globally situated oppressors. This conscious music and the perspectives it offers are frequently tied to the religious practices of Rastafarianism by performers like Capleton and Sizzla. In addition, artists who are known for either slackness or conscious music often transgress the boundaries between the styles or combine elements of both within single songs. Praise and condemnation are often contextualized within the doctrines of Rastafarianism and Christianity as well as in specific rules of sociality, including the strategic utilization of reputation and respectability, which exist within the intensely intimate setting of the overcrowded ghetto. These rules include not living parasitically by utilizing other people's resources, and not spreading gossip about neighbors.

According to Steven Feld, "Music is the most highly stylized of social forms, iconically linked to the broader cultural production of local identity and indexically linked to contexts and occasions of community participation" (Keil and Feld 1994, 269). Below I will attempt to capture one "occasion of community participation" in order to better understand the complex relationship between dancehall music and downtown culture, but I also want to more generally discuss broad lyrical themes. Charles Keil, in a transcribed "conversation" with Steven Feld entitled "Commodified Grooves," asserts, "I think some of these styles or traditions have autonomy or authenticity in their play-place or workplace or neighborhood or locality. There they have their own integrity, and then the recorded thing is just a memory device" (Keil and Feld 1994, 296). In the next section I set about to destroy the integrity of the songs I wish to consider in order to use their lyrics as an analytical device rather than their recordings as a memory device. Tearing lyrics away from their sound and their participatory context gives only an incomplete sense of their meanings to both their authors and their consumers without the benefit of an understanding of how they are received, digested, enjoyed, and utilized (LaBennett 2011).

With these comments in mind, I want to briefly examine the dancehall oeuvre as a primer that lyrically instructs listeners on how to be "the best" of that which they aspire to be in terms of a celebrated "badness" or an exemplary "righteousness" under conditions of poverty or newly acquired wealth. In the "deviance" of using "violence and lawlessness as a means to an end," the "badman," as he is known, "carves out his own space and finds his freedom and actualization out of the confines of marginalized spaces" (Hope 2006a, 119). Here, a measure of freedom can be found by rejecting the standards of polite society, which can also have social and economic benefits within the confining context of ghetto communities. However, badness and righteousness should not be viewed as polar opposites because in life they often blend together, just as the categories criminal and citizen are openly acknowledged to overlap within downtown culture, and, in fact, there is a connotation of glory and reputation associated with badness. Additionally the music's "transcendental and often ambivalent images . . . reflect dancehall culture's propensity to traffic in ambivalent representations of self and personhood, which often resist efforts to homogenize," and which, I would add, unsettle endeavors to dissect dancehall's content into clean analytical categories (Hope 2006c, 127).

Famed DJ Bounty Killer's song "Look" expresses this duality by speaking from the perspective of an impoverished criminal addressing his more affluent victim when he sings, "Look into my mind, can you see the wealth? Can you tell that I want to help myself? But if it happen that I stick you for your ring. Don't be mad at me, it's a survival thing." Continuing with the theme of looking, Bounty Killer describes the subjectivity of a gunman, explaining that he can feel the fear of the person he is robbing, but wonders if the victim is more afraid of the assailant's "hungry face" or of the gun he has hidden at his waist. Bounty then humanizes his gunman character further by having him wonder aloud about if the victim can imagine the gunman's children and understand what it means to him for his family to live with hunger. This turn then allows Bounty Killer to assert that the acts the character commits are justified by the fact that for people from poor areas, robbing and killing are a necessity for survival, finally concluding that his character has resolved to die rather than "live like dog."

In this song, the blurry quality of what might be considered morally right or wrong is skillfully demonstrated. Here, the criminal commits acts of violence and theft as a means of survival for himself and his family. This badman is ambivalent about the deeds he does to others, obviously engaging in an internal struggle regarding his and his victim's mutual humanity. In the lyrics, Bounty Killer, as criminal, seems also to be weighing to what degree his victim is actually the perpetrator of a different sort of violence. This is violence enacted through living in comfort in an environment of poverty and not feeling concern for the poor man's "hungry face" but only for the gun "bulging" in his waist. At the same time, Bounty Killer indexes his criminal as a struggling neoliberal subject who wants to "help [him] self." Ultimately Bounty's criminal, both somewhat nobly and out of defeat, resigns himself to death rather than his current subhuman existence.

The ambivalence of Bounty Killer's badman must be contrasted with other variations on the badman theme, which are an unbridled lyrical celebration of coldness and brutality within the narrow structuring limitations of normative badness policed by the enforcement of sexual boundaries. Mad Cobra's "Dem Fi Goweh" narrates a story about a fake gangsta who comes to Mad Cobra's territory, making threats and bragging about how many people he has killed. Mad Cobra sings, "Claim him a gangsta and nah help no yute, Come pon ends and come threaten 'bout shoot, last bwoy try that, tell yuh di truth, Mek people see him inna black and white suit." Mad Cobra's response to the imposter's effrontery is to call out the self-proclaimed badman by saying he identifies as a gangster but fails to help other youths from his crew, which is an indictment of the fake badman's reputation. He thereby implies that the fake badman lacks either the resources a true badman should possess or proper respect for other ghetto youth. Cobra then tells his listeners what will happen to people who claim they are bad when confronted with his "real" badness, which is comparable to that of Saddam Hussein and soldiers in Beirut.[13] The end result is the fake badman left in a "black and white suit," dressed for his own funeral.

Such badman lyrics often lay out the rules of a perfect badness, which can include a lack of concern for life, including one's own life; not issuing idle threats, but taking action against enemies; and a sense of self-reliance; as well as a particular relationship to women, who can be viewed as softening or polluting or, under certain circumstances, strengthening in their supportive and nurturing ghetto domesticity. Elephant Man, in his song "Bad Man," lays out the rules of badness by telling listeners the things a real badman will and will not do. "Badman don't bathe (Badman don't bathe), Wid dem baby modda rag (Wid dem baby modda rag), Badman dweet hard (Badman dweet hard), Mek she go round go brag (Mek she go round go brag)." According to these lyrics, a badman won't bathe using his child's mother's washcloth, indicating the polluting nature of women, particularly women who are menstruating or who have just had sexual intercourse. This sentiment is reiterated in the phrase "Shotta clothes don't wash wid gal underwear," which would translate to "A gunman's clothes do not get washed with women's underwear." This coincides with a general concern over what is "clean" and "dirty." Being clean can refer to hygiene, health, and a state of purity in a religious sense, while being considered dirty is an insult because it refers to bad hygiene, disease (sexually transmitted disease in particular), or a general lack of cleanliness and can also indicate a state of spiritual dirtiness. He then goes on to say that a badman has "hard" intercourse, suggesting both stamina and a degree of roughness, so that his sex partner will go out and brag about his skills.

Hard intercourse is often contrasted with the practice of "bowing," the patois term for oral sex, which is considered a dirty and taboo act and an indication of a lack of sexual skill.[14] If a man lacks the strength and prowess to please his partner through penetration, he has to resort to bowing. Deciphering an additional layer of meaning from the cultural taboo around oral sex, Saunders has suggested that, given dancehall's role in guiding behavior, taken over from the guidance of the church and the state, that there is a second reason for this preoccupation—oral sex is a non-"productive" activity; here sexual "wuk" and reproductive "work" have been symbolically fused (Saunders 2010). By this logic, a man that engages in oral sex is demonstrating a lack of "ambition," meaning that it signals him as a bad citizen because, without reproductive wuk or productive work, "the state cannot maintain itself, its citizens, and its identity" (Saunders 2010, 108). This argument provides further credence to my assertion that Kingston's urban improvisers have creatively interpolated the tenets of neoliberal globalization. In this case, the sexual deviance of a bowers corresponds with the stigma of nonproductivity that has been associated with poor populations in order to explain away the inequalities they suffer as a natural outcome of their own pathological behavior. Perfectly in line with dancehall culture's contradictorily resistant and normative role, the local symbolic interpretation of male engagement in oral sex not only shores up reproductive heteronormativity in relation to sexual practices but also seems to internalize the idea that sexual and economic marginalization is rooted in the deviance of those being excluded. Vybz Kartel's "Pussy Jaw" instructs women on what to do if they encounter such an unambitious man. "If a di pussy jaw sen on nuh hang on. Thou shall not si di batty and take on. Gal run di boy weh blow you like cow horn, mek him know badman a fuck you from now on!"[15] Vybz Kartel tells women that if they encounter a man who "blow you like cow horn," that is, a pussy jaw who engages in oral sex, then they should send him on his way; and he adds that anal sex (and homosexuality), also nonreproductive, is also proscribed, by stating "thou shalt not see di batty and tek on," in the quasi-biblical language of a church sermon. Throughout the song the man who engages in such behavior is also equated with a "batty man." He then suggests to women that they tell this type of man they are now having only the desired and socially acceptable form of intercourse that Vybz Kartel, a badman, can provide, "a fuck," thereby insinuating that he has stolen the pussy jaw's woman using his sexual skill. As a real badman with a reputation to protect and a rigidly defined set of masculinity affirming sexual standards, he would not engage in such taboo acts.

Homosexuality, proscribed in Jamaica, is a taboo that a prototypical badman will not tolerate, reflecting a ubiquitous concern within Jamaican society where homosexual acts are still legally prohibited as well. It is the preoccupation of many hardcore dancehall songs and has created international controversy, which has drawn the attention of human rights organizations, resulting in concert cancellations and boycotts. In an instantiation of market values and cultural values, Buju Banton has been heavily censured in the global marketplace for his song "Boom Bye Bye." Spragga Benz's "No Funny Guy Thing" similarly expresses the DJ's consternation for a man who is not attracted to women, but who instead pursues sexual relationships with other men. He DJs the lyrics, "Dem nuh want nuh woman, to girls dem say no, but when dem see another man dem light say go. Father God government dem wan overthrow, but dem ago get a fatal blow." Spragga justifies his position, as someone who will not "bow down" to (a double entendre that indicates both social accommodation and the act of oral sex), or pursue friendship with, a homosexual, by suggesting that they are going against the Bible and "Father God government dem wan overthrow." He goes on to say that homosexuals should stay away from a badman because they will be risking their lives, thereby reinforcing heteronormativity, justified through the righteous invocation of Christian values. Also significant to the importance of homosexuality as a taboo in dancehall culture is that dancehall masculinity has been rigidly formulated in relation to patriarchy as a powerful identity. Men are supposed to be sexually and physically powerful and to engage in contextually appropriate violence as a means toward maintaining reputation, in part because they are excluded from the economic power that goes with legal employment.

Given that women are positioned as weak as well as weakening and potentially polluting in relation to men, "if a man engages in sexual activities with another man he becomes feminized and thereby loses masculine dominance and power;" and "further to condone male homosexuality is to reveal an ideological overview that legitimizes . . . the feminizing and subsequent loss of power of men" (Hope 2006b, 79).

Women as Lyrical Objects

Unsurprisingly, dancehall songs about women also tend to buttress patriarchal gender norms using lyrics that judge them on their attractiveness, sexual abilities, and respectability. This is often done by contrasting a woman with other women whom she might consider her competitors for male companionship, thereby positioning male attention as a prize to be vied over. As noted earlier, this positioning by the male lyricist does not define the experience of the female dancehall participant, who may well attend a dance for the empowering thrill of rejecting or ignoring the sexual attention of male partygoers. One example of this type of song, also by Mad Cobra, is "Ever Tight," which sings the praises of an attractive woman who is physically and sexually fit. Mad Cobra comments that the women who talk badly about the hot woman must be "pharmacy rat," indicating that they buy creams with which to bleach out their skin. This line is a double criticism in that "chat" is something to be looked down upon, whether it consists of talking negatively about others out of jealousy, or spreading gossip. When chat is particularly vicious and conducted in the presence of the object of ridicule, it is called "tracing," a practice that has feminine connotations and which is a feminizing insult when applied to a man as in the phrase "you trace like gal" (you trace like a girl). The second criticism in the lyric is the implication that the women bleach out their skin. This is a widespread practice in Jamaica where light colored skin is a prized attribute, reflecting a standard of beauty shaped by European ideals, which has created the need for the patois term "brownin," to describe an attractive light-skinned woman.[16] Women who bleach their skin, particularly if they do so ineffectively, leaving their faces several shades lighter than the rest of their bodies, are often ridiculed both in daily discourse and in dancehall culture. The derogatory term "monkey" is often applied to such women.[17] Mad Cobra delivers the lines "Good body gal well ever hot, yuh never flop. Mek di world know seh when yuh hot, yuh jus hot. When certain gal a chat, dem a mussi pharmacy rat. Face look brown an di rest a body black." In the end, Mad Cobra concludes that these women's bodies look like the chassis of old cars requiring a visit to the "body shop" and that the appealing physique, personality, and sexual skill of the woman that he praises will keep him with her because she holds him "like a knot," both literally, in a sexual sense, and figuratively, in the sense that she can keep his interest.

Lexxus's song "Halla Halla" praises and condemns women based on a different set of criteria when he DJs, "Respect to di gal dem weh independent, weh wuk dem owna money and a pay dem owna rent. Nuh utilize dem dolla and nuh squanda a cent, dem deh gal deh have up some hot apartment." He gives his respect to the gals who are independent because they work for their money, pay their own bills, and do not spend foolishly. This type of woman is then contrasted to a set of women Lexxus "can't take." These women are "idle," meaning they do not work or actively pursue a better future, and whenever they hear the sound system play ("pan a knock") they want to go off to enjoy themselves, wearing revealing clothing ("skin out") and dancing ("bruk out pon riddim"), only to get up the next day and continue with their idle ways and self-reinforced poverty, echoing the normativity of neoliberal multiculturalism that I have gestured toward throughout this book.

As these examples illustrate, beliefs and tensions around womanhood and female sexuality are the focal point of many dancehall lyrics contextualized within a patriarchal understanding of the role of women and then refracted through the realities of a masculinity crafted in relation to histories of exclusion and marginalization. The praise of women ranges. Sometimes the celebration is of women as people, particularly in relation to a celebrated feminine domesticity. These women include mothers and nurturing wives and lovers. Other women are elevated as attractive, healthy bodies, and as apt sexual contenders, where "male identity negotiation" takes place in relation to the "female sex organ, feminine sexuality, and the female body" within dancehall culture (Hope 2006b, 50). The condemnation of women consists of depicting them as inferior to men, and dangerous, potentially polluting, physically unattractive, degenerate people. This focus on women reflects the male dominance of the genre and continuing gender based inequalities within Jamaican society that are exacerbated by the material vulnerabilities men face as they also struggle to create a space in which they can be socially valued within a system that has ideologically justified their exclusion. It is, then, understandable that gender inequality is particularly acute among the urban poor, and that this inequality finds expression in dancehall, not because of some pathological backwardness, but because of the contemporary conditions in which poor people are forced to exist.[18]

Though female dancehall performers and dancers enjoy subjectivity in the context of dancehall culture, it is largely a male-defined arena, and much of the content of the music expresses a view of women derived from the marginal masculine position. Tellingly, one day when I was in the studio at Wicked Times while one of the engineers mixed a new song, some young men who were apprentice studio engineers commented on Tanya Stephens, an extremely popular female DJ at the time, enthusiastically commending her verbal skills by exclaiming "She write like a MAN!"

The discourse on womanhood in dancehall includes widely held Jamaican attitudes toward women, and also reveals a bind in which there are contradictory models of ideal womanhood. While a woman's ability as a lover is celebrated in many dancehall songs, female sexuality remains ambiguous. The ideal woman is a good lover but hasn't had many partners, and there is a fine line between being skilled and being cheap. A woman who is known to be involved with more than one man at a time is condemned as a "skettel" or tramp.[19] Meanwhile, men who can have many women at one time are celebrated, and, in addition, a good woman in the view of dancehall is one that will remain loyal to a man if he provides for her, even though she knows he is not faithful to her. This can be seen in the idea of the "number one gal." Number one gal status in dancehall is viewed as something for a woman to be proud of because it indicates that she is either the wife of a given man, or at least the woman that he comes home to, shares most of his resources with, and has children with.

The sharing of men is not uncommon among working-class women, though it is not considered an ideal arrangement.[20] Sometimes the companionship and additional resources lead women to deem these relationships worthwhile, though they are also known to create potentially violent situations between the women involved. This type of violence is called "matie war," with "maties" being the designation for a pair of women known to be romantically involved with the same man.

Women in Dancehall

Women are both subjects and objects in dancehall, though, as it is a male-dominated genre, the subjective position often takes a backseat.

There are a few female dancehall performers who contribute a woman's perspective through their lyrics. This is not to say that a woman's perspective is always one that challenges male supremacy. At times female performers do manage to challenge the "it's a man's world" perspective utilizing a masculine bravado to assert their position as women who are in charge of their own lives. However, there are also lyrics written from the female perspective that matter-of-factly express the relative inequalities between men and women in a way that is accepting of the status quo. For example, Cecile's song "Respect Your Wife" admonishes men who have a wife that if they are also involved with other women, referred to as "concubines," they need to make sure the concubines know that the wife is in charge and if they overstep the boundaries she will physically confront them to ensure they learn their lesson. She sings, "This a fi all a de man dem, especially the promiscuous one dem . . . When you have you gal dem, dem fi respect your wife. When you have you gal dem, mek dem know dem no control your life."

It is important to note that Cecile, as wife, is not asking her spouse to stop carousing with other women, which might be seen as an attack on his masculine privilege. She is also not suggesting that she should, in turn, go and find herself other men to be with, because that would detract from her reputation as a woman. Cecile is asserting her badness by threatening repercussions on the other women if they do not adhere to the unwritten rules of number one gal status by boasting about beating concubines.[21] Her reputation in this context is not predicated upon being the only woman, but on being the wife and not the concubine in a hierarchy that revolves around a woman's status in relation to men.

Tanya Stephens, the DJ the apprentice studio engineers referred to as "writing like a man," puts a clever twist on the matie scenario in her song "Tek Him Back," in which she addresses the wife of her lover, singing about the times when the wife would call her phone and swear at her, demanding that she stop seeing her husband. The twist comes when Stephens explains why she *really* needs to end the relationship in the following lyrics, "'Cause him a refuse fi look a work, so him pockets stay bruk. Cyann mash hands, but a war him a chuck." Here, Tanya Stephens, who begins the song as the triumphant and powerful matie whose seductive appeal means that she can have any man she wants, resorts to begging her lover's wife to take her husband back because he is a subpar partner, falling short of working-class Jamaican standards of normative masculinity. This man is criticized for not looking for a job and never having any money, as his first weakness. She then goes on to say that he also doesn't know how to fight but is always going around making threats that he cannot back up with action, an indictment of his reputation as man. She creates an amusing irony by demonstrating how "one girl's treasure is another girl's trash" and admitting that even a powerful and triumphant matie, who has freedom of choice and can steal men from their wives, sometimes make mistakes, stealing a man that turns out to be of little "value."

Slackness and the Female Performer

Georgina, a performer who is having some success breaking into the dancehall industry and who has been touring internationally with Wicked Times's co-owner and most successful performer, Mr. Mention, highlighted the gender and class implications of being a woman and a dancehall artist during our interview at Wicked Times. Georgina is in her twenties and described herself as having grown up in a middle-class family. While attending school she decided she was interested in pursuing a career as a singer, which put her in a difficult position. According to her account, going into the music industry in Jamaica meant going into dancehall, which was not encouraged by her family or her school. She told me that a lot of white children and "very uppity people" attended her school, so the only music that was encouraged was gospel or R&B, which is not a viable route into the local music industry. It was only once she reached high school that more opportunities opened to her through school competitions and group projects, which led her to participate in an amateur singing group that performed R&B and some reggae covers by culture artists like Bob Marley and Marcia Griffiths. The group also had one member who would perform in a more DJ or hip-hop style.

Georgina's description of the group's dissolution is telling of both the class-based differences in women's roles and the perspective that middle-class women often have with regard to their working-class counterparts. According to Georgina, "Women are very crabby in this country and the mindset a lot of the time with women, which is like I said, a lot of women don't get through in the music industry in Jamaica, is that you have to have a baby or you have no sense of purpose, and you have to go home at 6 o'clock in the evening and cook dinner for whoever is the man that's coming home to you and what not." She then returns to the issue of work ethic, claiming that this domesticity on the part of women became an apparent barrier when she worked on group music projects with other women. "The other three girls were not from the same background that I was and when I was willing to be at rehearsal on time and to be at rehearsal over-time they had to go home and cook and clean and blah blah blah. And there was never any leeway for anything. So that ended and I ended up in another group." Here Georgina expresses a commonly held sentiment among uptown women, who often have more leverage in their relationship to men than working-class women and who, in general, are more indoctrinated with Western feminism, which includes a more flexible conception of gender roles, though they also might be more constrained by ideas about respectability. Where uptown women may be more inclined to define themselves through career aspirations, she suggests in her response that the working-class women with whom she worked defined themselves as women through motherhood and caring for men. These values impacted the work ethic of the group, and while Georgina's statement sounds like a value judgment, it also illuminates a tension where working-class women, even as children, tend to have a great deal of responsibility within their households, often being kept indoors to study and do chores, while male children are allowed much more freedom and are, in general, subject to less discipline, which can also be interpreted as less parental care than the care and nurturance received by Jamaican girls (Chevannes 2001; Sargent and Harris 1998). Middle-class families are more likely to have employed "helpers," who take on household chores and cooking, leaving women with less domestic responsibility and providing them with the opportunity to focus their energies on school, work, or other pursuits. Georgina went on to describe the other ways these class-based differences affected the new group she formed, stating, "The Jamaican music industry requires that you do a lot of studio work and it's supposed to be free. Nobody wants to pay you when you're just coming up, so you have a whole heap of sweating to do and begging and groveling and putting in work to get back what you want from it." Complications arose when, after about four years together, one of the group members wanted to start earning money for their effort, but no one was offering to pay them. In the end the group dissolved because Georgina grew frustrated when opportunities would arise that they couldn't take advantage of because one of the members was insistent on being paid.

The issue of nonpayment for studio work that would fall into the category of paying dues to the industry is characterized by Georgina again as a problem of work ethic. Her perspective focuses on the issue of impatience with the process and glosses over the different practical needs people from different class backgrounds may have in terms of income. Working-class Jamaicans are often characterized as valuing immediate gains over longer-term returns. While this is a commonly held stereotype, it contains a grain of truth that can be understood only in context of the immediacy of need within ghetto communities.[22]

Later in our interview, Georgina indicated the entwined nature of class and gender in the dancehall milieu when I asked her what it is like working in a male-dominated environment. Her response points to class-based differences in the ways women use their sexuality, as well as the power that respect and affiliation have in curbing inappropriate behavior in a professional setting. She began by explaining to me that it's likely that many of the women that have achieved success in the music industry have had to "sleep with this producer and that producer." Following up by indicating that she has never slept with a producer to get head ahead, Georgina revealed, "I've been approached maybe once and it was after I'd already done work with the producer and I told him straight, you know, if that's what it's gonna take for you to continue to work with me, then forget it." Claiming that her response was due to her background, she also indicated that her refusal to engage in sexual exchanges might be part of the reason she hasn't managed to break into the music industry. She said, "I am not a *dancehall*, dancehall artist. I don't know if I'll ever be a true dancehall artist because I have not lived the life that dancehall is reflective of." Describing her work as "reggae singing," she explained that being the protégé of high-profile and well-established producers automatically elicited a "certain amount of respect" because she is considered "their artist." She said that the producers working at the studio that she primarily records with all knew her from her association with her famous mentors, "so they are not going to ask me for or be too forward with certain things." Once Georgina started going out to find producers to help her get more deeply involved with the dancehall market, she was no longer sure about what the future would hold, but indicated that "at this stage enough people know my name already to at least want to hear what I have to offer." She lamented, "A lot of the time before they'd hear me do something and it wasn't dancehall enough or they didn't know how to place it or you know, whatever, but I don't know. I guess I'm going to see from here on in." Georgina resolved that she would have to adopt a "new outlook" on her career now that she had come to the realization that, "going into the singer's market is a lot slower than into the dancehall market."

Throughout our interview, Georgina implied that it is her class background that keeps her from exchanging sexual favors for professional ones and went on to suggest that this may also be a barrier to her progress as a singer in such a male-dominated industry. However, she also recognizes that it is her working relationship with two well-known male producers that has helped create behavioral limits around her in relation to other men that she works with because of the respect that has been earned by the producers and which is now extended to Georgina in a proprietary way as their artist. I then asked her directly how her background has affected her career, and she told me, "I got cussed the other day because I wouldn't do a slack song and that is what women in dancehall are supposed to do. If you aren't doing what Lady Saw is doing or what Cecile or Tanya Stephens, you're either cussing men, or telling them how wonderful you are in bed or telling them how horrible they are in bed, and that's not stuff I care about." She reflected that she felt it did not make sense for her to try to get into a style that she was not going to pursue over the long term, commenting, "because if I even did one song, I couldn't do another one." She continued, "It wouldn't be written by me, it wouldn't be reflective of me, so it's kind of pointless. I'm more of an issues person, issues or drama. I write a story line about something, but I'm not going to get into the 'skin out' and how many man I've rode through or whatever else it is." Returning to the issue of genre in the Jamaican music industry, in this quote Georgina highlights the problems she has faced as a woman who is trying to maintain her own authenticity, as someone foreign to the ghetto milieu, within the context of popular music that is driven by ghetto culture. In attempting to maintain what she views as her own feminine dignity by not writing explicit content ("skin out") or about conquering men sexually ("how many man I've rode through") she has slowed down her own career because she's overtly rejecting that which is expected of her as a woman within the dancehall genre in favor of traits more widely associated with a middle-class female rendition of respectability.

In addition to performing as singers and DJs, there is a large space within dancehall culture for women to "model" and dance. These roles feature competition between groups of women in the case of modeling, or individual women in dance. Modeling consists of women dressing in the latest fashions, completely styled from hair to toes. The women that look the best and express the most confidence gain recognition as the best modeling posse. Dancing involves great attention to personal appearance, but there is also a physical aspect to it. These competitions have been institutionalized within dancehall culture through annual Dancehall Queen contests, in which women compete with each other, being judged on their fashion, dancing abilities, and attitude. This competitive dancing is explicitly erotic and requires great physical strength, agility, and self-confidence because many of the moves are quite acrobatic, some involving the dancer supporting herself with her head and arms with her legs in the air. The attention attracted by skilled female dancers has led to the suggestion that "women have successfully used the dancehall as a stage on which to create space beyond male control;" however, the events at the dance that I will describe later in this chapter demonstrate that this "success" is not a decided one (Stanley Niaah 2010, 140).

Keeping a Dance

Street dances are a form of entertainment and celebration deeply embedded in the culture of downtown communities. They are often described as a release valve for places where the restrictions and pressures of everyday life can be overwhelming, giving people an opportunity to enjoy themselves and escape from whatever problems they may be contending with while also redefining the spaces they inhabit. However, the reality of poverty can play a role in dance attendance because people may feel ashamed if they cannot afford a new hairstyle or new clothing to wear to a big event.

While admission is generally not charged at street dances, the expectation is that patrons will support the host by "buying out the bar," making sure that the dance is profitable by purchasing beverages or food that are up for sale. Hosts who choose to "keep a dance" generally count on making money in this way in order to defray the costs of hiring sound systems that provide the music and in the hope of making a profit.

As I mentioned in Chapter 2, the keeping of street dances is linked to community systems of power and respect. It requires funds and prestige to successfully keep a dance because if a host is not well respected, people can choose not to attend, thereby humiliating the host by "flopping" his or her party and causing them to lose the investment in the entertainment and refreshments. In addition, the success of a dance is a reflection and reinforcement of the host's prestige in that prestigious hosts will be able to hire the top-ranked sound systems to provide entertainment, demonstrating their wealth and social connections, and also making a dance more enjoyable. Prestigious hosts will be able to guarantee the safety of their guests to a greater degree because they will have access to community security networks and it will be well established that any criminal acts at the event will be considered a disrespect, which will result in negative repercussions against the perpetrator.

More than reinforcing the host's prestige, street dances reinforce community power structures as well as commonly held sets of values, while also claiming public space in a way that defies the hegemony of the state and of the Jamaican elite. With reference to Juju performance in Nigeria, Waterman has suggested that the performance provides "a metaphor of social order" and that "musical sound conditions temporal experience and establishes a normative context for ritualized social interaction" (C. Waterman 1990, 213). This analysis is useful for looking at the structure and importance of street dances in Jamaica as well, even though a street dance and a Juju performance are different types of events and take place in very different cultural contexts. The street dance has a less *formally* ritualistic role in Jamaican society, though there are elements that can certainly be identified as public rituals, which are held in relation to significant events, and are created with a prescribed structure of action and specific symbolic value to their participants (Stanley Niaah 2010, 90).[23] Most obviously, street dances are often associated with major life events such as birthdays, memorials, or public holidays. In addition, a street dance utilizes public space in such a way that familiar crossroads or stretches of pavement are transformed from a means of getting from a person's yard to the local shop into a closed space cut off from automobile traffic, which is a site for celebration. Notably, this control of space is created by the sound systems that stack up their large speaker boxes to create both physical blockades to traffic and walls of sound which carry the music and chat of the selectors, announcing the dance throughout the community and beyond. A street dance also follows a standard format that relates to local status hierarchies while "conditioning temporal experience" through the selection of particular styles of music as the event progresses.

I will use the example of a particular street dance I attended in Guy Town to illustrate my point. This dance took place on a Sunday night at the end of November 2002 and was held to celebrate the birthday of the top man of "security corner."[24] The familiar stretch of road that divided Guy Town Square from the community Youth Organization building was blocked to traffic by two towers of speakers. One tower was placed directly in front of security corner, where a metal barrier inhibiting unwanted traffic and potential assailants would normally stand. The second tower was placed at the opposite end of the street on the corner where I conducted much of my research. This arrangement turned Guy Town Square and the expanse of road into a dead end. The sound system set up a green-and-white-striped tent on the sidewalk in front of the abandoned building that Krystal had at one time referred to as the sex house. The event featured two major sound systems that are well recognized throughout the country. There were two turntables and a mixer under the tent on a long narrow table with boxes and boxes of records stored behind. The men who operated each sound system shared the turntables, each playing their own sets of music. There were two makeshift bars set up by nailing wooden planks together to create counters. Each counter was tended by a few local community members, including Mita, who sold beer, stout, rum, and rum cream, and a sugary imported bottled vodka cocktail, which had recently become popular, throughout the night.

The sound systems followed a standard street dance formula by playing American soul and R&B from the 1970s and 1980s early on in the event. At this point, it was about 10 p.m., and the only revelers were a sparse crowd lingering on various corners abutting the street. The local "madman" danced alone in the center while Krystal's eleven-year-old son and a friend mocked him by imitating his dance moves. As the music permeated the community, a slightly larger crowd gathered around the periphery of the street, and men began driving through the blocked-off area on bicycles, motorcycles, and scooters, and the selectors eased into Jamaican oldies, which included some softer sounding reggae and culture style tunes. The party continued to grow in population, and the sound systems played songs that were aimed at a female audience. These included love songs and then harder dancehall that celebrated women's sexual abilities and appearance more explicitly.

The selectors showed their respect for all the key members of the local power structure, including Dads, the area leader, and his crew, and Mr. Lee, as well as the head of security corner on this his birthday, by saying for each, "Big up" and then his name, thereby announcing their presence over the loud speakers and highlighting them as particularly important guests. One selector, upon seeing me and an American exchange student I had brought, with our unexpected white skin, also bigged up visitors and foreigners. Krystal then approached the selector, in a typical street dance gesture, and had my guest and me bigged up as "sexy queens."

Finally, once the dance was in full swing and the square packed to overflowing with groups of men and women, the selectors switched to hardcore dancehall geared to a male audience, including that with more violent lyrics, songs that were currently at the height of popularity, and American hip-hop that was getting regular radio and television play. The party reached its height at around two or three in the morning. The peak party energy was sustained via skillful selection by the sound systems, a combination of liquor and ganja, and the arrival of some special guest entertainment. The blocked street was used as a runway of sorts, with cameramen filming women "wining their waists" in their best clothes and new hairstyles. People danced and "profiled," or posed, in their party finery for the two cameras that had been hired to memorialize the event. These videos would then circulate within the community in the coming weeks so that attendants could remember the night, look at themselves on a television screen, and, at least among the group of women I viewed it with, gossip about the other women they saw on the tapes and critique their clothing, dancing, and physiques.[25] Two women, in particular, stole the show with their Angela Davis–esque party costumes, which included fluffy round afro wigs and tailored blue denim retro-1970s ensembles. They were clearly enjoying the limelight and even underwent a change of attire as the night progressed. The other star of the show was a short, heavyset woman in her twenties who the mic man called Fatty. She was a local woman with a reputation for skillful dancing. A circle of people formed around her as space was cleared for her to perform. When she began, Krystal grabbed me by the hand, pulling me toward the crowd to insure that I would get a good view of this special show. The woman stooping at the waist, hands on her knees, pushed out her buttocks and moved in time with the rhythm. The crowd was filled with a mixture of awe at Fatty's skill and glee at Fatty's size and shape, which were not a predictable combination. Krystal commented to me with a laugh in her voice, "She can dance!"[26]

A little later a car and its driver, utilizing the only path open to traffic, pulled up to Guy Town Square at the height of the festivities, and Nadia, a local reigning dancehall queen known for her innovative self-presentation, emerged from the backseat, making a dramatic entrance with her female crew. She wore a sheer shirt with no bra, tight white jeans, and a blue thong that showed over the hips of the pants. The crowd buzzed in recognition of her arrival, and she soon found a member of an up-and-coming dancehall group whom I'd seen on a local music video show to dance with. She wrapped her legs around the youth's waist and hung upside down with her head nearly touching the asphalt and rotated her hips. It looked as if the youth was struggling to appear composed while enduring Nadia's athleticism. They were the center of attention for several minutes as they moved to the music.

The sound system then highlighted the DJ skills of some local youth by "running a rhythm" for them to perform over. One performer was Blake, who I later interviewed regarding his work with Wicked Times. As they performed, the crowd stopped what they were doing, turned toward the performance, and gave them their undivided attention, flashing cigarette lighters in the air in approval of the DJ skills on display.

Once the selectors returned to playing tunes, a crew of ten to twelve youths, led by the youth who had danced with Nadia, gathered in a cluster. They moved forward in formation toward the cameraman, who was backing up in front of them, and performed coordinated dance steps as they glided down the runway/street in sync. The dancehall performer among them was clearly the leader, and, as they danced, he demonstrated new moves for the other young men to follow.[27] Krystal's "sister-in-law," a hilarious woman in her fifties, provided comic relief to the display of cool, youthful, masculinity and style by joining the cluster of men and attempting to imitate their gliding steps for the camera.

The party continued until the sun came up. At about 6 a.m., Nadia climbed the huge stack of speakers set up near security corner. Once at the top, the light of dawn behind her, she proceeded to stand on her head and arms and "wine" her lower body in the air. The selector narrated the performance. She opened the button and zipper on her pants, revealing more of her thong and an impressive, rippling set of abdominal muscles that could have belonged to a body builder. The mic man said, "Yes, [Nadia], take off those pants." She slid them off, turning away from the crowd and gyrating her buttocks and thighs. She then slithered face down on the top of the stacks, mocking intercourse with the speaker. She turned again, revealing her buttocks, while the mic man told her to show them the expression she has on her face when she has sex. She indicated that she doesn't "make up her face," pretending she's not in pain. She demonstrated that she just "takes it" by shaking her head and waving her hands, making her face into a grimace and slapping her buttocks onto the top of the speaker box. She eventually climbed down, having gained the attention of the entire crowd, and made her way to the selectors' tent, where she proceeded to hang upside down from one of the metal supports, shaking the tent and alarming the selectors and crowd that she might pull it down, injuring herself.

In this performance, Nadia is exhibiting behavior in some ways beyond male control, with her initial domination of her dance partner and then by scaling the speaker stack, drawing the entire party's attention to her skillful, erotic, display. However, the selector's narration over the microphone in the end guides and interpolates the action using the male gaze. Nadia, in this role, speaks with her body, while the selector speaks with a masculine voice.[28] She was given $5,000 for her performance because the sound system had offered that sum to the woman who could win the wining contest. Then the selector offered $20,000 to any woman that could beat Nadia's performance, but no one took up that challenge. Nadia's payment for her work as a dancer evokes Donna Hope's analysis of sexual display and female labor in the dancehall: "many of the economic and other rewards reaped by the women in the dancehall come directly from men in an exchange that serves to underpin and legitimize the sexual identity of men and their superior position over women" (Hope 2006b, 75).

In addition to offering up the opportunity for women in attendance to capture the top prize from Nadia in the wining contest, the mic men also told the crowd to raise their hands, wine their waists, and flash their lighters for a number of different reasons throughout the event. For men, it was if they "love pumpum," (meaning vagina) and "have nuff gal." Women were to make themselves known if they "na dash wey belly" (have not had an abortion), if they "have pickney and you body na mash up" (have children and still maintain an appealing figure), and if "you pumpum tight." They also made a general call "if you na HIV positive." Sound systems use these strategies to get the crowd excited and engaged in the street dance because if a person were to fail to make noise, flash lighters, and dance when any of these calls were made, they would be admitting to shameful or socially unacceptable traits. This strategy both serves as an easy way to raise the party's energy level and gain praise for the sound system, and simultaneously solidify the group into a community who, at least superficially, share the same values.

It must be kept in mind that this particular dance was kept on a school/work night, and whether residents liked it or not, they would be awake until dawn unless they could sleep through all the noise. There were few children at the event; however, Krystal's children were out on the square for most of the night, and neither of them went to school the following day. While her children enjoyed the party, Krystal joked that they could sleep at school. Others went directly from the dance to work and directly from work to bed. Alesha went down to her yard, a few lanes away, in time to wake her children up for school. My American guest and I left at about 6:30 in the morning, and, reportedly, once we'd gone, some gunshots were fired and the police came to shut the dance down. When I talked to Frass at Wicked Times the following day, he said the studio was deserted due to "too much party last night." The local soccer team had also won their match, so there was additional cause for celebration.

As the above description demonstrates, street dances reinforce status hierarchies in a number of ways. The ability to successfully keep a dance relies on the host's ability to mobilize his or her resources, including money, respect, and the potential for the use of violence, in order to both display and solidify personal prestige. It is a display of wealth, both monetary and social, that in turn generates further wealth. The host provides a service to the community through entertainment, and the partygoers show their gratitude toward the host by spending their resources, displaying further respect, and withholding potentially disruptive behavior during the course of the event.

Status hierarchies are also reinforced through public displays of respect, which take the form of big ups that identify who the key power brokers are in the area and which can be looked at as a ritualized practice within dancehall culture. In addition, the format of the event itself can be viewed as a mirror of ghetto social structures that also strengthens their power through collective, public performance. A dance, at its start, draws only social outcasts and children. People who are included in the mainstream population know better than to arrive at a street dance too early, and especially esteemed guests will not appear until the event is well underway. The participants arriving in the next wave are itinerant, using the open space as a venue for displaying their ownership of various modes of transportation, such as bicycles and motorcycles. Eventually, the soundmen target their selections to draw women to the event, whose mere presence helps the dance to attract more men. Only once the general crowd has reached its peak will the celebrity guests arrive and special forms of entertainment take place.

Public display further comes into play in the street dance setting when mic men appeal to the crowd as individuals to audibly and visually demonstrate that they belong to the larger collective. This is done by purposefully choosing accepted social categories with which members of the crowd will want to express affiliation. As shown in the above description, these prideful categories include men who love women and sex, people who can demonstrate their independence by not wearing borrowed clothing to the event, women who can jump up and shout proudly because they've never had an abortion, and people who are disease free.

Conclusion

Dancehall lyrics, participation in the genre, and public consumption of the music all point to a relationship in which dancehall music and ghetto communities are, in a sense, coconstitutive. The music is an expression of the ghetto, but the worldview and practices taking place within the ghetto are also reinforced through the lyrical content of the music, through the practice of creating the music, and through the ways the music is utilized and enjoyed both publicly and privately. However, Das and Poole's discussion of the ways in which the "margins" are actually constitutive spaces also needs to be reinvoked here (Das and Poole 2004). It can be seen through P. J. Patterson's "poor" choice of words at the National Arena, and through the relationships between area leaders and members of Parliament discussed in Chapter 1, that ghetto communities contain political populations central to the operations of the state and have created in dancehall a form of expression that has become central to the public discourse around what Jamaica, as a nation, is and should be. So while Jamaican dancehall and Jamaican ghetto communities may construct and reinforce each other, they also interrupt the normative imaginary of what the Jamaican nation is and shape the ways in which the Jamaican state must operate.

CHAPTER 4

"Got to mek a living"

Dancehall as Industry

Wicked Times, as a dancehall production company, exists at the intersection of a physical and ideological divide—Kingston's uptown and downtown. In the minds of most Kingstonians, regardless of class position, the boundary between uptown and downtown, called Halfway Tree, signifies class and cultural differentiations among residents of the Kingston Metropolitan Area. A representational boundary has been fashioned from class-based residential settlement patterns, which shape the city's social geography and the local language of class difference. Beyond this sociopolitical location, the company also creates a connective node that transgresses the local through Wicked Times's participation in the multinational music industry. The production activities of Wicked Times link Jamaica, as a space of creative production and economic paucity, with the global economy, in pursuit of foreign investment and expanded consumer markets for dancehall music.

Only by first examining the current state of the music industry as part of the Jamaican national economy can the significance and complexity of Wicked Times's location be fully understood. Wicked Times is a fundamentally local company that developed in downtown Kingston and which grows out of the long history of Jamaican musical culture. This locus requires a level of operational versatility that allows the company to bridge the ghetto milieu that fosters the creation of dancehall and a business milieu that requires an understanding of professionalism both locally and abroad. Finally, the marketing of dancehall music to overseas audiences becomes a crucial issue for the success of the company. In particular, the way overseas marketing gets addressed at Wicked Times is indicative of the professional maneuvering necessitated by Jamaica's position within global economic and cultural hierarchies, and of the impact that position has on the company and its performers with regard to career-building strategies.

While many researchers have effectively focused on the imperialism of the multinational music industry and "First World" celebrity musicians' treatment and promotion of "Third World" performers, here I am more interested in looking at the ways in which Jamaican performers view their own relationship to the global market for music and the multinational music industry that controls its production and distribution (Wallis and Malm 1984; Keil and Feld 1994).[1]

Additionally, rather than taking on the issue of musical "creolization" as either an artistically invigorating phenomenon reflecting the free flow of people and ideas in the present period, or as another by-product of colonialism, slavery, and, presently, the global inequalities of neoliberalism, I am choosing to treat it as a context confronted by musicians and artists that necessarily includes all these possibilities (Appadurai 1996; Keil and Feld 1994). This perspective emphasizes the relationship between the artistic choices and career decisions made by performers situated in economically peripheral, but creatively significant, localities such as Jamaica.

The relationship between artistry and commercial opportunity has been characterized as a strategic negotiation of market values utilizing local cultural values at a time when locally crafted music enters an uneven global marketplace (Saunders 2003). A comparable set of issues has been examined in the realm of pink collar employment in the Caribbean through the analysis of personal style as a practice of self-presentation, which serves as a mediator between the local and global in the formulation of new kinds of selves for female workers in Barbados (Freeman 2000). The preoccupation with "professionalism" versus "vibes" at Wicked Times reflects the position of the company as a node that connects local and global markets, as well as the revised position of the dancehall industry in the eyes of the Jamaican government.

The Jamaican Music Industry

There has been a noteworthy shift in thinking with regard to the music industry within the Jamaican government over the past fifteen years. Since 1996, music and entertainment have been included as part of the country's National Industrial Policy (Witter 2004, 57). Steps have been taken to monitor the earnings potential from entertainment enterprises that had previously flown under the radar. This is not to say that the reluctance to promote dancehall as a valued product of Jamaica as a nation has been alleviated. Current struggles over national symbolism and branding often have debates over the value of dancehall music as a product of the urban working class at their center (Mussche 2008). However, the recognized earnings potential for Jamaican music led the country's leadership to institute a three-phase plan in 2001. The policy's intention is to bring all entertainment-relevant government ministries together to craft public policy, to create an Entertainment Advisory Board which links public and private interests in order to help formulate entertainment policies, and to establish an entertainment division of the Ministry of Tourism and Sports in order to implement industrial policies (Planning Institute of Jamaica 2002). As part of this effort, the Private Sector Development Program, a 28.67 million euro, five-year initiative launched in 2005 includes the Jamaican Music Network under the management of the Recording Industry of Jamaica, a private sector organization (PSO), alongside more traditional production sectors like agriculture and tourism, as a target for assistance. Jointly funded by the European Union and the Jamaican government, the program has three focus areas: enhancement of national and enterprise competitiveness; PSO empowerment; and enrichment of access to corporate financing (Panadeiros and Benfield 2010, 44–48). These measures were introduced after research indicated that the 218.8 million Jamaican dollars contributed to the gross domestic product by the music industry in 1992, according to the World Bank, were a mere drop in the bucket, representing only 0.03 percent of the total GDP (Jamaica Promotions Corporation 1996/1997, 13). Though notoriously difficult to track, various estimates of earnings potential suggest that the market value for Jamaican music as an export could potentially reach $2.5 billion dollars in U.S. currency (JAMPRO 1996, 59). According to 2005 data, music, theatrical productions, and opera, categorized as a group, represented 0.21 percent of the Jamaican GDP (V. James 2007, 294). Accompanying this potential contribution to the GDP, Jamaican economist Michael Witter has also estimated that the music industry contributes in the range of twelve thousand local jobs concentrated among populations with few recognized skills and an average of only 10.3 years of formal education, directly enhancing the economic environment within poor communities and directly supporting approximately forty-three thousand persons (V. James 2007, 245; Witter 2004, 37, 56).

The new attention to the music industry's earnings potential has often been supported by reference to global economic shifts that favored service-oriented economies over those reliant on manufacturing or the extraction of raw materials (Anderson, Kozul-Wright, and Kozul-Wright 2000; Bourne and Allgrove 1995). Arguments in favor of modernizing the music industry through better regulation, newer information and communication technologies (ICTs), and professionalization are usually accompanied by the implication that these changes will also constitute a step toward the modernization of the Jamaican economy as a whole. It has been suggested that, in addition to modernizing the industry, the use of ICTs might allow music industries in developing countries to bypass the dominion of the international music industry, which has been monopolized by a small number of conglomerates located largely in the United States and Japan that control 70 percent of the market share (Kozul-Wright and Stanbury 1998, 10; V. James 2007, 235).[2] The promotion of reggae music as an authentic expression of Jamaican culture has also been advanced as an enhancement to the marketing of "Brand Jamaica," which will, in theory, encourage tourism and the purchase of other Jamaica-identified exports (Bourne and Allgrove 1995; Jamaica Promotions Corporation 1996; Mussche 2008).

The three-phase plan was designed to diminish obstacles to the successful cultivation of the industry's earning potential, which include ineffective copyright control and insufficient repatriation of artists' earnings to Jamaica, as well as a general lack of institutional support and regulation for the entertainment industry as a whole. However, patterns within the music industry itself, including disorganized trade associations and general secrecy around business practices and earnings, make understanding and developing the industry's potential a difficult project (Kozul-Wright and Stanbury 1998; Witter 2004).

The concerns of the Jamaican government around the creation of an effective framework for the cultivation of reggae music as a revenue-bearing part of the national economy focus locally, as the three-phase plan indicates, with an eye toward bridging local production and international markets. This focus requires an awareness of both local production practices and the international division of labor that has been established for the production and distribution of music, which begins with recording; then proceeds to manufacturing, marketing, and distribution; and finally concludes with retailing (Kozul-Wright and Stanbury 1998). The management and talent at Wicked Times, one of an estimated two hundred Jamaican recording studios, possess an acute awareness of the class-based socioeconomic dynamics of Jamaica, dancehall production as a creative process, and the music industry as an international commercial enterprise. This awareness is, in many ways, enhanced by the company's rootedness in Guy Town, among the ranks of urban improvisors who maintain a unique interpretation of neoliberal productivity and entrepreneurship as a mode of survival in relation to the exclusionary practices of economic globalization.

Locating Wicked Times

Wicked Times's offices and recording studios are located well above Halfway Tree, the area that demarcates the division between uptown and downtown both physically and ideologically. This location is a long way from the company's humble origins in a tiny office in Guy Town, though it is only a short trip by car between the two areas. According to the company origin myth, as told by Dads, the company's CEO, the seeds of Wicked Times were sown when he began working with a sound system that was attached to a neighborhood repair shop where he was receiving electrical engineering training after having left high school because of financial constraints. At this time he began "hanging around the sound." Dads eventually received permission to be a more formal member of the sound system, working his way up from the bottom by helping at dances and lifting sound boxes onto trucks as a way of gaining access to the events. He explained, "Now, eventually you start to take part in a musical situation. You know? So we continue being around the sound and learn sound and [. . .] we have now additional experience toward the musical aspect. Because then you start get how a selector select his tune, what type of tune them come for, and then we start interact with musicians and start interact with artists so you start to develop that culture." It was while traveling with the sound in this capacity that Dads met the key people, children in their early teens at the time, with whom he would construct his now internationally known company. His ghetto-based networks and social skills (reputation) created the springboard for what was to come. He recounted attending a performance competition where he "met these likkle youth name [Mr. Mention] and [Bizzy]." The two boys from Baymore won first and second place.[3] Dads described meeting his longtime business partners for the first time: "So I went over to them and introduced myself to them as part of the sound because the people I was there with, the owner of the sound and all them people, them always like when me talk. [. . .] So we invited them to come down and so that is where we start have a serious dialogue with artists." At that time, Bizzy and Mr. Mention started coming around on a regular basis. Then, according to Dads, "one day the same person [who ran the electronics company and sound system] says to me, 'Why you always ride up and down and a ask other people to write songs for them? I think you is capable enough that you can write songs for them!' You know? So hence I wrote one of the first songs for [Bizzy] and then we start that there." At that point it was 1987, and the three decided to launch a record label and coined the name Wicked Times. Dads referred to Wicked Times proudly as "a collective venture between myself, [Mr. Mention], [Bizzy] and [Loverman]." He added, "So far the three artists are still with me." This conversation speaks to the importance of positioning within ghetto-based social networks. Dads, as a youth who is around the same age as the newest dancehall performers, is able to relate with them in a way that enables him to make connections for the sound system, which the older operators may not be able to make so easily. However, it is only with the guidance of a more experienced mentor that Dads is convinced to take the next step by writing lyrics and cultivating this set of young men as "his artists." This relationship seems to have carried on into adulthood for Dads and the artists because now, as a mature and successful performer with Dads as his primary producer, Mr. Mention told me that "[Dads] is the man with the idea, I am de man wid de paycheck!"

The symbiotic nature of Wicked Times as a company owned and managed collectively by a foundational set of performers interrupts standard music industry horror stories of performer exploitation at the hands of their unscrupulous management.[4] The distinction can be linked to the normative social relations of reputation and respect that Dads and Mr. Mention share owing to their comparable upbringing in ghetto communities. However, Mr. Mention also told me that this was an arrangement that took time to develop. His version of the company's history takes his own quest for superstardom as its starting point. In our interview, Mr. Mention highlighted the fact that as a street smart ghetto youth, when talking to Dads about working together, he was cautious about acting on empty promises. His socialization had taught him that unfounded loyalty and other missteps could set the hard work he had already put into building a reputation off course. Therefore he needed to be convinced, even as a young teen, that something concrete would happen before he could wholeheartedly sign on to the project.

Superstar status don't come to you, you have to go out there and work for it. So, that's exactly what I did. You know? I went towards making a company because I had met [Dads] since I was eleven years of age. You see it? And he have been a friend of mine for years, but I never was taking any talk from [Dads] because you know as a ghetto youth I do not tek promissory note and promises. You seen? I have to definitely see wha happen. You see wha mi a seh? And mi seh "alright we can move on dis." So, [Wicked Times] start and then I become the spokesman for the company. So we have [Bizzy] and we have [Clark] and we have [Loverman]. Seen? We deh deh now try fi mek a team out a nuttin.'

Dads remembers the early days of the company as a scramble for opportunities to perform, which led to new connections as well as a level of financial discipline, which led to larger offices, because they were operating out of a small room in Guy Town and they didn't have bookings for the artists. He described Mr. Mention and Bizzy as being on a "wild goose chase," searching for opportunities to perform. The endeavor gained momentum, as Dads recounts, "and then we was to where we needed to have a base for ourselves so, 1994, when [a prominent dancehall producer] moved from [the building that housed his company] and the fact that we usually hang around [the company], we asked the owner if we could get the office space and he [afforded] us with the privilege." Dads explained that "from there on we started same way to put our resources into good use and not being the fact that you see a bunch of youths weh love party and we use our money to buy pure champagne and living a wild life. We never go that route there. [. . .] We put our resources safely for a rainy day and save and save until we saw weh this place was selling." Referring to the current office building, Dads told me that they entered into an agreement to buy the property, "licked it down," and after demolishing it, rebuilt the studios from scratch. The latest incarnation of Wicked Times studio sits on a cul-de-sac that juts off of a high traffic avenue covered with strip malls, gas stations, and chain restaurants. The cul-de-sac is a prime location for spotting Jamaicans famous in the music industry that "pass through" Wicked Times to use the studio, talk business, or visit with friends.

When approaching the Wicked Times complex, a visitor is confronted by the high front gate bearing the company's insignia and the adjacent security guard booth. By peering through the green metal bars, a passerby can see the selection of flashy cars driven by the company's performers and executive board, which are often being washed in the front drive. Alternately, a visitor might see a cluster of young men sitting on a truck bumper and talking with the company's co-owner, and most prominent performer, Mr. Mention. This might be a visitor's first glimpse into the diasporic reverberations that take place between North America and the Caribbean and that are an integral part of Wicked Times and the dancehall industry in general. These reverberations are, in part, reflected in modes of dress and in consumption preferences, which are influenced by the stylistic choices made by African Americans in the hip-hop industry (Gilroy 1993a, 1993b; Hall 1996; Mercer 1994; Thomas 2004, 2011). They often take the form of tastes regarding preferred car makes and models and clothing brands. However, styles adopted from hip-hop videos and other media featuring African American celebrities always have a unique Jamaican twist, such as a variation on the fit of the clothing or pairing of styles, and are not taken on wholesale. It is important to note that these stylistic choices are meant to index a specifically working-class African American aesthetic of affluence rather than a European, Euro-American, or even an uptown Kingston one.

Looking past the social scene in the driveway, the viewer's eye is confronted with a multistoried stucco complex painted a characteristically Caribbean pastel color. The balcony on the upper story of the complex is decorated with an enormous portrait of Mr. Mention, which appears to watch over the front of the property with a romanticized, windswept majesty. Those unfamiliar to the elderly security guard are briefly questioned at the gate before being admitted into the compound via a swinging door for those on foot, or through the large sliding gate for those arriving by car. Visitors then approach the main entrance, which is equipped with a door buzzer so that the receptionist can identify people through the tinted windows and admit them while still seated behind her desk. These features speak to a general necessity for uptown businesses and homes to be well secured in the high-crime environment of Kingston but also reflect the company's unique position as a place of affluence linked to places of poverty through the dancehall genre.[5]

Upon entering the reception area, the visitor may feel the cool blast of the air conditioner and notice a large wood-and-glass curio cabinet, which prominently displays all the awards that have been given to performers at Wicked Times. The cabinet includes a Grammy Award along with numerous plaques and trophies issued by the local entertainment industry. There are also soccer trophies awarded by Wray and Nephew, a Jamaican rum producer, for the greater Perry Town area's champion team, over which Dads presides. The reception area is outfitted with comfortable leather loveseats and features a large oil painting depicting an apparently lifeless Bob Marley lying in the arms of a grieving woman. The side tables are scattered with industry magazines for the perusal of waiting guests.

After passing through the doorway of the reception area into the brightly lit and open central administrative space with its cool tile floor, there is a stairway going up to the second story, where Dads' sequestered office is located. Looking straight ahead past the desks of the public relations manager and her assistant, you can see the sliding glass door that separates the employee's lounge and two studios from the administrative space. Crossing a small outdoor walkway from the studio section, you see an open but sheltered area designated for smoking marijuana, which is not permitted at the front of the building. The second part of the complex across the walkway contains a gym; a lunchroom, complete with private chef; and a bathroom with shower. These amenities serve as an additional reminder of the company's origins because they are designed to fulfill needs such as access to regular hot meals, physical fitness equipment, and facilities to enable good personal hygiene, which may not be readily available to some of Wicked Times's staff members and many up-and-coming performers.

A Home Away from Home

In my interview with Natural, a DJ who, though born in Kingston, is now a Canadian citizen who returns to Kingston yearly to perform and record, he described in personal terms how he contends with the income gap at Wicked Times as someone who, himself, grew up with few resources. He told me,

> Jamaica has a lot of poverty. Jamaica have a lot of money. There's people here who are wealthy, but the gap between the wealthy and the poor is so wide! [. . .] 'Cause, I see people that I get depressed when I see them because I just hate to see certain thing and, like, these people want to do better, but it's just like they don't have the money. There's people who can't even find dinner for the evening or the morning so.

He explained that sometimes when he comes to the studio he gives away his money: "I probably have a thousand dollar in my pocket and there's guys that come to the gate sometimes and you know they're hungry. They don't have bus fare to go home and a guy come to you and like 'just beg you a hundred dollar' [. . .] and you know this guy's hungry and you end up giving it away and you know this guy wants to get into music." Natural's description of himself as someone who gives away pocket money throughout the day grows out of the same set of values around giving, respect, and reputation that I detailed in Chapter 1. He goes on to identify with the hungry dancehall hopeful as someone who may not be able to take advantage of career opportunities when they arise because of the physical impact of their poverty on their day-to-day activities. "It's not like he wants the music more than you because we both want to be successful in whatever you want to do, but you feel more pity for that person because he can't find something to even eat. I see guys here and know that they're hungry and like if they get a chance to go sing a song, I think, 'How is he gonna sing it?' because you probably have a headache or something!" The thing he likes about Wicked Times is that they provide a lunchroom where all the employees can have free cooked food every day. He continued, "[Wicked Times] has a couple plans that I haven't seen in Jamaica and it's working out because sometimes a lot of these guys come to get lunch and stuff like that. So that's what I like about [Wicked Times], there's good things here." He told me that Wicked Times feels more like a family than a business enterprise, providing the example, "sometime some young guy could have a problem because a couple young artist here. We'll always if you have problem, everybody put together like, okay, get him this, get him stuff, if he need something to get for a kid, or something, this and that. Sometimes they come in with no bus fare to go home so they could ask for a bus fare to go home and stuff. It's hard. To me it's hard, hard, hard." In the interview, he emphasized that the combination of poverty and pursuit of a dancehall career is a particularly difficult one. While the payoff from a successful career can be quite high, there are no guarantees. To him, Wicked Times's recognition of these problems and their efforts to ameliorate employees' and performers' difficult living conditions set them apart from other companies.

Loverman, one of the founding performers at Wicked Times, who is also a company shareholder, indicated as well that the company was like a family when I asked him how it was different from other studios. His response suggests that beyond family connoting a system of shared support, it also implies shared responsibility, hearkening back to the values of community support and giving that residents of Guy Town stated were part of their culture. He echoed Natural's statement that the company is more like a family saying,

> We're close. Very, very, close [. . .]. Each man know what type of part they're playing where the company is concerned and you know whenever anybody step out a line you know we round up a meeting and you know we discuss it and put everybody back in place again. So you know is a whole different ball. You know we don't allow [. . .] things to just happen like that, because whenever you allow things to just happen like that it will get out of hand.

He told me that within the company, "everybody feel as if we all are one, but yet still we don't really mek nobody put their foot over the boundary. You know what I'm saying?"

Blake, the up-and-coming performer whose career I discussed in Chapter 3, described the studio as his "second home," which reinforced a feeling I got from the performers and employees on my visits. He said, "Well, this is [Wicked Times], my second home, you know, ca here suh mi deh everyday [because I'm here every day] and mi even deh yah so more often than my home [and I'm even here more often than at my home], ca dung a mi yard mi just go dung a night time go sleep [because I just go down to my yard at night to sleep]. Seen? And come up back early a morning. Seen?" When I asked Blake if he had everything he needed at the studio in terms of a second home, he responded with a smile and a boastful enthusiasm in his voice,

> Yeah, everything, everything! You have two studio, you have a big studio and you have preproduction where like you find a idea you just get your riddim and go round there and play your riddim until you got it good! You go into the big studio. Yeah, it's good up here. And here, you know, waiting room. Kick back and watch two TV and wait on your friend and you have the lunchroom up there and you have the gym . . . little weight lifting.

As Blake's description indicates, Wicked Times has the feel of a clubhouse where people can work, or just relax and watch television. It is largely the male performers who spend the whole day at the studio working on music and socializing.

The few times I saw female artists there, they were taking care of specific business-related tasks, or working on particular projects in the studio. Members of the upper management are generally locked away in their private offices, in contrast to the lower-level male employees who work in more public spaces at the studio and who are usually age-peers with the younger performers. The few female employees tend to fill administrative roles in the organization, including receptionist, administrative assistant, and public relations manager.

When I sat with Lena, the neatly dressed and well-composed public relations manager, at her desk, I asked what it was like for her to work in such a male-oriented industry and environment. She told me that, "as a woman now, the women that are well known tend to be aggressive. You look at the ones who are really prominent, you know you ask anybody on the street if they've heard their name and they have, are very aggressive. Very, very, bitchy kind of people." She went on to say that female artists are few and far between, so the ones who are in the business need to be tough because it's hard for a woman to get respect. Of her own experience, she said, "I have been hit on by just about everyone I can think of, you know? And there are different levels of it. There are people who will say 'bwoy' . . . and there are people who will try to force you. And I guess that occasionally women who get bitchy, get bitchy because there have been more people trying to force them. I think they had to develop a very hard skin." Her comment references the prevalence of male romantic/sexual pursuit of female professionals within the dancehall industry, which at times veers into the realm of sexual coercion or "force," demonstrating the patriarchal control over women that is a significant component of ghetto masculinity; the culture of dancehall spills over into the business environment in ways that harden female participants, shifting their personalities away from any sense of feminine propriety or submissiveness and making them, in her words, "bitchy." Lena was doubtful that she would ever reach the level of "a Dads" because she was "not ready to curse bad words and be boisterous and flamboyant and I think I am a proper person and I would like to stay that way. And I don't think a woman can make it like that, but I am going to try! But those are the difficulties." Here Lena makes an important point about women in dancehall. As mentioned in Chapter 3, the female dancehall persona is derived from a working-class idea of womanhood and is also modeled as a counterpart to the male dancehall persona, both characterized by the flouting of upper-class ideas of propriety and restraint (Cooper 1993, 2004; Pinnock 2007). She echoes Georgina's statements from Chapter 3 when she indicates that a woman, in particular, who is a "proper person" may face additional difficulties when trying to break into the male-dominated dancehall industry (see Hope 2010). However, as Freeman has noted in her study of pink-collar informatics workers in Barbados, "the models held up as 'respectable' are changing . . . out of local economic and cultural conditions," which raises the possibility that as more women enter into the dancehall industry as professionals, definitions of respectability will shift to accommodate this new set of employment opportunities (Freeman 2000, 235).

"Maleness" permeates the studio, which is a gendered space where competitive and affectionate verbal jousting between men is a standard style of interaction (Cooper 1993). For example, while I was interviewing one of the performers in the employee lounge, Frass, the assistant public relations manager, burst into the room. The artist I was talking with told Frass that we were in the middle of an interview, and Frass replied, "Yeah, but I've got the OVERVIEW!" The cleverness of the quick response bested the artist, who had attempted to establish his own importance because he was being interviewed, and provoked laughter and approval for Frass, who had successfully taken him down a notch within earshot of others. This creativity, play, and competition also translate into the production process itself, as I experienced after witnessing recording sessions and other, more casual, aspects of the artistic process.

Making Dancehall and Making a Business

Creating dancehall music is often a collaborative enterprise and the studio becomes a venue for sharing ideas and practicing creative wordplay. As a highly valued form of communication, this wordplay, when applied to writing lyrics, makes dancehall a verbally intricate and inventive genre (Cooper 1993). Younger artists and some nonperformer employees at Wicked Times practice lyric writing with the hope that their work will be adopted for use by more established performers as they formulate new songs to record. Though performers have different methods for writing lyrics, they will often use current events and descriptions of their surroundings as inspiration, in addition to the sets of stock themes that have become standards in the dancehall genre (see Chapter 3).

Blake described the process and studio politics of recording a new song, which begins in the preproduction studio, before moving into the main studio, where the artists continue their work with the assistance of the engineers. He indicated that if the company management believes in an artist they, will grant access to the studio prior to hearing what they have been working on. Turning to his own status as a recording artist, he said,

> Them know seh, "alright, [Blake] can deliver and come up with the stuff wha them waan hear," them will trust you dat wey deh, seen? But if not, you know the management haffi go hear what a gwaan first. Seen? Like me now, dem know mi can do my thing, seen? [. . .] And mi na DJ no foolinish, so you know dem just give me the go. All mi haffi do a just link up with the engineer and then we just do something.

When the producer or management come to hear what the artist is working on and like what they're hearing, they will make sure the public also hears it. In his words, "Him like it, you know it gone! [laughing] Him a go push it, trust me." In the above conversation, Blake emphasized artists developing a reputation within the Wicked Times community and earning a level of respect, which then allows for relative freedom in the recording studio. Then, only secondarily, will the management become involved in the process if, upon hearing the track, they decide it will be marketable for the company.

Building a Rhythm

Just before my scheduled interview with Mr. Mention, Clive, a well-established performer who is not a member of Wicked Times, but who uses the studio at times, showed up to work on a rhythm with Simeon, one of the younger studio engineers. I was able to join them behind the thick and weighty wooden studio door, in the cool, damp room, which is carpeted floor to ceiling and soundproofed. Clive welcomed my intrusion and explained to me that they were building a dancehall rhythm. When I heard the track, I knew that they were working to capitalize on the Indian sound, borrowed from South Asian dance music called Bhangra that had become popular, first in hip-hop beats, and then as part of the dancehall rhythm repertoire.

Once he and Simeon had adjusted some of the computerized drums that sounded like tablas, Clive experimented with some off-the-cuff DJ-ing over the rhythm track. He then had Simeon DJ over it as well. Clive then dragged several other young men into the studio and played them the rhythm, which reverberated throughout the equipment-laden room, to which they exclaimed, "Bumbo!" an expletive that, in this case, expressed ecstatic approval. One of the youths then told Clive that he was a genius. Clive explained that he wanted to create three new rhythms, each different than the other, mentioning that after a recently popular rhythm he'd produced, people were expecting something different from him. He indicated that everyone was trying to do something that incorporated the sound of hands clapping now that a rhythm called Diwali, which used that sound, had become a dancehall favorite. Referring to the rhythm he and Simeon had just finished, he said that the introductory part left listeners not knowing what to expect. He asked to have Mr. Mention sent in to listen, and one of the youths quickly went to get him. Mr. Mention appeared through the studio door, taking a seat by the mixing board and listening quietly to Clive and Simeon's creation. Clive tested how his lyrics might work over the rhythm, while Mr. Mention vocalized a few of his characteristically entertaining percussion noises over it. They experimented with the new beats and exuberantly danced around the periphery of the studio. After Mr. Mention departed, Clive announced that if he and Mr. Mention were to be on a rhythm and make two strong tracks, the rhythm would "buss" ("bust," meaning it would be a hit).

The management's understanding of this creative process influences the business practices at the studio, which is why, according to Dads, Wicked Times is reluctant to rent out studio time. When I asked if Wicked Times rents out their facilities, he explained,

> No, not on a full wide scale rental basis, because we believe that music [. . .] is a situation where it just hit you at any time of the night. We don't want to be renting the studio and then a song hit you with one hour and you just want to record and then you have to stop someone session. We rather that the studio lock and if anything of that nature happen we can quick to capitalize on that.

It is important to note that when Dads referred to inspiration hitting a resident artist, he did not suggest that the artist would have to wait to record, but that the artist would have to interrupt the booked studio session of the renter to "capitalize" on that moment. In talking to other performers who work at Wicked Times, it became clear that there was also an internal pecking order for studio use, with Mr. Mention having the first priority. Both of these practices can be linked to the importance of the concept of ownership, which seems to have particular salience with members of the black working class, who prize independence and self-employment.

A further indication of the importance of ownership arose when I indelicately asked Mr. Mention what he felt the difference was between working at a local studio as compared to a foreign studio. He was quick to correct me, replying, "Well, I don't *work* with a company in Jamaica. I *have my own company* inna Jamaica." Ownership allows the management, company shareholders who are largely top-level dancehall performers, a high degree of control over the music they produce, the profits they earn, and the composition of the company itself.

The management strategically surround themselves with employees they know to be trustworthy, some of whom have been cultivated through the education efforts Wicked Times sponsors in Guy Town. When I asked Dads about the staff at Wicked Times, he told me, "Well, basically we have a roster of about twenty-eight, broken down into sections, we have engineers, we have chef, we have administrative staff, and you have maintenance staff." After telling me that approximately 60 percent of the staff is drawn from Guy Town, he referred to "the fact that you grow up with these youths and you are around them and you know their capability because you see it. [. . .] What I believe in, you know, it's just opportunity. Opportunity where I have to look back from where I come and the fact that we come from there and the youths dem just need the privilege." He then followed up, "We believe that if they are capable, then why not give them that privilege? So our road manager, our assistant manager, our public relations officer, you know, the chefs, all of them come from [Guy Town]."

Part of Dads's brilliance as a businessman is his knack for assembling a wide range of people from different backgrounds and with an array of skills, who can fill the variety of positions necessary for things to run smoothly at Wicked Times. This composition is critical to the functioning of the company within Jamaican society given that dancehall is linked to illegitimacy and indiscipline in the imagination of a public that is raised on the value of meritocracy through education. The varied personal strengths, which can be thought of as social capital, combine to create an environment that is both acceptably professional and deeply connected to its ghetto roots, an essential combination when creating and selling dancehall to local and international markets.

A perfect example of Dad's skillfulness as a businessman is his employment of a lecturer from University of the West Indies. This lecturer was introduced to Dads by one of the faculty participating in the adult remedial education program in Guy Town, with the knowledge that the lecturer was interested in becoming a dancehall performer. The lecturer became a guest instructor in the men's education classes and became familiar with Dads, thereby gaining access to Wicked Times's studio. Dads utilized this arrangement strategically, appointing the lecturer spokesman for Wicked Times. In this capacity, he became a public face for the company. As a former ghetto youth who now has a PhD, the lecturer is authentic yet respectable and, therefore, the perfect ambassador to address the media and wider public. It also does not hurt that this particular lecturer grew to be widely celebrated in Kingston as a rags-to-riches success story, placing him among the ranks of Jamaican public intellectuals. He served as a public example of social mobility into the middle class through hard work and education, values that ideologically justify his new status and global citizenship. The lecturer's skillfully fashioned subjectivity is highlighted by his elocutionary practice of switching between patois and Standard English in his presentations and by his public assertion that listening to Mr. Mention's music helped him to toil through the PhD program he completed in the United States.

Professional Vibes

The public face of the company has been carefully cultivated both through the choice of employees who are encouraged to interact with the media and through the publicizing of development activities in Guy Town as a "model" community fostered by Wicked Times.[6] Among employees who have primary media contact are Lena, the public relations manager, who is a middle-class woman in her late twenties, and Winston, a member of the executive board from Guy Town, who is in his forties. Both of these employees emphasized the importance of professionalism at Wicked Times, which I found often gets contrasted with vibes, the feeling and energy necessary for making good dancehall. This distinction was particularly apparent when I asked about the studio's working relationship with companies based in the United States. Lena described a style of professionalism at Wicked Times that is tempered by the "laid back" culture that exists in Jamaica, suggesting that, given Wicked Times's global reach, the company had not attempted to simply replicate foreign business culture. Instead, by melding Jamaican commercial and social practices with advantageous foreign ones,

Wicked Times had created space for employees to engage in the "exploration of alternative subjectivities" (see Freeman 2010, 229). The company created an institutional culture that should be described neither as "conformist" nor explicitly "resistant," but as a new kind of business culture crafted in relation to the contemporary opportunities and constraints created by entrance into a global market for the consumption of their dancehall product.

When I asked Lena about VP Records, a Jamaican-owned, US-based dancehall distribution company that Wicked Times and most other Jamaican production companies work through to access US-based expatriate markets, she replied:

> And while I think [Wicked Times] is the most professional, we are still laid back compared to them! We are comfortable. [. . .] Just to get a website domain name transferred has taken [. . .] nine months of negotiation and it is hard to prepare for that! Most of the people in our industry have no formal education. [. . .] I have the benefit of a college education. I started work before I left school and I finished the year but I didn't do the exam. It's laid back. They tackle Friday like Monday morning! It's difficult. So [Winston] is the one primarily responsible for international relations.
>
> I think [Wicked Times] tries very hard to appear professional and responsible. We are professional, we are going to handle it a different way. We are not going to handle it this way. We try to set the trend for people to follow. We stumble and fall like everybody else but we try. [. . .] We have rules here, no shorts in the office, no cursing in the office, we invite other people in the business that we respect to see what we do, because it helps the industry as a whole with the American aspect, the European aspect, that is the market we want to tap into. The Japanese are on a whole other level of professionalism. They show respect. They don't have casual Friday! Not to say that we are going to give up our culture, which is why we have the smoking corner around the back, but at the same time we are always trying to be more professional.

Lena's statement emphasized the need the dancehall industry has to create professional reputations in which they are seen as easy to work with while simultaneously maintaining a comfortable working environment for their range of employees and not giving up their culture. The concept of professionalism has been indexed as a code that suggests "presentation as bound up in a particular worker 'mentality'" that, "implies that the way one looks both reflects and shapes one's work ethic and productive capacity" (Freeman 2000, 215). Lena's statement about casual Friday both contrasts the formality of overseas industry and suggests a heightened level of productivity bound to a conception of work ethic. By this logic, her mention of the smoking area highlights the maintenance of culture, where the consumption of ganja in Jamaica can be a religious sacrament for Rastafari; a medicinal treatment; and a source of vibes and inspiration for artists creating dancehall.

Winston reiterated these differences during our interview with the implication that they are, in a sense, cultural. When I talked with him about his experiences in the music industry after leaving Guy Town, he explained that he had worked in radio, as the general manager of one of the first stations in Jamaica with an all-reggae format, before joining Wicked Times, where he now oversees marketing, public relations, and contract negotiation. Shifting between the working environments of the Jamaican music industry and those of overseas companies has not been a radical change for him, he claims, because he has had broad exposure to the corporate world. When he described the industry in Jamaica, he used words like "organic," "naturalness," "go with the flow," and "vibes," which he posed as a "West Indian thing." In contrast, he described the industry in the United States as "regimented," "systematic" and "methodical." He also spoke of "difficult business practices" and "timelines," indicating that Jamaican businesses were "not keen on those types of operations."

Artistically, the difference among these settings was posed slightly differently. When I talked with Natural about his experiences working in the dancehall scene in Canada versus in Jamaica, he told me, "It's different. It's way different. The thing about it is that the potential to earn more money is there than here, but to get the real good work out is here! It's like you can do reggae from there but it's not as effective as to be able to do it here." To Natural there is something about Jamaica as a setting that is conducive to creating better dancehall music. This point has also been emphasized by researchers investigating the earnings potential of the Jamaican music industry for the economy as a whole, with recommendations that encourage state investment in the tacit knowledge and creative capital that are particular to Jamaica as a form of domestic capital that will enhance the contributions of the industry to the overall economy (V. James 2007, 311). Natural supports these recommendations when he talks about the economic bind that provides counterweight to the idea that the "real good work" comes out of Jamaica. His qualification is based on the greater abundance of financial resources available to performers working abroad. I asked him why he thought the divide between earning potential for artists and the production of the real good work existed between North America and Jamaica, and after briefly pausing to consider my question, he replied.

> One is because reggae is like a native thing. It's not just something you just get up and do. Like someone in Europe or someone someplace can say, okay, I like reggae, I'm gonna do some stuff in reggae. It just doesn't sound the same as from here because it's native. It's a culture thing here. So it's like when you're in Jamaica you're born in it. You grow up with this in your blood. So there's a passion here to do it.

He then told me that when foreigners pick up reggae, they do it to make money, so for them it is less about passion and more about being able to make a profit off of it. He continued, "so it brings a different feeling in the music because here like there's more passion, and not only passion, but in Jamaica and in reggae there's so much competition so it brings out more in you to be good. Like because we're around [Mr. Mention] and stuff now so, you are in one of the best reggae environments so it kind of pulls you, pull money." With this statement, that reggae is a cultural thing in Jamaica and one that is in the blood, he suggested that there are also so many passionate creators of reggae in Jamaica that it pushes aspiring performers to make better music. He associates the embeddedness of reggae, as a Jamaican cultural tradition, with a passion that goes beyond the desire for money, the factor he identifies as the motivation for non-Jamaicans to participate in the genre. He also suggests that these differing motivations make non-Jamaican-made reggae sound different than the local variety.

Natural then told me about how he feels when he is at Wicked Times working on his music, as opposed to working on it in Toronto. "It's good for me because I'm in the groove here. It's still in me. I feel what I'm doing and stuff. It's not like it's out of me and stuff like that. And vibes, I think [. . .] you can keep your vibe wherever you are. It depend on your mood and how strong your mind is and how focused you are." He repeated his point about keeping the Jamaican vibe, which seemed particularly important given his current residence in Canada, "'cause I think your vibe can be with you wherever you go, it's just that you have to be a strong person mentally or a determined person or you have a lot of passion for what you want to do. Then you could have that vibe wherever you go. But when you do the song here, to me it comes out better." Here he describes a person keeping their vibe when outside of Jamaica as a struggle, which might relate to immigrants' experience of loss of identity and cultural authenticity in their new place of residence, even though Toronto is a city with a large West Indian community (Averill 1994; Hall 1990). As a dual citizen, Natural exists in a complex location because, as a Canadian, he can now enjoy the benefits of guaranteed health care, a stable economy, and a higher standard of living, while simultaneously gaining prestige in Kingston as a person who has made it. However, in terms of dancehall, this new location can also detract from his authenticity as a performer because he is no longer a Kingston ghetto youth and now speaks with an accent tinged with North American intonations. To combat the impact of these factors on a person's vibe, Natural identifies the need for mental strength, determination, and passion, which will keep the person's vibe with him even if he leaves the island.

According to Natural, dancehall made in Jamaica will not only *sound* more authentic in this formulation but will also be more appealing to the foreign reggae enthusiast because it was created at the genre's wellspring. What he refers to is the cachet that "Product of Jamaica," as a mark of authenticity, contributes to a dancehall recording. His statement resonates well with the concept of Brand Jamaica. Beyond the soul that working in Jamaica contributes to a performer's sound, there is also marketing to consider. Natural said,

> It comes out with more soul to it and then the thing about it is that people who listen to reggae around the world or people who like to buy reggae [. . .] when it's from Jamaica, they give it more attention. They're like, "You know what?" If there's a couple CDs there and they're like this one's from Jamaica, this one's from Canada, this one's from the States, this one's from England, they're like, "I want to take this one that's from Jamaica because that's where reggae is from, so this must be better than all of these."

He identified this cultural branding as a basic advantage of working out of Jamaica but added, "So doing it from here can help be a better, better benefit for you financially and, probably, as a reggae artist, if you're big in anywhere else and you're not big in Jamaica, you probably feel like you're left out." Another component of this authenticity, according to Natural, is recognition among Jamaican artists. Ultimately, however, he concludes that the local and the international are both crucial components of a successful artist's career. The Jamaican artist needs international opportunities in order to achieve significant financial success, while the artist abroad requires Jamaica as a cultural and musical reference point in order to make good dancehall and maintain an authentic image. "You know, it's like I'm popular in England, I'm popular in Canada, I'm popular somewhere in Europe, but you're not popular in Jamaica, you feel left out. You're like, 'I'm not really a reggae artist because I'm not amongst the best in Jamaica, my name is not called amongst . . . ' So you feel like you're second to those who are coming from Jamaica. So there is a lot of advantages and disadvantages." Natural acknowledged that success on the global market is the primary goal for many Jamaican artists, while those overseas perceive Jamaica as a fundamental cultural root for the music. He said,

> But, I think artists here when they are working they think, "Okay, I have to make myself popular enough, have to get good song, so I could go tour overseas to make good money to set myself up real good." While people over there think like, "Okay, I'm going to try to work from Jamaica or try to get work from Jamaica and stuff." So there is something here and there is something there so, but when you put them all together it works out [laughing].

He then raised a widely discussed concern among dancehall artists regarding the limitations of international success given that foreign listeners do often not understand their accents. The terms of this debate are often the financial and career advantages of having an international following, which requires the adoption of more Standard English, versus the idea that abandoning Jamaican patois as the primary language of dancehall is the equivalent of abandoning the music's roots as well as its core following among the Jamaican working class. Natural brings up Shaggy, a Jamaican American performer who has had numerous international hit singles, as someone who has been able to successfully cross the divide between dancehall and pop music. He also mentions No Doubt, a Los Angeles–based band that started off playing ska in the punk rock scene and who successfully incorporated the dancehall sound into their best-selling album. No Doubt recorded much of their album in Jamaica and included guest appearances by dancehall performers such as Lady Saw and Bounty

Killer on two of their tracks.[7] In regard to the language issue, Natural said, "The problem with most reggae artists is that we're not understood when we talk. Like our accent sometime give outsiders a problem. Like, they're like, 'What is he saying?' So—especially with Shaggy—Shaggy is from the reggae family, but he has the accent, the clarity, so people [. . .] know what he's saying. So he sort of hit big and No Doubt saw that this music could go all the way up there." He described the language barrier as a "border to cross," one that "reggae artists are not crossing most of the time." One of the reasons he gave was that many reggae artists are dropouts from school. He said, "They come from a poor family. They come from little communities where there's not much and you have a sound or a voice and just get lucky and you did some work. You put in some hard work and you get your voice so other people like it. But not all reggae artists can say, 'Okay, what could take me to the next level.' Not all of them can say, 'How can I be accepted everywhere?'" Natural also explained the lack of crossover success by many reggae artists as a reflection of where they've come from. "Most of them aren't doing that because is like the money they getting now, 'Okay, I never see this money in my life. My family never see this money, so this will be all right for me. I don't care.' You know, but somebody like No Doubt they think that 'Okay, we need to go to the next level.'" Natural attributes the failure of many reggae artists to cross over to international markets to a lack of vision for the future and a focus on present survival, which is a trait heavily attributed to the Jamaican working class (Chevannes 2001; Harrison 1988). Artists who have lived in dire poverty but who can now provide sufficiently for their families become satisfied with the level of their careers, whereas the US-based No Doubt, he suggests, is always pushing their career forward regardless of the abundant wealth they have already attained. The US-based performers simply see more possibilities and fewer constraints. This contrast relates to Jamaica's position within the global economy, which can create limitations for Jamaican businesses and performers by curtailing their own expectations for success through the creation of more palpable barriers such as trade limitations, stringent visa regulations, and vastly disparate currency exchange rates.

When I asked people at Wicked Times about working with the larger multinational record companies, their responses reflected a consciousness of their music as a product. As people who have lived with few resources, rather than focusing on the idea of selling on international markets as "selling out," they often highlighted international popularity as a career-building opportunity that would keep them employed and able to support those who depend upon them.

As a career strategy, performers must strike a balance where they can maintain a local fan base with dancehall that is more attuned to a Jamaican ear for music and that is created with an awareness of the way dancehall is used socially in Jamaica. The result of this artistic formulation may not be a sound that appeals or makes sense to mainstream international audiences.[8] Simultaneously, and sometimes inadvertently, they also create songs with a more internationally popular appeal by incorporating pop or hip-hop sounds and delivering lyrics in a fashion that is clear and understandable to speakers of Standard English. On this point, Loverman told me,

> Well, working with the industry here, you see, inna Jamaica is a grassroots. You know, this is where it build. This is where it start from, you know, and inna di States now they grab on to everything that current. You know, they keep close in touch with Jamaica still, you know, and it not much different still because, you see, Jamaican market for the dancehall is there wide open, big! You know what I'm saying? So is not much difference, you know?

He said that it was after crossing over that there is a big difference in the choices recording artists might make, recognizing that style and sound preferences can be different for consumers outside of Jamaica. "Because you know they don't used to certain sounds which you know normally hit in Jamaica and don't on an international level. You know what I'm saying?" These choices are spoken of strategically rather than as artistic choices in a genre where success and survival are closely linked. There is the recognition of dancehall music as artful entertainment and its production as work rather than as strictly a product of creativity.

When I asked Loverman specifically about his own crossover success, which included a song that gained popularity on U.S. pop and urban music charts, he said,

> Now we even more fragile than anything else before because people are expecting better things again. You know what I'm saying? So, even though we don't really look pon it like seh we was concentrating on going crossover, but now we haffi more concentrate pon, "yo!," because the language barrier is there and they beginning to understand what we are saying now. You know ten out of a thousand Jamaican artists get the

chance to get visa to have opportunity so you know you got to nurture it and nourish it and mek sure, try your best.

Commenting that he and his partner had developed a dedicated fan base, he told me,

> So, you know, we have to be careful about what type of song dem that we're coming out with next time. So we have to keep it on that level and still keep it dancehall because this is what they know [Loverman] for, dancehall. You know, nuttin' na change. We don't haffi string go to hip-hop on a hip-hop beat or a rock beat you know. Nuttin' na wrong with trying a little experiment, but you know stick to the root that the people know you.

The fragility of the artist's relationship to their local and overseas fan base as well as international markets for dancehall requires successful crossover artists to make careful choices about the songs they release. Loverman characterizes this position of success as a rare opportunity for a Jamaican artist, which must be cultivated and cared for. Listener cultivation must include consideration of what artistic choices will appropriately nurture the financial and business aspects of a career. To him, musical experimentation is okay, but it is important not to stretch too far beyond listeners' expectations. This is particularly true if the experimentation ventures into a realm like hip-hop or rock, which might appear to be a shortcut to mass appeal, forsaking an artist's Jamaican roots. Here, a lazy approach to music making aimed at accruing financial benefits may, in actuality, have the opposite result when fans are turned off by the choices an artist has made.

It is notable that Loverman, a DJ, and his artistic partner, a singer, have had great success in overseas markets due to their pop-oriented style, which is also beloved within Jamaica where consumers are usually open to musical hybridity as long as it is enjoyable. There seems to be less of a hang-up about a rigidly demarcated authenticity here than in places like the United States (barring the requisite "authenticity" entailed by adhering to narrowly defined working-class Jamaican gender norms), where popular culture connoisseurship frequently becomes a key component of subcultural identity formation.[9] However, as Saunders has argued, when an artist like Buju Banton, with great crossover success, is censured for expressing local values that come into conflict with the beliefs of some global consumers, claims to the expression of cultural values can be used as a "means of mediating the hegemonic force of market values in the age of global capitalism" (Saunders 2003, 96).

When I asked Dads about marketing at Wicked Times, he also indicated that understanding the market was a key aspect of the success of a crossover single and that the company, as a collective, determines which new songs are appropriate for the market at any given time. I asked Dads if the company has a dedicated marketing department, and he replied, "Not really. Um, we have nobody that specialize on that aspect. You know each department . . . whatever aspect or whatever marketing plans come aboard we tackle it collectively." I asked him if he had ever seen a project going in a direction that he really didn't like, or if he had ever thought, "This won't represent what we are trying to do very well." He responded, "Correct, right, because, as I say, collectively we make decision and sometimes we have a project and we say, 'Okay, we going with this song,' and then immediately the trend in the music business change. Then you know seh you have to pull back and go with the trend. You know? So hence we always leave that as a collective thing where we say, 'yo! We don't feel this!' You know? 'Mek we go with that next one there.'" When I asked Loverman about "going with the trend," as Dads put it, he gave an example of a recent crossover success that was not cultivated to its full potential because its prospects were not fully recognized by the company at the time of its release. After I raised the issue of cultivating a path for music being released, I asked him more specifically if the company will pitch a project in different ways with that path in mind. With regard to his own work, he replied,

> What with this last track? Um, [laughing] the good thing about it, it was a hit song. The bad thing about it, they didn't expect it to go pop so they didn't have the stragedy to market the pop. And then again now, what bad about the whole situation—didn't have Atlantic [Records] at the time. They were just out there on their own. You know and Sean Paul barely catch the edge a it. You know they come in the nick of time for Sean.

He said that if Atlantic had come two or three months earlier, he and his partner would have been, to use his emphasis, "*IN* the mainstream." He continued, "You know, because Atlantic come in now, so they know where to put it and where they have all the people them who know about pop. You know VP they don't have a clue about pop, so that was the big downfall for that song. Yeah. But it's all good still. We can do it again!" Loverman suggests that the timing of his song's release was poor because VP Records, who worked on the distribution, had not yet joined forces with Atlantic Records, a much larger company with greater resources and an understanding of non–West Indian markets for pop music. Sean Paul, the greatest dancehall crossover success story of the past fifteen years, is held up as an example of what can happen if your sound and your timing are right. Sean Paul, according to Loverman, gained recognition at exactly the right time to be promoted by Atlantic and achieve unprecedented mainstream market success. Loverman also detailed the different advantages of being distributed through a Jamaican company versus one of the larger international companies. Referring again to VP records, he recounted their credentials within West Indian communities in the United States.

> I was a kid when those guys were in the business and they migrate and go to the States. So they know the business and they know the market. So them have the organization where they put somebody in California, somebody in Florida, one in Boston. You know, street teams . . . They always drop wherever the dancehall youths, wherever the Jamaicans, are 'nuff, 'nuff, 'nuff. So they have different-different street teams all around in the States now so they more understand the dancehall.

In contrast, he explained that Atlantic Records has more financial resources to put into the marketing of an artist and better connections with large chain retailers. "They provide more funding, more places that the music didn't reach before. [. . .] Atlantic know all these crevice and corners [. . .] so they know where to put them, yeah. And they have the money to come in with the big video and, you know, spend it on the street team, spend it on the radio, so . . ."

Mr. Mention's comments also support this view. "You have different-different company, like VP is a great company fi Reggae, but VP take you but so far. See what I'm saying? And you have [the international company I'm signed with] now, which is a very huge company, but they are not as great as VP because VP know reggae. [The international company] know pop music. So you see is a whole different thing. So [the international company] tek you pop, introduce you to some white people that didn't know you." He continued, "You're gonna play in the areas because now you a di product. Now you're everybody. That's what [the international company] do, you know, tek you to higher level, but when it come to keeping it real, it's VP and [Wicked Times]." This cultural and business distinction between dancehall and pop continued to come up in my interviews at Wicked Times, but before exploring this facet in greater detail, I will first explain the business relationships that exist between Wicked Times and the multinational record companies that they partner with for North American and European album distribution.

As Dads described these partnerships to me, Wicked Times "owns" a performer like Mr. Mention. When they enter into contractual relations with a larger recording company, on the day of the contract signing, that company is responsible for all recording that is done by the artist during the contractual period. Concerts and other appearances are still the sole responsibility of Wicked Times, meaning that the larger company owns only the recordings of Mr. Mention, while Wicked Times "owns" the artist himself. Therefore, if a promoter wants Mr. Mention to perform, they don't go to the larger company, they have to come to Wicked Times, who manages Mr. Mention, in order to book his appearances.

When I asked Dads about Wicked Times's working relationship with international companies, he described Wicked Times's contract negotiation strategy as active and assertive. The management and performers negotiate to get what they want out of a deal whether their goal is a particular career building strategy or marketing angle. This measure of control is significantly different from many other accounts of music industry dealings that highlight exploitation and victimization. I am not suggesting that these business relationships operate on terms of equality but would like to emphasize Dads's perspective as a Jamaican music industry CEO. Here, these relationships are posed as opportunities that are entered into carefully, but willingly.

> We tell them what we want for them to amend it in the contract because we mek them know that you cannot market a [Mr. Mention] like how you would market a Michael Jackson. You know, it's two different culture. You know, and most of these A&R from international companies, they only used to the American R&B and having a reggae act on their roster, they have to be careful. And you cannot allow them to dictate the pace or to path the career of your artist. You has to come on board with what you want the path of the career of your artist.

Dads also reiterated that the cultural distinction between pop and reggae is a crucial one when establishing fruitful business relationships with international companies. When I asked him to elaborate on his assertion that marketing Mr. Mention was a different task than marketing Michael Jackson he told me:

> As I said, both are different cultures, seen? [Mr. Mention] do reggae, Michael do pop. Hence, how you approach the type of music, which radio stations you go first to, you know? You have to be careful if you go urban or you go to pop or you go straight R&B, you know. Which of the station dem? How you position this act, as straight dancehall or as urban act or you position this artist as a pop artist. And you can kill a song. Which songs come first? Which tune is supposed to hit the marketplace? . . . and all of these things. So it is a whole collective decision you have to make and careful!

According to Dads, selection of the proper media outlets to carry a reggae song is crucial to its success and, in addition, the selection of the first single to be released must be done carefully because a misstep can destroy the chances an album has for good sales. The wrong decision in these matters can potentially destroy a performer's future recording and distribution prospects. Among the critical issues in marketing, he emphasizes determining which genre the single might fit with most comfortably. This problem hearkens back to the debate around the commercial designation world music, which, both academics and enthusiast have argued, often serves as a deterritorialized dumping ground for any music that is considered exotically non-Western (Connell and Gibson 2004; Keil and Feld 1994). Reggae, up until very recently, could not be marketed on its own terms outside of Jamaica because it did not fit cleanly within any of the standard genre designations. Currently, dancehall music is most often paired with urban media outlets that also favor hip-hop and R&B. These outlets can be contrasted with pop-oriented outlets that might be more likely to serve populations interested in alternative rock formulations that include some selected hip-hop and R&B crossover acts.[10] Marketing decisions, under such circumstances, are particularly tricky and, in addition, for a company located in an economically weak country, the stakes are particularly high. Here Dads reiterates that all major decisions are made collectively at Wicked Times, a strategy that both pools the company's knowledge base and distributes the risk among the interested parties.

Beyond the risk of being saddled with the burden of poor decision making, Wicked Times also takes steps to minimize the risk of a poor business match. Agreements must be reached whereby an artist's authenticity with their Caribbean fan base is not compromised when an American or European company takes them on. Companies outside of Jamaica may have greater access to resources but may just as significantly lack an understanding of Caribbean musical performance, participatory practices, and gendered mores around propriety.

> Any time we sign a deal with a company with any one of our acts we always have to maintain our roots! So we always have to say to them seh, "Jamaica and the entire Caribbean is our territory!" So that has to be incorporated in any agreement that we make . . . We also have clause, exit clause in the contract, where we ask that in case you don't do nothing for our artist in a six-month period then the artist can reverse and be back with [Wicked Times]. So these are the types of negotiation that we enter into . . . Also, fortunately, with [Mr. Mention, Bizzy, and Loverman], they are all shareholders of [Wicked Times]! So we don't look 'pon them only as an artist, they also have investment in [Wicked Times]. They are part of the management. They are part of the directors.

Exit clauses are a standard part of all contracts that may be utilized in the event that an artist does not receive the necessary support from the larger company with which they have signed, or if the marketing match is simply not a successful one. In addition, performers who are shareholders have a vested interest, not only in the promotion of their own careers, but also in the success of Wicked Times as a whole. Hearkening back to statements indicating the company is also a family, this shared interest keeps individuals from "stepping out of bounds" for their own benefit, though it is also clear that those performers that bring in the most revenue also enjoy the most clout within the company. They must be kept happy because the delicate balance between what they give and what they gain with regard to the company can be easily tipped.

Conclusion

Wicked Times is a company with an internal politics shaped by local social relations and human needs, and determined by the requirements for operating a successful dancehall production company within an unequal global marketplace. These internal politics are deeply rooted in values of respect and giving, which I have shown are of central importance in communities like Guy Town.

From the perspective of the performers and staff at Wicked Times, Jamaica's relationship to the marketplace affords both strong limitations and rare opportunities. The actions taken within this framework are considered strategic business and career choices rather than as simple exploitation, though it is clear that the rules of the game are not generally ones created on Jamaican terms. The grounds upon which strategic choices are made are regularly justified as cultural in nature, rooted in Jamaica as the fertile soil where the vibes that produce reggae are cultivated. Business decisions are made in the spaces between vibes and professionalism, which can be ideologically mapped on to the spaces downtown and uptown as well as local and foreign. Though vibes and professionalism may seem mutually defeating in some senses, it is their combined strengths that are being capitalized upon by Wicked Times and the government of Jamaica and that are also being exploited by the multinational recording industry. The melding of vibes and professionalism might be most elegantly summed up within the Planning Institute of Jamaica's use of Brand Jamaica to describe their marketing and export goals and their efforts to transition into a functioning service economy.

Accompanying the government of Jamaica's long-term plan for neoliberal economic shifts, which include enhanced governmental support of private enterprises like dancehall production, is the widespread privatization of care for the Jamaican citizenry. Such shifts in governance and economic strategy are reflected in Wicked Times's emphasis on channeling of some of their business profits into long-term community development projects, projects that are facilitated through Dads's participation in well-established community patronage arrangements. In Guy Town, community development strategies employ a similar combination of uptown and downtown, vibes and professionalism, which I will discuss in the next chapter.

CHAPTER 5

The Contradictions of Neoliberal Nation Building in Jamaica

Community Development through Dancehall

Some critics/analysts will ask what is there to show for a decade and a half in office by this Administration. I do not believe that we need to say a great deal about improving physical infrastructure. As regards the economy, we now have one which is more open, more competitive; more diversified than any time in our history.

This means that contrary to utterances, some of which I heard on Tuesday, we are better placed than most of our peers to meet the challenges of globalization which has resulted in painful adjustment processes, creating "winners" and "losers."

We cannot stop the changes brought by globalization even if we don't like all of them. And where our national interest is threatened we will continue to defend it. Furthermore, we struggle not only on our behalf but also for other countries. Nonetheless, we intend to be amongst the "winners."

The winners are those who are educated and trained, motivated, flexible and involved in activities producing goods and services of quality and at a price demanded by the external world.

It is our task as Government to make more and more of our people, and indeed the whole country, "winners"—not because it is a noble objective but simply because we have no option as the global trends will continue whether or not we are on board.[1] (Davies 2005, 1)

One of the development strategies adopted by P. J. Patterson's People's National Party government during the first half of the decade was to make more of the Jamaican people economic winners through the establishment of partnerships between public and private entities. This strategy, in part, aimed to incorporate, educate, and discipline the poor urban black populations that inhabit communities like Guy Town. These community development projects were part of a larger national development program that, as the above quote by the finance minister identifies, admits the inevitability of the global economy in the success or failure of Jamaica as a politically independent nation. With a critical reluctance, the crafters of Jamaica's future resign themselves to carving out a sustainable economic niche for the small, peripheral, and predominantly black-populated former British colony.

The grassroots community development programs in Guy Town, instituted by Wicked Times in conjunction with nongovernmental organizations, the University of the West Indies, and the member of Parliament, served as one part of a People's National Party agenda of nation building based on the empowerment and incorporation of disenfranchised black populations. The programs included remedial education classes focused on imparting a disciplined masculinity on at-risk youth. Youth who are classified as at-risk are thought to be more likely to engage in violence and crime as a solution to the everyday challenges of poverty. Therefore, remedial education programming included dispute resolution and verbal communication techniques intended to provide alternative strategies for the young men to draw on during times of conflict. The programs also taught history rooted in Pan-Africanism and assisted in the implementation of small-scale income-generating enterprises. The design of the remediation also fits in with attempts to redeem populations viewed as possessing a pathological culture that naturalizes their exclusion in global citizenship within the logic of neoliberal multiculturalism. However, since the Jamaican state's caregiver role had been significantly curtailed with the adoption of neoliberal governance strategies, members of the controversial dancehall industry and organized criminals were two of the few private entities with a vested interest in creating ghetto-based social safety nets. The outcome was that the community-based projects in Guy Town were riddled with the same kinds of contradictions that beset Jamaican nation-building efforts more generally. The at-risk youth are taught to emulate model citizenship practices, but a less nation-friendly community citizenship rooted in illicit activities, local power hierarchies, and a ghetto-based normative masculinity is simultaneously being reinforced.

As Arturo Escobar has argued, development is an "act of cognitive and social domination," engineered by the organizations that design the projects (Escobar 1991, 675). However, projects may simultaneously afford participants the opportunity to make new choices that may not have been previously available.[2] The critique of development has been, by and large, based on the study of initiatives to modernize production activities among rural peasants. Attempts to change production often end up radically altering peasant lifeways (Escobar 1995; Ferguson 1990; J. Scott 1998). The urban context that I am examining, in a country like Jamaica, presents a slightly different set of issues. The country was *created* by a colonial encounter, founded on the introduction of enslaved Africans and the relocation of British administrators and planters (Trouillot 1992).

The population of Guy Town was decisively shaped by rural-to-urban migrations that took place in the 1960s, which resulted in unplanned urbanization and Kingston's famed shantytowns. Urban community development in this context does not disrupt any asserted primordial tradition, though, as indicated in previous chapters, Guy Town's residents possess well-established modes of sociality and economy. The development model employed in Guy Town is also not one that interrupts a whole way of life because the primary focus is not a fundamental reorganization of production (J. Scott 1998). The blueprint for the Guy Town projects can be more appropriately described as one that offers new possibilities for the integration of area residents into a pre-articulated community and national vision shaped by postcolonial struggles to carve out space in the global economy.

Programs advanced the People's National Party's nation-building agenda by attempting to discipline the unruly space of the ghetto—a place that from the state's perspective emanates crime and violence while jeopardizing tourism and foreign investment. However, the implementation of the projects through partnership with the dancehall industry, purveyors of a genre created by ghetto residents and rooted in their sociality, created deep contradictions. Community citizenship in poor urban areas and hegemonic national citizenship, as well as global citizenship, are in many respects ideologically antithetical. The at-risk youth of Guy Town were simultaneously taught to create a well-publicized image of model national citizenship by exhibiting self-control, positive relationships with agents of the state, and an admirable entrepreneurial spirit despite adversity. At the same time, their community citizenship was also being reinforced by programs that bolstered their loyalty to local systems of informal governance—often linked to illegal activities—and a normative masculinity rooted in reputation and marked by the use of violence and the fathering of children with multiple women as key status signifiers. Continued participation in necessary aspects of community citizenship thereby undermined the image of stability the program organizers sought to promote and also compromised the state's authority to govern.[3]

The educational programs, designed largely by University of the West Indies faculty, were aimed at teaching the young men communication skills, self-discipline, and pride. These elements are considered essential for youth who are at-risk. Additionally, the programs had turned Guy Town into a model community, which for a period of time became the darling of the local media. This aspect of the development program required extensive public image management. Here an insider and outsider narrative was developed, which I discovered only over a period of months after the outsider façade could no longer be maintained for my benefit.

The narrative produced for the public was one of victimization, exclusion, and struggle against discrimination and brutality as well as perseverance in the face of desperation. It depicted the Guy Town youth in a light that minimized the complexities and contradictions of everyday survival in favor of a respectable image of rehabilitation, idealized national citizenship, and worthiness for global citizenship. This duality can be treated as a manipulation of development's cognitive and social domination. The lived contradictions of community development in Guy Town create a unique space for participants to creatively manipulate both local and national citizenships, reputation, and respectability, providing greater access to a variety of crucial benefits.[4] However, despite the additional benefits, the administrative design of the programs and their relationship to local community structures ultimately continued to undermine residents' full incorporation into the nation. The programs do not successfully weaken the need for informal community governance, crime, or vigilantism and, in fact, reinforce undemocratic community hierarchies. Therefore, community development hinging on already existing social relations does not so much contribute to the construction of the Jamaican nation through greater local enfranchisement but, instead, reinforces ghetto communities as semi-autonomous mini-states within the larger nation.

The Opening Ceremony

As I approached the newly completed Guy Town Skills Center to attend its opening ceremony, I had no idea how much time I would eventually spend within its pastel cinderblock walls. Initially, the ceremony was to be postponed because of a funeral in the community, which I later learned was that of Martin's father. In the end it was held anyway because the planning and scheduling had already been done. A number of prominent guests were in attendance, including representatives from a few participating national and international nongovernmental organizations and several anthropologists from the University of the West Indies, as well as a selection of high-ranking government officials.

There were rows of neatly arranged plastic chairs in the building's small paved courtyard, beyond the wrought-iron front gate mounted on the concrete-block wall in an attempt to form a secure enclosure. The chairs faced a long folding table outfitted with a microphone and seats for the presenters. Dr. Wilson, a professor from the University of the West Indies, and instructor of men's remedial education classes in Guy Town, presided over the ceremony, introducing the guests and commenting on the proceedings. As the dedication began, a prominent Kingston reverend performed the opening blessing before giving way to the Guy Town Youth Organization's secretary, the only female executive board member, who explained the programs offered by the Youth Organization and described the black history lessons that members of the adult remedial education program were learning before turning the microphone over to Minister Oliver, the member of Parliament. He notably changed the tone of the event by chiding the community, telling them that this was a second chance for the Skills Center, which had been robbed and vandalized in the past. He asserted that if the building were broken into again, everyone in the community would know who had done it, implying that the whole community would be implicated in the crime if it were allowed to occur. Then a representative from the Jamaica Social Investment Fund, which had partnered with the university and the community to have the center built, spoke about the organization and the success of the Skills Center construction, which included the creation of two classrooms and a computer laboratory and library.

Afterward, the university lecturer, who would eventually become a spokesperson for Wicked Times, performed a "cultural presentation." He DJ-ed two original songs, one about guns not making people men and the other, a tribute to his mother, about how he was now a university lecturer even though he had come from the streets. Given that Dads, the president of the Youth Organization, was also in attendance, much talk was heard about whether he and the lecturer had met, with the subtext that Dads might be able to help him build a music career. The vice president of the Youth Organization then spoke, commenting that if the event had been a tragedy of violence in Guy Town, the TV cameras would have been everywhere, but, since it was a positive event, there were no television cameras, only photographers and newspaper reporters. The center was then opened with a ribbon cutting, and guests were invited to tour the facility while catered food and music were offered.

By this time it was after 6 p.m., and a crowd of community residents began to gather outside of the gates. Their appearance was in stark contrast to the neatly dressed guests who were enjoying the food inside. They didn't enter the confines of the courtyard, however, but hung around the periphery observing the goings-on and hoping someone might share a helping of fried fish.

The design of the Skills Center speaks to the role that this type of community development is to play in Jamaican national development. Its chalkboard-clad classrooms, computer lab, and library, chosen instead of workshops with tools and sewing machines, assert the direction in which Jamaica is planning to go and the role that urban communities such as Guy Town are envisioned to play in that process. The skills being cultivated in the center are not the typical production skills toward which the Jamaican poor have generally been guided. They go beyond furniture making, sewing, and catering, to enhance national agendas that extend out from mere economic initiatives to social ones promoting stability and new economic skill sets that incorporate information technologies. In some ways, training in information technology may put the proverbial cart before the horse in communities such as Guy Town, where many residents lack even basic education, but it does coincide with the explicit goals of development that the PNP government had set its sights on. According to Prime Minister Patterson, during an address to CARICOM (Caribbean Community), the Caribbean has entered into a new ballpark with respect to development and incorporation into the global economy. Here, instead of development entailing the archetypal struggle of men attempting to more and more efficiently tame nature for economic gain, Patterson indicates that it must be "technology driven and alliance ridden" (Patterson 2000, 7). While the alliances Patterson alludes to are reminiscent of classic labor strategies of collective bargaining, here the union is a union of Caribbean and other global South nations assembled in order to leverage political power in economic negotiation with other nations such as the United States and those of the European Union located in the global North.

Technology in this context is not employed toward the transformation of natural resources into economic ones through production. Instead, the construction of a technologically driven economy requires the production of human resources via the transformation of the Jamaican citizenry by the state and private development entities into useful contributors to global capitalism. This distinction is necessary for Jamaica's transition from an industrially oriented economy into the service economies in demand by the First World whose own economies are now constructed upon investment and outsourcing of jobs such as phone banks and other types of customer service apparatus to Third World nations.

Former British colonies are uniquely situated to fulfill this niche in the global division of service labor because of their use of English, as has been seen in India among other locales. However, the inability of a large segment of the Jamaican population to effectively communicate in Standard English has proved a sizeable stumbling block. This is the segment of the population that is also most desperately in need of gainful employment and incorporation into the body of the Jamaican nation from the perspective of the state.

Building "Better Communities"

Most of my conversations with community members left the impression that Dads was solely responsible for the construction of the Skills Center, even though a large sign at the gate clearly listed a range of sponsors from outside the community. This sentiment is an extension of a deeper tension related to local loyalties and the goals of community development, which must be teased apart in order to better understand the impact of privatization at the local level in a setting like Kingston.

A good place to start is by looking at the origins of the Guy Town Youth Organization during the 1980s and the way the organization has developed into an imperfect bridge between local and national, public and private in the present. As Dads described it, the Youth Organization was an outgrowth of a desire for political representation. He told me,

> so, being in [Guy Town] as youth, we founded the [Guy Town] Youth Organization in 1989. That was founded on the basis that we as youth saw where our community was neglected by the political [. . .] and we figure out seh we should be getting equal attention like anyone else from [the area]. So hence we approach the former member of Parliament [. . .] for dialogue and he stated that he won't be speaking to us unless we are an organized set or organized body.

They formed a youth club in order to facilitate a dialogue with the MP. According to Dads, when the club met with their MP they communicated their desires for Guy Town and initiated a productive working relationship. He continued, "In 1989 we stated that [Wicked Times] in its green time. What we can do back for people who support us through the years? So we come up with a situation and say how much of the youths from the ghetto can't afford a stage show, and our artists are some of the artists where they support we throughout the year, so hence let us give a free concert!"

It is a desire for care from governmental entities among a group of youth in the community that provided the catalyst for the establishment of the Youth Organization. The member of Parliament's insistence that an organized, unified, voice exist before he would listen to community members' demands led to the need for an organizational structure such as a club.

Among the group of eight or nine youths who were on the corner on the day in 1989 that the member of Parliament toured Guy Town, was a woman, Lorraine, at the time twenty-four years old. When I talked to Lorraine about her perceptions of Guy Town, as a woman who had grown up in the community and who was now a prominent employee of an international development agency, she indicated to me that when the Youth Organization was founded, she was elected its first president. When I asked her about being a woman and a community leader, she told me that she'd always gotten the support of her peers despite the fact that the community was male dominated. I suggested that it might have been because she was better educated than many of her peers at that time. She agreed that this might have been one source of support but also indicated that she had always been confident and had a reputation for being a woman who "loved to talk." Her participation in the Youth Organization eventually launched her into a career in social development, leading her to earn a master's degree from the University of the West Indies.

My conversation with Lorraine somewhat challenged the predominating narrative of Wicked Times's community concert because, by her description, the primary funds that enabled the Youth Organization to hold the free concert as well as a "treat" for the community came, in part, from a donation from the member of Parliament who initially demanded an organized community voice. This issue hearkens back to the recurrence of Dads being identified as the sole benefactor for community projects, regardless of the multitude of sponsors that might actually have contributed. In a sense, the development story in Guy Town is being privatized through community discourse to a greater extent than the actual development process has been.

Dads has been the president of the organization for the past decade, even though, having long reached his midthirties, he may no longer qualify as a youth. This fact complicates the democratic nature of the organization, whose members have been elected by club participants. There is a deep sense among community residents that without Dads, there would be no Youth Organization.

The member of Parliament's request for an organized voice from the community and the establishment of the Youth Organization in response coincides with a Jamaican tradition of community-rooted clubs as a development strategy that pairs British philanthropic practices with political values that can be linked to anticolonial struggles and Garveyite/Afrocentric ideologies. These strategies were first instituted in rural areas and townships, having grown out of the agricultural cooperative movements of the late nineteenth century (Bryan 2002; Girvan 1993).

D. T. M. Girvan is a key figure in promoting the community center model of development that has been the trend in Jamaica since the 1930s. His work within Jamaica Welfare, an organization founded with the support of the People's National Party's leader Norman Manley, institutionalized the "Better Community" approach to development. This approach was developed utilizing training Girvan acquired in Europe and Canada and incorporated development strategies that were favored by the United Nations (Girvan 1993). Significantly, the cooperative approach was initially designed to combat the individualistic tendencies of capitalism in favor of a more collective and mutually supportive sensibility. Girvan's brief training at the Horace Plunkett Foundation in Ireland would have exposed him to anticolonial strategies aimed at protecting Irish farmers from the economic advantages held by the British in a setting of widespread market deregulation.[5]

The concept of building better communities was based on the fostering of collective action toward community accomplishment and was first implemented in an urban setting in the 1960s by the Social Welfare Commission in western Kingston (Girvan 1993). This approach focused on assessing "felt needs" in the language of the United Nations. The goal was to establish community councils that would utilize "key people" of influence in any given area. Projects were to encourage "character building" through self-help and attempted to treat both social and economic factors as enmeshed in the fabric of communities in need of development. These community programs, which created internal systems of governance, worked toward educational, health, home improvement, and income-generating activities. The communities were not considered isolated units but were nodes in a larger network of neighboring endeavors called "zones" that then stretched out through urban and rural areas alike. Though the felt needs of these settings might be radically different, the development vision was unified around a sense that each area had a specific role to play in the overall development of the Jamaican nation. The development of the nation as a whole would also have particular impacts on the development of specific localities based on how they fit into the bigger picture.

The Perry Town Community Council can be looked at as a more direct outgrowth of this sort of development scheme because it was incorporated into a long-term community revitalization plan that included the construction of an amphitheater as one piece of a greater effort to transform the proscribed area into an entertainment mecca, and it is less immediately associated with patron figures like Dads. However, the Guy Town Youth Organization can also be viewed as an example of this style of development that demonstrates how such programs take on their own character once actualized in situ.

The organizational structure situates the Youth Organization as a point of contact between Guy Town and other development-oriented institutions. It provides external organizations with a means of enlisting local youth in wider development initiatives, including conflict resolution training programs, public health education initiatives, and police programs that educate populations in citizens' rights.

It is the quirky nature of the Youth Organization when it is observed in practice that reveals the tensions of implementing this development model within the power-laden sociality of a contemporary ghetto. The specificities of the ghetto as a context contribute an added layer of meaning to the United Nations' term felt needs. Dads asserted that the Youth Organization always had a "consultational" approach, where there are regular meetings with the citizens of Guy Town. During their regular Monday meetings, for example, the executive board of the club might ask, "What you would like?" or "What we can do fi unnu?" Dads explained what might happen if the group gets something other than what they've requested:

> And then now if they say let's go the route of having a playing field [. . .] that is their decision, so when they have a playing field they will

cherish it. But if [. . .] they want a basketball court and you give them a netball court, they will destroy it because they didn't want that! So we always consult with them and whatever task they want we to take on, we always take on that task to the fullest and whatever we can achieve for them, we go for it.

As Dads explains it, beyond felt needs providing a means of understanding community deficiencies, felt needs are also crucial to program success given that residents often have strong feelings about what they want and equally effective ways of sabotaging unwanted interventions or efforts that they feel do not meet their needs (J. Scott 1998).

There are also more passive forms of protest. People can vote with their feet, making the decision to not participate. In Guy Town, participation is somewhat influenced by the locality of community members' residences. Those who live closest to the Youth Organization clubhouse seem to feel a greater affinity for Dads and receive the most direct benefits from him. Those residing on the outskirts are more likely to feel disenfranchised and are less likely to participate actively in club activities. Beyond this aspect of participation, there is also the issue of immediate gratification, which was recognized by many people as a barrier to residents' sustained participation in club activities. Dads identified this issue as a major influence on membership numbers. He said that every Monday they held a quorum, and membership during that time hovered at around forty people. He then told me, "When we started we had a membership of over eighty. But you know some people think again that being a part of the organization is an alternative [. . .] for finding employment and we are saying that we are nongovernmental, nonpolitical organization. Our basic interest is the interest of the people of [Guy Town], so hence we are not, or cannot, provide full-fledged employment! So our membership now stand at a little over forty." He suggests that, initially, people would join the club to access resources that he was not necessarily able to provide. Though some club members receive employment at Wicked Times or are given stipends to take care of maintenance of community resources, such as the shared restrooms, the clubhouse, and Skills Center, there is not enough work for everyone. This issue of instant gratification creates an unexpected outcome in terms of club membership.

A Youth Organization Populated by Middle-Aged Women

The first Youth Organization meeting I attended was overwhelming. I hadn't yet spent much time in the community, and my taxi man's expression of panic at being in Guy Town in the dark and not knowing his way out heightened my own sense of anxiety regarding what I was doing there. However, upon meeting Martin, my worries were somewhat eased. He appeared outside of the clubhouse and directed the taxi man out of the community. He then guided my assistant and me into the club meeting room, which was outfitted with a chalkboard in the front, rows of plastic chairs for club members, and bulletin boards in the back that displayed the artwork of club members as well as photographs from special events, such as graduation ceremonies. Martin sat next to me and waited patiently as I conversed with my research assistant. Finally he got my attention, introducing himself and saying, "We need you."

They began the meeting by collecting dues, which consisted of $20, or whatever sum people could afford, logging the contributions in the attendance registry, and gave my assistant and me a special introduction. I was expecting game night to be mostly men, but, curiously, the room was packed with women.

They used the business segment of game night to ask if I would be willing to teach a class for women in the community. Martin explained to club members what a PhD and cultural anthropology are and apologized for the fact that women had not been included in the current remedial education programs, saying that it had not been his idea. The vice president then explained that the young men had decided that women in the classes would be too distracting for them and that, in addition, they would prefer that the women of the community not know that some of them were unable to read. After I'd agreed to lead weekly remedial education classes for the women, game night resumed.

Tonight would be a "penny concert," meaning that a person could donate $10 or some other small sum to the club in order to have the right to ask another club member to perform for them. The selected person had to follow the command or pay double the money to get out of performing. The participants were making each other sing and dance and, as a newcomer and white-skinned foreigner, I was not exempt, having to demonstrate my subpar dancing abilities to the room full of club members.

At first I was shocked by the demand of money for participation in Youth Organization activities, given the acute poverty of the area. However, I soon came to realize that these small contributions were intended to cultivate responsibility, self-respect, and a sense of investment in the organization while simultaneously providing discretionary funds for the club, even though nearly all club activities were funded through Dads and Wicked Times.

Over time I began to understand that it was largely women that regularly attended the club meetings and, eventually, it was explained to me that when Dads is leading the meetings the room is packed with young men. However, Dads has many responsibilities and interests, including his company, his political career, and the soccer team he organizes, which take him away from the club for stretches of time. During these periods it is largely the women who will attend without Dads's attention and resources as a motivation.[6]

"When the baby cry, who look?"

From its inception, the club has also been affiliated with Wicked Times, whose first attempts at giving back to the community took the form of the free concert and, over time, evolved into the more systematic and ideological development project. Dads told me:

> We think that even the fact that we have been an organizational structure in [Guy Town]. We also think that small projects where we can finance most of the youth them because, then again too, you a say to one "don't do that, don't go there, don't go into crime" but yet still, when the baby cry, who look? You know a man is desperate. Him not going to just sit idly and let desperation kill him. So hence, we started some small projects which is the callaloo farm [. . .] and we supply the community more on that basis and then outside of that you have people who have restaurants and other establishments weh need to put dung, comes in and buy it. We have a [concrete] block factory. We think it's time for we to get rid of some of those zinc fences from the community, so we started a block factory to remove the zincs and replace them with some concrete wall. You know, and also the youths dem can use it as some form of earning to make blocks and they would sell it and the money would go to them as long as they can replace back the materials. You know, and we were going the route of trying to have a bag juice factory and a little bakery, so that's still in the pipeline.

The projects Dads describes are based on principles of self-reliance through income generation as well as pride based on the dignity of work, beautification of the community itself, and the fulfillment of basic community needs. These tenets are closely linked to Black Nationalist ideologies, which emphasize the importance of black ownership, pride, and responsibility as well as social welfare tenets of character building and, most recently, neoliberal precepts of entrepreneurialism and self-reliance. Community betterment initiatives also contribute a sense of belonging or community citizenship to participants and are indicative of a favorable productivity.

However, the reality of the two primary income-generating projects was far more complex than the aspirations for them as expressed by Dads. The callaloo farm was only intermittently operational during my initial research period. In addition, after the apparatus for making concrete blocks was purchased, it was realized that the quality of the blocks was too poor for home construction, and that they were suitable only for the replacement of the zinc fences that encompass many community residents' yards. Even given these setbacks, the executive board of the Youth Organization, who managed the public image of the community, would tout these as successful initiatives. It was only those more familiar with the circumstances of the organization and the community who were likely to know that these efforts were, in fact, foundering.

These same ideals of self-sufficiency and betterment are systematically incorporated into the long-term remedial education classes offered by associates from the University of the West Indies. The classes began when a group of youths from the club approached a professor from the university whose students were assigned the class project of conducting assessments of the community. The group requested that the professor assist them in organizing a set of classes for adults that would help them recuperate the opportunities many of them had lost because of early attrition in the formal school system.

The seminal narrative of this program as told by the founding professor and his students highlights the incipient thirst for learning that was sparked by an unjust incident with the police. According to several youths I spoke with, the danger of illiteracy for the area's young men was made clear to them when one of their friends was arrested for a burglary he had not committed. While in police custody, this youth, who could not read, was asked to sign a document. The youth blindly signed the document, not knowing until afterward that it was a confession of guilt. The youth, according to this narrative, was wrongly convicted because of his inability to read. Illiteracy had rendered him powerless to help himself.

The education project grew into a larger effort that provided homework support for children currently attending school, guided by older, academically successful area youth, as well as the adult remedial classes lead by university faculty and students. Dads asserted that education was vital to community improvement, so they started a homework center for the younger children, coordinated by the Youth Organization's vice president. He boasted that during first year the program ran, 100 percent of the youth that took the GSAT examination passed. Continuing on the importance of education, Dads told me, "We are seeing that most of the youths dem one to one speaking to them they are illiterate or semiliterate. So we come up with program for them [. . .] because we think going the route of a JAMAL kind of stigmatize and most of the youth don't want to be associated with JAMAL because, 'oh JAMAL, a pure dunce people go a JAMAL.'"[7] The solution to this stigma was to "come up with a pretty name" and to get the program endorsed by the University of the West Indies. He explained that "one of their lecturers was the coordinator until he went to the university in the U.S. and then [Dr. Wilson] take it over fully and he's present at the training and also at the Youth Organization and he's also the coordinator of all the educational programs in [Guy Town]." Soon the programs outgrew the Youth Organization clubhouse. The classes include the homework program Mondays to Fridays, which meet after school from two to five p.m. and adult education classes on Tuesdays. Dads described the adult programming indicating, "we have [. . .] a specialist in illiteracy, you know, so she design programs for slow learners. On Wednesdays we have maths and it's one of the two students from the university." However, the centerpiece of the program for Dads was the history course. He told me, "And then now, on Saturdays we have [Dr. Wilson] give us history. A wide cross-section of political education, them get things on Steve Biko, C. L. R. James, Marcus Garvey, you know, African, so basically most time what we realize is that what we do is to introduce the same program to the youth as what they taught at the university. So it was a big privilege for them." The black history orientation of the programs was often highlighted to the public, the idea being that these lessons would show young men that they possessed a heritage to be proud of and also demonstrate the great achievements that have been made by black people despite the adversities they faced. In addition, when viewed from a nation-building perspective, the classes ideologically bolstered the black leadership of the

People's National Party and reinforced the national identity PNP representatives were carefully advancing for the country as a whole.

Socializing Responsible Men

In describing the prospects for area youth, Dads emphasized the need for exposure to new ideas and contexts as well as positive role models.

> Now them try to learn to socialize and them start to go outside of the area because most of the youth them come from the community, them live in the community, them go to school in the community and them die in the community. So they don't even know as far as Constant Spring. And we think that for us to have a safer society, then we have to make role models out of these youths. Youths have lack of role models because often times people who come from the community don't look back at the community, isolate themselves from the community, so these youths at times, don't know who make it and who are successful entrepreneurs who came from their side, so hence, they only used to the [dons and criminals] and all of these things. So they only say to themselves that we want to be like a [don], but as more of these people come back to the community, mek them see seh I didn't have to go the route of being a criminal, seen? I am like you. I started out same way as you, but I dedicated to education and see it? I have a nice car. I have a house and the youths them say to themselves seh, "yeah, see who mi want to be like?" So that is why . . . you know, the lack of role models. Half the time people are too ashamed to state where they're coming from. You know, you have to be proud of where you come from!

Toward this end, the educational programs for young men were designed to instill a sense of pride of place and heritage, including a class-based pride and critical thinking skills that would enable students to question many of the messages they are sent about themselves on a daily basis.

Upon learning that I would be guiding women's education classes, Dr. Wilson invited me to attend the regular men's class in order to get an idea of the format, material, and classroom environment. The class began at about 9 p.m. on Saturday night and opened with the singing of the Jamaican national anthem. On this particular evening the university lecturer was conducting the second part of his guest lecture. He worked to impart students with an understanding of the study of anthropology that would enable them to take a step outside of their own lives, a challenge for most people, but a particular challenge for young men who may rarely leave the confines of their small community, and to look at their day-to-day decisions in a more critical light. He talked about the meaning of culture, socialization, and worldview and then challenged the class to apply these concepts in order to understand how they have each acquired their own set of views. He then pushed the class further in their thinking by suggesting that, given that view points are socially acquired, class participants can step back and think about their own perspectives, which will allow them to utilize selectivity and self-awareness in their daily lives. He introduced the concept of reflexive identity construction. While working with these difficult and highly academic concepts, he simultaneously managed to conduct most of the class in Jamaican English and established a great rapport with the students.

The discussion ended with a conversation about what it means to be a man and how a person can choose to react in different ways during confrontations to diffuse a situation or to save face, preserving reputation, without resorting to violence. Once the idea of saving face was introduced, there was extended debate about whether a man had to hit a woman who disrespected him by telling him to "suck her out."[8] There was disbelief on the part of the class that a man would be respected if he did not physically discipline the woman who had attempted to humiliate him. The lecturer suggested that a man can construct himself in such a way that the challenge does not affect him. From this position of power, he can walk away without comment, making the woman who hurled the insult look like "an idiot." This assertion raised doubts among the young men, who wondered aloud if this strategy could work in a crowd of people without the insulted party appearing weak.

I noticed that during the discussion the students were also testing the lecturer. For example, one youth asked, "What if someone were to come to you and say . . ."; then the student proceeded to describe the *exact* attire worn by the lecturer and indicated that the choice of clothing made him look like a batty man.[9] The comments were posed in such a clever way that the speaker was not directly insulting the lecturer, but was instead describing a situation in which *someone* was insulting the lecturer. It was an extraordinarily subtle device.

Eventually the classmates started insulting each other jokingly, calling each other restaurants and chefs.[10] Tempers flared, and the lecturer intervened, telling one of the students that he could have responded differently to the jokes and asking him to come up with a new response to being called a chef. He also suggested that they were taking part in a very creative process when coming up with insults and jokes, which was a widely utilized strategy among the university personnel designed to make the young men recognize moments in which they employed their intelligence in ways that may be undervalued by the wider society and by the men themselves.

The class concluded with the announcement that the past weekend had been the three-year anniversary of the classes and that this perseverance was a testament to the strength of the students. Dr. Wilson told them that they were doing what people on the outside never thought they could do and showing the world that they were wrong about ghetto youth. He then said that the program was now being tested for use in other communities. They applauded themselves for the achievement.

At the very end of the class, an older woman in her sixties, who I later learned was a community activist, Martin's mother, came in and asked if the class would be open to her since she loved learning, and she gave a short speech about how programs like this gave strength to the community and showed outsiders that there was more to the area than they think. At the time it did not occur to me that this intervention was actually a form of protest, given that women had been barred from the classes, and an alternative was not currently being offered for them. It foreshadowed a deeper set of issues that emerged in my discussions with community residents with regard to the education programs.

In my conversation with Lorraine, she indicated to me that she had distanced herself from Youth Organization participation over the past year and a half. There had been a conflict, and she reported that the organization no longer reflected her beliefs. Women were not being given priority in the program, which was unacceptable because, to her, men and women are equals. She found that initiatives she had recommended were not being given consideration, whether owing to lack of capacity or for other reasons, and she did not feel that things were "the way they used to be." Lorraine explained that community perception was that the organization was in decline compared to where they were a year and a half ago because of the "kind of leadership" that was presently in place. She told me that there was a general perception of exclusion that had not previously existed. However, she had not entirely ruled out reestablishing participation because there were people in the community that had asked her to come back.

In my experience with the organization, her perceptions were fairly accurate. Once we reinitiated the women's remedial education classes, it became clear that they were not of primary interest to the organization's leadership. One of the first obstacles we confronted as a class was that babies had been banned from the classrooms. This was an acute problem in that many of the women who signed up for class were young mothers who had been forced to leave school because of pregnancy. These women did not necessarily have access to childcare that could be relied upon with the regularity that would be required to attend classes. As a group, guided by one of the women from outside the community who had organized the women's classes in previous years, we voted to overturn this rule and to allow babies in the classrooms for the period in which we were using them. At times this decision turned my agreeable, male research assistant and coteacher into an impromptu provider of childcare, who would look after a few students' babies while they took tests or completed assignments.

In addition, whereas the men were given incentives to attend class, including small sums of money from Dads that would pay for an evening meal, the women attended class of their own volition, in the hopes of gaining literacy, or finding an entry into stable employment. This impression was supported by my observation that when Dads was not in the community, the number of young men who attended the evening class dwindled in comparison to attendance numbers when he was in the area. However, as depicted to the public, the classes were an expression of the ghetto youth's thirst for knowledge. My desire here is not to diminish the achievements of the Guy Town development projects, which were in some individual cases personally transformative, but instead to try to understand the narratives that were developed by insiders for an outside audience.

Inside Meets Outside

In early October a group of representatives from the Youth Organization were invited to speak to some American exchange students who were attending the University of the West Indies for a semester. The topic of discussion was to be "Life on the Corner." Martin and three other young men from Guy Town were the regularly appointed representatives to the outside. Martin invited me to accompany the group, and I met up with them on the university campus prior to the beginning of the session.

In preparation for the meeting, the group discussed how they would respond to particular issues that may arise. Notably, one youth asked what they should say if the question of guns came up during the session. They established that their rote response would be that they had handled guns and knew everything about them, but had never fired one. The need for the establishment of such a guideline was a clear indication that, had the truth been told, their answers would have varied widely. However, the admission that some of the club members had, indeed, fired a gun would have undermined the successful veneer of discipline and rehabilitation (respectability) that the Youth Organization attempted to cultivate for the benefit of outsiders.

During the session, the four men sat in the front of the small room, which was largely populated by white women in their late teens and early twenties. They talked extensively about male socialization in a tone that reflected back the research and teaching that the UWI professors had conducted among them.[11] They discussed the greater discipline that girls were subject to in the home as well as the greater affection they received from parental figures. They explained that boys were encouraged to spend time on the corner learning how to protect themselves, whereas girls tended to be sheltered in the home. The session concluded with a reception that included food and the opportunity to socialize in a less formal setting.

After the program ended, we walked over to Dr. Wilson's office to pay him a visit. On the way, the men talked about the T-shirts two of them were wearing, from a pro-abstinence safe-sex campaign, that had been given to them during a public health training initiative they'd been invited to attend. Playing on the lyrics of the currently popular song "Love So Nice," by Junior Kelly, the brightly lettered slogan read, "If love so nice wait until the time is right." One youth teased the other two about the shirts, suggesting that they were "no fucks" and, as such, questionable in their manhood.[12] One of the youths then replied that just because he wears the shirt does not mean he is waiting on having sex. This joking went on for a little while as we continued on our way. It was interesting to me that the two young men would choose this forum as the appropriate time to wear the T-shirts they'd been given, as opposed to some other attire. It was yet another clue that a skillfully manipulated and well-understood public image was being created. This image elegantly covered the far more complex and contradictory reality of Guy Town youth, who are at once being elevated as participants in the struggle to create a model ghetto community, and who, simultaneously, must take part in the much messier lived contradictions of day-to-day life in that community, which include the pressures to perform their masculinity in culturally specific ways that detract from the desired external image of a sanctioned self-discipline.

Organizational Tensions

Some of the problems with the community-centered approach to development in the context of Guy Town emerged during the planning and implementation of club activities and, in particular, the summer camp for preschool- through high-school-aged children. The strategy of using key people from the area in leadership roles idealistically creates a level of independence, community sensitivity, and personal responsibility. In some instances these goals were actually accomplished when the key people involved had community improvement as their primary incentive. However, this approach can also provide status and resources for participants pursuing self-interested motivations. Two Youth Organization executive board members, in particular, represented these poles. One of the two consistently lead weekly club meetings regardless of other executive board members' lack of attendance. He fielded member complaints and constantly attempted to organize new activities that would keep the dwindling membership interested in club participation. He did the majority of the work and received very little recognition in return. At one point he managed to find full-time employment on a night shift, which prohibited him from running the meetings. Rather than picking up his slack, the other executive board members made excuses as to why they would also be unavailable. In addition, those at the apex of the organizational structure regularly undermined his planning of initiatives. He would research and begin to plan events without Dads's explicit approval or participation. Though the club was recurrently encouraged to operate independently of Wicked Times, Dads, as the club's president, had ultimate veto power, which he used frequently if the plans did not meet his standards. His investment in the standards for club-sponsored events was understandable, given that the organization's reputation was inseparable from his own, but this arrangement did thwart any sense of independence for the club.

The second executive board member was rarely present at meetings but was always given the most prestigious roles in the organization's activities. One of these roles included coordinating the Youth Organization's summer camp, which was really an academically oriented summer school that included weekly fieldtrips to sites around the island so that the children could leave the confines of the inner city and enjoy the beaches, waterfalls, and amusements that were typically closed to them because of lack of transportation or other resources.

Some issues came up within the community around the management of the summer school with accusations of child favoritism being made, particularly in relation to which children got to go on fieldtrips and which children were sent home for bad behavior. The teachers were largely community residents but not necessarily club members, and they were well versed in the area's interpersonal politics and in the reputations of their students' parents.

The other key community issue that arose out of the summer camp was fee payment. The fee for three weeks of camp was three hundred dollars per student, which, at the time, was the equivalent of approximately six U.S. dollars. The teachers were told not to mention fees to the external organization that funded the camp because they were not aware that any fees would be charged. By the third week of camp, a policy had been established by which students were sent home from class and barred from the excursions if their complete payment had not been made.

Beyond this questionable practice, there were also accusations floating around that the coordinating board member had been stealing the dues that were paid during each club meeting. The controversy was compounded when speculation was circulated about the improper appropriation of funding for the summer camp. It was suggested that a large sum of money beyond the fifty thousand dollars that had been expected for the summer camp had been granted to the organization. Some community residents were saying that they thought the coordinator was going to keep the remainder of the money for himself and rumors were spreading about who had "leaked" the information about the sum that had been granted, though to my knowledge all the teachers and organizers of the program were aware of the sum.

One executive board member suggested that club members demand accountability over the club finances. The funds for summer camp were not all accounted for, given that the teacher's stipends were a fraction of the total sum and that very few supplies were available to teachers for their classrooms. In addition, the daily lunch—which largely consisted of a drink dispenser full of reconstituted artificial fruit punch and sandwiches made from canned meat, or on better days, patties consisting of meat- or vegetable-filled pastry, and which was allegedly paid for using the three hundred dollar fees that had been collected—was not provided consistently because of "lack of funds." The other overhead costs were for bus rental and to supplement entrance fees on fieldtrips.

Power relations in the area were such that the problem was never directly confronted because of the potential for repercussions against accusers. Instead, the problem was addressed only via the aggressive circulation of gossip about those at the center of the controversy. Many club members saw this misappropriation of club funds as a betrayal, given that they had contributed their limited resources, which could have been put to better use, to the club as a communal resource only to have the funds allegedly supplement particular insidious individuals' own reserves.

It was in this context that community residents' frustration with the local power structure began to surface through the agitated gossip that was being circulated. It became clear that residents were reluctant to directly confront the inequalities of the system and that they felt generally powerless to make changes, even though the organization was purportedly a democratic institution. Here, as with other aspects of the Guy Town development project, patterns were in place that reinforced the local power structure through daily practice. At the same time, ideologically, attempts were made to educate area youth, in this case, to succeed in the formal school system, thereby incorporating them into the Jamaican nation as potentially productive citizens. Here, residents, in a sense, confronted "double domination," asserted through local community relations as well as official national structures, which are simultaneous and interconnected, but also often paradoxical.

Conclusion

If the rights and responsibilities that constitute citizenship within the Jamaican nation and within Guy Town are entwined, and yet in conflict, the community development programs there are complex and contradictory endeavors. Given that the dancehall music industry is the primary private benefactor in Guy Town, and that dancehall is a masculinist genre, which was unapologetically created in a male-centered cultural context, programs prioritize young men under the guise that they are more at-risk and that their development will result in an improvement of conditions for women. However, it is also the case that the loyalty and participation of young men, in particular, is crucial to the maintenance of community power structures.

Programs officially encourage citizens to resolve conflict using socially acceptable verbal strategies. However, for the sake of survival, informal community security is also supported utilizing illegal weaponry and the power of brutality as a resource toward the protection of Guy Town's population. While participants are instructed in national membership in an attempt to fashion them into neoliberal citizens through the prioritization of participation, self-control, and personal contribution, they are also necessarily participants in illicit networks and systems of community governance that are all but compulsory for citizenship in Guy Town and the wider area.

Issues of class and culture are critical to understanding the intricacies of development through dancehall. Dads's participation in bourgeois business and political networks does make new resources available to Wicked Times and to Guy Town, as a community, through the new points of contact that are forged. However, even though Dads, at times, attempts to strategically deploy an air of bourgeois respectability, particularly within the context of his political campaign, it does not seem that he wants to transform himself culturally or socially into a fully bourgeois subject (see Freeman 2000).[13] Even given the resources that he and the performers he works with are able to command, it is not an upper-class brown identity that they choose to cultivate. The markers of success that they adopt are instead those of African American hip-hop moguls, who largely retain a distinctly and purposefully black working-class sensibility. Beyond the consumptive preferences, trappings of success such as fashion, jewelry, and expensive cars chosen under this sensibility, he and his cohort also retain a deeper set of socialized cultural values based on concepts of giving, loyalty, and respect that are intimately linked to an urban working-class sense of community and the democratic socialist values of a prior political moment.

Residents of Guy Town, while desirous of resources that make life enjoyable, or in this case, merely possible, are reluctant to give up their own language and social practices in order to acquire them on the terms of the dominant culture. The diversity of the newly forming middle class may provide a space for upward mobility, which will allow distinct class cultures to be bridged, bolstering the construction of a culturally, politically, and economically "black"-dominated national vision on the part of the People's National Party. However, as part of that enterprise, the incorporation of the Guy Town youth into the Jamaican nation ends up being a superficial or even performed process. Residents have learned how to obtain resources through image cultivation while simultaneously participating in practices and networks that undermine the state's authority at the local level. Additionally, the state's tenuous grasp on the governance of garrison communities has led to reliance on local power hierarchies, including informal systems of justice, as an extension of state power because the local systems are more well informed and efficacious in their response.

The superficiality of Guy Town's incorporation into the Jamaican nation is further reinforced by the privatization of the development discourse among Guy Town residents. Even initiatives that were sponsored by government agencies and NGOs were most often attributed to Dads and Wicked Times as the conduit for funding and other types of resources. Since norms of giving relate to the cultivation of loyalty among ghetto residents, this attribution reinforces residents' commitment to local power structures rather than to the Jamaican state. The result is a corroboration of the disenchantment with electoral politics and cynicism regarding state-sponsored benefits and elected officials, regardless of the deep, but abstract, party loyalty that became clear during election time. This tension creates a space for play where community residents are able to manipulate both structures for immediate benefit under conditions in which their life choices are also molded by them. However, the long-term benefits of these arrangements are questionable. The young men who graduate from the remedial education programs undoubtedly benefit from enhanced literacy and new critical thinking tools, but the lack of growth in the Jamaican economy means that there is not employment available to accommodate them.

CHAPTER 6

The Long View

Looking back at the declining heyday of the Guy Town development projects ten years later confirmed many of the concerns I initially identified in the development programming back in 2002. Though Dads was unsuccessful in his election bid for member of Parliament, he has continued to rise through the ranks of the PNP, and the change in focus has caused him to withdraw from development activities in Guy Town. Dads's withdrawal soured his relationship with the wider community, whose loyalty dwindled with the passage of time. It was expressed to me that Guy Town was no longer a safe place for Dads.

Dads's beneficent support of the security corner gunmen, which I was ultimately told did include supplying firearms and money to encourage participation in the men's classes, was withdrawn. Because Dads's infrequent presence in the community seemed to be creating conflict, the police eventually warned him to stay away from Guy Town completely. Upheavals in the local power structure resulted in long spans of gun violence and retribution that birthed a new variation in personnel within the informal system of justice, including a new private businessman who stepped in as a sponsor. Notably, this upheaval and the ensuing conflict were not drawn on political lines but were instead rooted in a power struggle over territory and access to resources within a stolidly PNP-affiliated area.

During my most recent round of interviews with area residents, when asked about the development projects, the decline was notably blamed on the change of government, with the JLP having less concern for PNP areas and the member of Parliament losing access to the JLP government's resources because of his PNP affiliation. The decline was also blamed on "the war," which led to the cancellation of programming when outsiders became even more reluctant to visit the potentially deadly community. However, from the perspective of a Youth Organization insider, I was told that the

Jamaica Social Investment Fund had continued to lead some scaled-down after-school programs using volunteer teachers from Mico College and had been planning a summer school up until the point that the Guy Town liaison was found to be misappropriating funds. JSIF allegedly blacklisted Guy Town once the misuse of funds was discovered.

When I ran this information by one of JSIF's representatives who lived in the community, I was told that Guy Town had not literally been blacklisted, but that with the global economic downturn there were fewer resources. When resources are restricted and services are cut, I was told, the community perception is that the service reductions are a form of punishment. According to my source, JSIF is still willing to work with Guy Town, but there would have to be a clear effort to clean house when it came to the liaising Youth Organization's leadership.

Globalization, Dancehall, and Jamaican National Development

Treating dancehall, nation building, and development together as subjects of inquiry provides an entry point into the contingencies of local, national, and global processes. Economic, cultural, and class-based struggles are of great importance in understanding neoliberal globalization's impact on weakly positioned postcolonial societies. By beginning to map Jamaica's active, if hesitant, participation in the current global moment, both in terms of the national economic vision and the place of disenfranchised communities within that vision, the complexity of postcolonial governance in a neoliberal age begins to emerge.

The task of national identity formation must be considered alongside the goals of global competitiveness, particularly in postcolonial societies that have historically been positioned to develop deeply dependent economies. Self-imposed economic austerity measures that prioritize servicing the Jamaican private debt burden over funding social welfare programs, followed by the global economic contraction of 2008, seem to be setting the poorer population of Jamaica adrift. While the social safety net is shrinking, the acquisition of training and credentials by individual citizens is supposed to transform them into agents of their own economic success. Given the lack of employment possibilities for qualified people and the lack of national economic growth, there is no concomitant increase in economic stability even for those who show the necessary initiative.

I have examined these issues ethnographically by focusing on local moral economies of resource redistribution, which are a central component of life among the Jamaican poor, tied into community power relations based on reputation and respectability, gender roles, the deployment of violence, and access to employment. Giving practices are rooted in a prior democratic socialist political period but have become deeply embedded in local value systems, in part, because of their compatibility with Christian values.

Ironically, these practices of economic mutuality take on a different tone in the neoliberal capitalist moment. Giving practices continue to coincide with the national agenda of the state. However, these acts of giving, rooted in a prior democratic socialist political moment's values, can now arguably be treated as the private initiative of individuals supplanting the need for care by the state. A similar analysis can be applied to the continued importance of private patronage and informal community power structures, which have been allowed to flourish in poorer communities that are largely disconnected from legitimate systems of benefit distribution and participation in wage labor.

As has been insightfully suggested in James Ferguson's recent work on South Africa, similar redistributive practices on the part of poor populations have started to be regarded as a tax on the working poor, who are unable to accumulate surplus resources because of their private obligations to ensure the well-being of family members and neighbors in the absence of adequate formal employment opportunity and state support. By thinking of these informal financial obligations as a system of taxation on the productivity of the poor, it is possible to begin the crucial project of envisioning alternative economic models that can be decoupled from the twentieth-century ideal of working toward formal employment for all. According to the Congress of South African Trade Unions, this inequitable tax burden calls for the implementation of a proposed state-sponsored "Basic Income Grant" providing a baseline of financial support for all South African citizens regardless of employment status or income level, which they would be free to use at their own discretion (Ferguson 2009).

While this particular proposal would not be efficacious in a country like Jamaica as compared to South Africa, the reconceptualization of systems of mutual obligation on the part of the poor as informal taxation certainly can open up new ways of thinking about social policy that can move away from the singular focus on formal employment as a primary solution to the problem of poverty. Young black men, who have been particularly pathologized within neoliberal multicultural ideological models, might benefit from the space this change would open up to develop a valuable masculine identity decoupled from the male-breadwinner norm that has served as a central preoccupation of industrial economic development planning. With a new understanding of what it means to make a living without formal employment, the weight of failure might be lifted off of a population that is simply too large for the Jamaican economy to accommodate, even with personal initiative and jobs training. However, such an ideological shift would require the abandonment of long-standing and globally circulated biases that have marginalized black family formations by pathologizing their nonnuclear composition and thereby "scientifically" naturalizing long-standing social and economic inequalities that can be traced back to the days of plantation slavery (see Thomas 2011). Such powerful mechanisms of social regulation will not perish quietly but will require a sweeping reorientation of Jamaican state policy to accommodate the possibility of continued high levels of formal unemployment within poor communities.

Neoliberal restructuring, imposed by the demands of the global economy via international financial and regulatory bodies, creates profound consequences for the least well-represented segments of the Jamaican population. In communities like Guy Town, these consequences are seen as a clear failure on the part of the state. Since Jamaica is in the midst of a political-economic transformation, the lack of state care previously received by poor populations is perceived as a betrayal. This change is particularly explicit in the Jamaican context because of the democratic socialist agenda that was pursued in a prior political moment by the People's National Party. The pursuit of egalitarian political and economic reforms as well as efforts at cultural inclusion initially attracted members of the black working class to become party supporters. Now, the same party that sponsored these initiatives, in a new political moment, has insisted that citizen's be "helped to help themselves" even where prospects of employment are extremely low. The end result is a dislocation of the nation from the state as the state loses legitimacy in the eyes of politically crucial poor populations who have become disillusioned with their party and electoral politics in general. These views are, of course, embedded in local understandings of party dynamics in relation to access to crucial resources, as well as intimate understandings of class relations as experienced through acts of discrimination.

Community residents continue to be nationalistic, proudly identifying themselves as Jamaicans and rooting for the success of the country as a whole, but this does not correspond to a deep commitment to the Jamaican state. Part of this disillusionment relates to a pervasive sense that the People's National Party has not been true to its established political traditions. Loyalty is then redirected toward those who do provide residents with a measure of security. In the Jamaican case, this has meant the solidification of local moral economies, the power of informal community structures, and the position of private patrons.

In an effort to incorporate, discipline, and improve the life chances of these populations, the Jamaican state has encouraged the implementation of community development initiatives that provide training and education to marginal populations. These projects can be looked at as part of a nation-building strategy that is educating populations to take pride in an understanding of their place in Pan-African history, while also instilling in them values of self-restraint and discipline. In part, these lessons take the form of redirecting participants who are seen as part of unruly and disruptive populations to nonviolent dispute resolution techniques. While the end result of programs is rarely gainful employment, programs do forward the national agenda in two key ways. First, the Afrocentric curriculum helps indoctrinate participants into the vision of Jamaica as a black-led nation. Second, the instruction of dispute resolution techniques, discipline, and self-restraint, if efficacious, would, ideally, quell the volatility of inner-city communities, which are primary contributors to national crime rates, a key barrier to the attraction of foreign investment.

Given that these education programs are undertaken at a grassroots community level, they too are imbricated with local systems of power. In this particular instance, local power dynamics prioritize the needs of men and require participation in the informal power structures that govern the area. Simultaneously, development projects were privately sponsored through the dancehall music industry, a genre created by ghetto residents, which is also an expression of their worldview via the crafting of perspectival fantasies and the reinforcement of cultural normativities. The content of dancehall often interrupts the imaginary of nationhood being set forth from above, whether by the state itself through the educational and criminal justice systems or through a national media controlled by Jamaican elites, and has become central to debates around propriety and the appropriate substance of Jamaican national culture.

In addition, the music industry itself is caught within this system of contradictions as it attempts to market its product. Here the reputation and class-based authenticity of performers is linked to musical authenticity. An artist's rootedness within a marginal community is significant to the desirability of his or her music in the global marketplace. However, professionalism is also a crucial attribute for Jamaican artists hoping to maintain productive working relationships with North American and European companies, creating the need for newly fashioned subjectivities. This bind corresponds to the bind of the participants in the remedial education programs. In order for residents to survive within their community, and for performers to survive in their industry, they must participate in that which development and professionalization programs attempt to eradicate. Ultimately, performers and community residents must learn to navigate and manipulate the symbols of both reputation and respectability in order to capitalize on the availability of crucial short-term resources.

Many of the issues I have raised in this study of Jamaica are exportable to other localities, and it is my hope that I have contributed to a comparative body of literature seeking to better understand the impacts of neoliberal restructuring and market globalization on countries holding a weak position in the hierarchy of nations. These countries are often also contending with their own internal inequalities and social tensions that are an ongoing legacy of the colonial project and which have now been translated into discourses about the deserving and undeserving poor that naturalize violence, exclusion, and suffering. This normalization of marginality uses neoliberal multicultural ideologies that locate the "failure" of poor populations to find a place in the global economy within racialized understandings of cultural inadequacy that justify their exclusion from global citizenship. Additionally, the need to attract foreign investment continues to limit the shape these nations can take and the vision of a future that they are able to forge for themselves. The strategies they use to carve a specialized space in world commerce restrict the life possibilities of their citizenry. Here it has been left to the residents of poor communities to eke out a living and to redefine the principles of neoliberalism in a language of their own—a language of urban improvisation. The resultant communities are constituted by the private financiers, entrepreneurs, and flexible subjects treasured by neoliberalism, but with a practical twist. Their activities are not limited to those characterized by state-sanctioned legitimacy. Instead, they operate in a context of legal demystification in which expediency trumps adherence to the law. This is a legal context that has been cultivated by the state itself, and, furthermore, its participants are still, ultimately, answerable to a calculating state that allows illegal but licit activities to continue, but only up to the point that the state's needs are efficaciously served (Galvin 2012; Roitman 2006). Might a revised concept of poor people's sharing practices that redefines mutual obligation as a form of informal taxation open up new possibilities with regard to Jamaican statecraft, governance, and nation building? Could loosening the legal restrictions on informal commerce or, even more profoundly, facilitating economically beneficial informal labor practices change the socioeconomic landscape for Jamaica's urban poor in ways that would, in the end, enhance the well-being of the country as a whole?

Regionally, there are resonances here with both Brazil and South Africa, where stark racial and class-based inequalities and processes of ghettoization have also contributed to the solidification of informal economies and high rates of violent crime. In these places there is also a similar and related crisis of masculinity, which is an observable commonality among poor populations living under circumstances in which economic policy and social inequality has produced limitations on the availability of employment and created profound income disparity. The inability to fulfill the provider role in families, regardless of the form those families may take, has created a vulnerability, which has fed the need for alternative, achievable markers of manhood. At times these new markers are in tension with national goals, contributing to high levels of violence and the proliferation of illicit enterprises, creating a sense of generalized chaos among citizens and outside observers. Fitting marginal and potentially disruptive populations into a distinctly defined, constructive, national vision of citizenship becomes the task of states as part of the effort to create stability, which is a prerequisite for foreign investment and economic expansion.

I will now return briefly to the place this book began, the Guy Town development initiatives. The programs, designed in accordance with the sensible Better Communities model, were riddled with contradictions because of the unique politics of garrison life. Rather than building the nation by reforming and educating residents, enfranchising all people of Jamaica by developing a web of interconnected communities created by local clubs driven by citizens and their own identified needs, the Guy Town projects met the short-term needs of strategic participants while failing to undercut the area's entrenched reliance on criminality. This limitation was, in part, due to a lack of employment opportunity and the use of local leadership hierarchies as the cornerstone of what was initially designed to be a rural development model. The use of local leaders is, in theory, an empowering development strategy. In practice, within the context of Kingston, a city of vast income inequality with a long history of political patronage and garrison politics, the end result was somewhat different than anticipated. The

Jamaican state has historically used the control enjoyed by organized crime as an extension of state power in communities that have been deemed ungovernable, thereby turning over community governance to local, informal justice systems. The outcome of this ceding of governance is a strengthened loyalty to local patrons, heightened suspicion of the Jamaican state, and the continued proliferation of informal community justice systems, which may contribute a degree of stability, but ultimately undermine the state's ability to govern its citizens.

The development programs therefore empowered those who already wielded disproportionate power within Guy Town. This elite group, closely affiliated with Dads, was given an even greater ability to make decisions on behalf the community and, additionally, to skim extra benefits from the projects. In the long view, at-risk area youth were not persuaded to put down the gun. Instead, area residents persisted in drawing their rights, responsibilities, and personal security from the informal relations of community citizenship and continued to experience alienation from the shrinking benefits of citizenship offered by the Jamaican state, despite community development efforts intended to bridge that divide. The continued state of disenfranchisement and lack of, or criminalization of, economic opportunity ultimately positioned those targeted for reform to use their education, not in a personally or socially transformative way but, instead, to redefine the principles of neoliberalism (entrepreneurship, self-sufficiency, privatization) in their daily practice. The initiatives were also ultimately unsuccessful in minimizing community violence, in particular because of the Jamaican state's continued utilization of informal governance in areas like Guy Town to maintain a sort of stability, an approach to governance that favors expediency over adherence to the law. Because of this enduring contradiction, youths that participated in the men's classes were able to employ their new knowledge during the continued recurrent periods of violence. Returning to Martin's thoughts on the matter, they had learned to "conduct the war more intelligently."

A more profound change will be necessary in order to transform the lives of those who currently must exist within these informal systems of economic exchange and community governance and to undermine the cycles of violence that continue to destabilize Jamaica as a nation. Those changes must begin within the state itself, whether they take the form of coalition building with other postcolonial nations in order to muster greater global influence, or through a far-reaching rethinking of what it means to amalgamate a population that, foreseeably, will remain perpetually poor. As seen in Guy Town, members of poor urban populations are already helping themselves as entrepreneurs, flexible subjects, and private investors, but personal initiative cannot conquer the problem of limited national economic capacity and unemployment. The current moment of global economic convulsion and reconfiguration might provide a productive milieu, freed of neoliberalism's ideological baggage as a universal panacea, in which to begin the project of rethinking how its precepts have been reinterpreted and applied in Kingston garrison communities in order to begin the development of fundamentally new approaches to the ongoing problem of poverty and violence in Jamaica.

Notes

Introduction

1. All the names of people and places have been changed, unless they are public figures whose public statements are being referenced. This attempt to anonymize people and places reflects my commitment to maintain the confidentiality of both the research setting and of the research participants. Guy Town is a space that is frequently embroiled in violent power struggles, be they politically rooted or based upon private motivations. Within these struggles, access to private knowledge can be used as a form of power. For this reason it was important to me as a researcher and to my collaborators in Guy Town that their identities be protected as effectively as possible.
2. To "have" in local parlance means that a person has access to regular sources of income and is wealthy relative to the low standard of living within poor urban communities.
3. "Baby father" is a term used to describe the father of a woman's children who is not her husband.
4. Martin's perspective expresses a familiar frustration among community residents who grew up with few resources and who often view themselves as having made better choices than others from their age group. However, it is important to recognize that there is economic and social stratification within ghetto communities themselves that might also provide advantages for some that others did not possess. Martin indubitably did work hard to achieve stable economic status, but he also had family support and other resources that some other community residents lacked. The perspective does, in a sense, reproduce ideological narratives that contrast the traits of the deserving and undeserving poor.
5. The role of the state in "dominated" countries might, in fact, be particularly important, even though their generally weak position may make the state appear to be less evident.
6. However, it is important to understand that in Jamaica what is being here characterized as "minority" culture is actually created by a marginalized majority.

7. Interestingly, it was often hard for people to racially-ethnically classify me, in part because my dark curly hair led some to believe that I was a "brown" Jamaican at the light end of the phenotypic spectrum. At other times I was variously called "whitey," "chiney," "Indian," "cooley-gyal," "England," "Canada," and even on rare occasions, "America." The rarity of this final designation is a reflection of the infrequency of American tourism in Kingston, which has been labeled too dangerous by the majority of American travelers, unlike the slightly more adventurous Canadian and European visitors.
8. "Garrison" is a term applied to areas with uniform voting patterns and a militarized power structure linked to a political party.
9. Wicked Times is a pseudonym for the dancehall production company in which I conducted my research.
10. The fathering of children with multiple women as a status signifier for some young men does not indicate the social endorsement of parental irresponsibility. In fact, men who do not contribute to the well-being of their children are in many ways socially stigmatized. It is important that the fathering of children with multiple women not be conflated with a lack of parental involvement on the part of the fathers.

Chapter 1

1. Thanks are owed to Don Robotham for pointing out that values around giving and generosity are prevalent throughout Jamaican society, even among the upper and middle classes. Through my research, I noticed that the form that these values take in daily practice is distinct in the context of ghettos, which are heavily populated, intensely public, and highly social settings.
2. Barry Chevannes identified sharing as one of the major values that is taught within homes in Jamaican ghetto communities (Chevannes 2001).
3. It is important to note that the shorthand of "uptown" and "downtown" representing a physical division in Kingston with concomitant racial and class connotations did not solidify historically until the late 1960s and early 1970s (Robotham 2003).
4. At the time of my initial fieldwork, fifty Jamaican dollars was the equivalent of one U.S. dollar.
5. Katrin Norris, in her book *Jamaica*, published in 1962, identifies similar practices among young unemployed Jamaicans. She refers to the practice

as "'scuffling' a share of the livelihood of friends or relatives" (Norris 1962, 11).
6. Wilson argues that shaming through gossip is a powerful social tool that can be used to attack and undermine a community member's reputation and respectability (Wilson 1973, 118).
7. Framed as a marker of manhood, Wilson describes the role of money in the signification of maturity, responsibility, and generosity, stating, "It is no good simply earning money, one must be generous with it, so being able to both earn and give (and lend) are proofs of manliness. Money is a means, not an end" (Wilson 1973, 152). By delinking reputation from masculinity, it becomes evident that these same standards apply to women, who also gain status and social capital through the redistribution of assets.
8. Other strategies for income generation include gambling, a widespread practice in Guy Town, and "throwing partners" which has been discussed by anthropologists as participation in "rotating credit associations" (see Ardener and Burman 1995).
9. Don is the colloquial title for the leader of informal power structures that often organize inner city communities. This title references the Italian Mafia. I will go into further detail about donsmanship in Chapter 2.
10. On more than one occasion during my period of research, criticisms of North American individualism were made in my presence by working-class Jamaicans who regarded this individualism as selfish behavior.
11. An example of these limits is the use of padlocks on refrigerator doors in private kitchens, which have been installed to keep unauthorized persons from consuming the contents.
12. The terms "big man" and "big woman" are terms of positive reputation applied with gender appropriate connotations. A big woman is usually a mature woman who is independent and treated with regard by other prominent community members, including men. This often also means that she has resources available to engage in socially appropriate acts of redistribution and generosity.
13. The use of this term in popular discourse additionally complicates Wilson's use of the term because when an individual is addressed with the word respect it often actually serves as a testament to his or her positive reputation as a community member, rather than referencing any European-initiated standard of respectability (see Wilson 1973).
14. The word is largely, but not exclusively, used in interactions between men, as in "respect, mi bredrin" or "nuff respect."
15. He also indicated that giving or lending relationships can become

contentious because financial arrangements are personal and at times become inappropriately public in such an intensely intimate setting.
16. One of the most striking examples of this that I encountered occurred when Krystal's son was admitted to the children's hospital with a broken arm. Upon visiting him with his mother, sister, and aunts, we were introduced to a young boy, who couldn't have been more than five or six years old. He was in the hospital after receiving surgery for a leg deformity that required him to lie on his back with weights attached to his ankles for an extended period of time as part of the recovery process. The group found out that this little boy was an orphan and were so empathic that every time they went to visit their own family member they would spend time talking with him and, even given their own financial struggles, managed to give him small amounts of money and a hand-me-down teddy bear that had been brought to him from Guy Town.
17. For more on this issue, see Chevannes 2001 and Wilson 1973.
18. The differences in romantic relationships within the context of Jamaican ghettos have been treated as a continuum with romantic love at one pole and prostitution at the other, with some combination of the two existing in the middle (Chevannes 2001).
19. "Mattress" as a name for a female indicates a reputation of loose sexual morals. This is a name I have fabricated in place of her actual nickname to protect the identity of the young woman. In *Crab Antics*, Wilson indicates that nicknaming is an important element of reputation in the Caribbean. However, given that his use of reputation as a social status that must be "minimally fulfilled," the nicknames he identifies are ranked as incrementally positive social markers and include royal titles such as "king" and "duke" (see Wilson 1973, 151). Many of these titles (with the exception of King) have largely been replaced by newer titles including "boss" and "big man." Mattress's story reveals that nicknames can also be applied to those possessing a negative reputation and who have not "minimally fulfilled" the requirements to attain social status.
20. My suspicion is that this woman probably has a diagnosable mental illness.
21. A derogatory term for a homosexual, which is a grave allegation among Jamaican men.
22. JLP is shorthand for the Jamaica Labour Party. Guy Town is affiliated with the People's National Party, and supporters of the JLP are often considered to be their enemies.

Chapter 2

1. Many thanks are due to Patrick Peterkin, who, while working as my research assistant as I became accustomed to the sound of patois and moving through my research community, insisted that I pay careful attention to the multiple patron figures that I would encounter in the area.
2. I will go into this feature of ghetto communities in greater detail in Chapter 3.
3. "Legitimate" is placed in quotes because these businesses often serve as fronts for criminal activities.
4. "Tribal war" is the name commonly used to describe the armed conflicts conducted between members of neighboring garrisons, which is posed as political rivalry in the name of party loyalty.
5. "Bleaching" is what it is called when people stay up all night talking. In this case it refers to the men in control of securing the area negotiating agreements about plans for protection.
6. Here "tall up tall up" and "short up short up" are being used in reference to large and small guns, the terminology coming from a dancehall song popular at the time which had an accompanying dance called the "tall up tall up."
7. Women's underwear is considered to be polluting to men, who avoid contact with it in any nonsexual context.
8. The distribution of work is a common strategy for patrons wanting to infuse money into the area, and one that will come up again in the discussion of the record producer's patronage.
9. The issue of PNP not doing anything for residents is one that came up often. When people indicated who it was that takes care of them, they usually indicated the record producer–patron, rather than other people active in the area. This is a clear indication of the slippage between a deep community value of party loyalty versus the dissatisfaction of many community members with what the party, which often takes the blame for the reduction of services on the part of the state, has been able to provide for them.
10. The area leader, who decades earlier had been a prominent record producer, now owns racehorses and is involved in other sorts of business enterprises. While I met him, and some of his associates, on several occasions, I was never able to interview him. The information I obtained about him is based on interviews and discussions I had with community residents and the member of Parliament who largely referred to him

abstractly and not by name. For this reason, I too will not refer to him by name and will discuss the role of area leader in the community without directly linking this role to any particular person's identity.

11. I have theorized the Anglophone Caribbean as a space of "legal demystification" introduced with British jurisprudence during the colonial era in relation to piracy tolerance. Throughout Jamaican history, both the British colonial government and the contemporary Jamaican state have permitted illegal activities that contribute to the state's ability to govern owing to their expedience. This setting allows for opportunistic manipulation of legally ambiguous acts for the accumulation of wealth and social influence among populations that have included privateers and pirates as well as area leaders and don figures (Galvin 2012).

12. When I returned to my field site, four months after the incident, residents of Guy Town were still speculating over what had happened, and rumors were circulating regarding the involvement of other prominent community members in the attack.

13. In Jamaica there is an intricately articulated set of adjectives used to describe combinations of skin shade, hair type, and facial features. "Red" is used to describe people of a light, freckled complexion.

14. Though there were at times men who would spend time on this corner, it was largely recognized as space belonging to an established group of women who could ask those perceived as interlopers to leave.

15. There are rules surrounding the appropriate circulation of gossip in Guy Town, also related to interpersonal respect and potential retaliatory violence. No one ever indicated to me that Dads was directly involved in violence or punishment akin to that which the area leader was known to engage in. In addition, it was clear that Dads, and the community, benefited from the protection of the men who inhabited the security corner, and that Dads turned a blind eye to certain activities they engaged in, but Dads's direct support of the area security or criminal activities they may have engaged in was not made evident to me until ten years later, once Dads was no longer a significant influence in the area.

16. Recent legal cases around the world, including the Steubenville, Ohio, case (see Pavlick 2013), have brought to light that rape culture is a prevalent facet of contemporary life in many patriarchal societies, not just ones that have already suffered a long history of sexual stigmatization.

17. It is not lost on the author that the pseudonym "Dads" highlights the patriarch role this patron plays within community dynamics, and the fact

that the name "Dads" is a common title of respect for men in Jamaica also indicates that this patriarchal sensibility is significantly woven into Jamaican society.
18. It is not uncommon for "downtown" businesses to operate sound systems as a side line. In fact, sound systems, which are mobile discos, were initially used by businesses to attract customers to their shops using popular music. They eventually split off from the retail industry, becoming legitimate entertainment businesses in their own right. For more on the history of sound systems in Jamaica see Stolzoff 2000.

Chapter 3

1. Kingsley Stewart has recently argued that, in fact, the values expressed in dancehall music are values that are held by wider Jamaican society, and not the vulgar aberration they are often deemed (Stewart 2002).
2. In addition, members of the black working class have taken advantage of opportunities for upward mobility and have successfully contributed to the formation of a diverse middle class, adding themselves to the ranks of the traditional Jamaican middle class (D. Gordon 1987).
3. When tackling issues of popular culture, I have found that many intellectuals attempt to recuperate the value of the genres they write about for audiences the genres are not intended for. My discussion of Jamaican dancehall comes from the perspective of both an outsider and a lover of the music. For this reason, I choose not to engage in the debate over the value of the music, as I believe the music's value is innately affirmed by the millions of people who listen to, dance to, and enjoy dancehall.
4. There are many excellent and in-depth accounts of the development of Jamaican popular music, with a focus on dancehall and its historical antecedents. Some of these books have been marketed to popular audiences (see Barrow and Dalton 1997; Foster 1999; Chang and Chen 1998). There are also several rich academic treatments of the development of dancehall in relation to Jamaican culture and society (see Stanley Niaah 2010; Stolzoff 2000; Hope 2006a).
5. Juggling sessions are dances in which a sound system plays music for a crowd using strategies that encourage dancing, whereas a sound clash is a competitive event in which two or more sound systems compete with each other to prove which has the most extensive and rare collection of music as well as the best skills in presenting the songs and the most clever emcee, who best entertains the crowd with his or her linguistic virtuosity. A sound clash ends with one sound determined to be the winner after

having "murdered" the other competing sounds with its combination of skills.
6. Songs are also promoted via the local radio stations, some of which have recently adopted an all-reggae format, departing from the previous trend of airing a combination of American pop music and religious programming.
7. Carolyn Cooper has suggested that this practice contributes to dancehall's "intertextuality" (Cooper 1993, 138).
8. Though rural poverty is more widespread and acute in Jamaica as a whole, the dramatic results of urban poverty have made it the focus of greater public attention. In addition, while the rural poor are often treated as a part of the dignified wellspring of Jamaican culture, the urban poor are often posed as a lazy and immoral lot. The Jamaican Left often tries to ideologically recuperate this group as a part of the Jamaican cultural "grassroots," and reggae and dancehall music have been incorporated into these discourses.
9. Loverman is referencing the US-based Latina, pop singer Jennifer Lopez's song, popular at the time of the interview, called "Jenny from the Block," when he discusses his relationship to his community of origin.
10. I do not want to overlook the fact that there are a limited number of success stories through participation in the music industry, and that such aspirations are, at times, unrealistic. However, there are numerous ways of participating in the music industry that can provide ghetto youth with steady employment, including working as security at events and moving equipment.
11. The "crisis of identity" suggested by Chevannes, which has resulted in a retooling of the roles of men in Jamaican ghetto communities is catalyzed by the very real and painful reality beyond the problem of relating with women. Men who do not have access to resources are forced to watch their children suffer physically, emotionally and socially.
12. The analysis of dancehall lyrics alone could fill several volumes. My aim here is to demonstrate some major themes as they relate to life in downtown Kingston.
13. While conducting fieldwork in the months shortly after September 11, I noticed an increased number of references to the Middle East in connection with the assertion of badness both in the context of dancehall and in daily practice. This included taxis adorned with large windshield stickers saying "Taliban" as well as idiomatic references to Bin Laden, Hussein, and "terrorists" in general.
14. There is much debate over the issue of oral sex, which is practiced by

some Jamaicans, but which is often spoken of as an American practice that is defiling Jamaica.
15. Notably, in referencing "cow horn" Vybz Kartel is referencing the abeng horn, which was a musical instrument made and used by Maroon populations.
16. The term "brownin" also can have class implications, where most naturally light-skinned women hail from the upper classes. Light skin can also at times be linked to the inability of a woman to maintain a home, cook, and care for a man because of its association with upper-class women, who often have hired "helpers" to cook and clean for them. In addition, it can also be associated with a "slim" body type, which may be unappealing to some Jamaican men who prefer a more curvaceous woman.
17. Donna Hope provides an extensive treatment of the issue of skin bleaching in her book, *Inna di Dancehall: Popular Culture and the Politics of Identity in Jamaica* (see Hope 2006a).
18. However, it is important to note that there is a gender gap being created in Jamaican society because women are gaining higher levels of education than men at an alarming rate. This is a reflection of the marginalization of Jamaican men, but also creates a tension, because males are largely still considered the socially dominant gender overall.
19. Disturbingly, a spate of dancehall songs, including one titled "Red Plate," by Mr. G., blames female promiscuity for the spread of HIV/AIDS. A "red plate" is a registered taxi cab, named for the official red license plate issued for taxis. Mr. G. compares a promiscuous woman to a taxi that has many passengers. This criticism of promiscuous women must be considered in conjunction with the standard celebration of men who have many sexual partners, and with the fact that an emphasis on practicing "safer sex" in dancehall is rare. The dissemination of this type of "local knowledge" is particularly worrisome because a woman's request for the use of condoms by her regular partner can be risky. It may be considered, by some men, as evidence of her infidelity.
20. Sharing of men between women seems to be prevalent throughout Jamaican culture, but it is more explicitly acknowledged among the urban poor.
21. Here wife or spouse does not necessarily refer to members of a marriage conducted through an official ceremony, but may indicate an established relationship, or common-law arrangement.
22. Faye Harrison has named this strategy a "present day survival orientation" and discusses it in detail in relation to what she calls "social outlawry (Harrison 1988)."

23. For an extensive analysis of dancehall's ritual performance geography see (Stanley Niaah 2010)
24. Sadly, during my second summer fieldwork trip, there was another memorial street dance held for this same man, who had been brutally murdered several months earlier.
25. This gossip included discussion of a young woman who had bragged to the camera that she was stealing another woman's man and who at some later time had ended up in a physical altercation over the man, in which the braggart matie had been stabbed.
26. Stanley Niaah argues that the dancehall is a space that, revalorizes "aspects of the body that are censored in the wider social sphere, including shape, size, age, definitions of structure, social utility and symbolic value," pointing to the valorization of women with a "visibly plump pudenda"; of "mampies," who are fat women, and of "marky marky belly," women with stretch marks on their stomachs, which serve as testimony to their fertility (Stanley Niaah 2010, 136).
27. Stanley Niaah, notes a shift in dancehall participation by the turn of the millennium, where couples were less frequently attending dances together in favor of attendance with friends of the same gender. At this same time male dance crews came to predominate the parties in ways that upset some participants' conception of appropriate masculinity. She writes of a party called Bembe Thursdays where "males were thought to be dominating the dance floor, male dance moves overshadowed those created by females and the dancehall was overrun by a new male aesthetic that ran counter to the normative social constructions of gender identity. It was not 'gender appropriate' for men to upstage women on the dance floor" (Stanley Niaah 2010, 142)
28. Thanks are due to Oneka LaBennett for recognizing the issue of bodily performance versus narration in my account of Nadia's performance.

Chapter 4

1. Steven Feld's analysis of "world music" performers as "wage laborers" for "First World" celebrities is particularly useful (Keil and Feld, 1994, 242).
2. This is an important observation when taking into account the major shifts in the global entertainment industry that have occurred based on the prevalence of the downloadable digital music formats that have gained popularity over the last ten years.
3. "Baymore" is a pseudonym for the area from which Bizzy and Mr. Mention come. It is another downtown Kingston ghetto community.

4. The position of younger performers at Wicked Times who have not yet "buss'd" (become popular) on the dancehall scene is slightly less egalitarian, where there is still dues paying to be done.
5. Wicked Times has not been impervious to violence. One of the company's foundational members was murdered in what was reported to be a "contract killing," which took place just outside the company's gates.
6. I will discuss these development projects in more detail in Chapter 5.
7. Significantly, the pairing of No Doubt with Bounty Killer went sour because of a conflict of values that might be attributed to the very Jamaican "authenticity" that Bounty Killer contributed to the project. Bounty Killer parted ways with No Doubt after the music video for their collaboration was released and he realized that his DJ-ing appearance in the piece overlaid images of a naked man doing gymnastics. The image broke a taboo over male homosexuality from Bounty Killer's perspective, and his insistence that the video be changed accordingly was not heeded by the California-based No Doubt.
8. The social uses of dancehall in "inner city" Jamaica are discussed in greater detail in Chapter 3.
9. Thomas has argued that given the tenets of "modern blackness" and the deterritorialized nature of the Jamaican nation in diaspora, it is adherence to these narrow gender normativities that defines Jamaican citizenship, where geographical boundedness no longer serves that purpose (Thomas 2004).
10. Here "crossing-over" does not refer to popularity in international markets, but rather "Euro-American" markets where hip-hop and R&B, it can be argued, might have initially been intended for African-American listeners.

Chapter 5

1. This quote is excerpted from the 2005/2006 "Jamaica Budget Opening Presentation" delivered by the minister of finance and planning on Thursday, April 14, 2005. The full address is available at *www.mof.gov.jm*.
2. These choices may coincide with the overall development agenda, or they may be unexpected by-products of the development process, which nonetheless create new possibilities.
3. It might be more accurate to assert that the programs reinforce normative gender roles in general. However, the reinforcement of a particular style of femininity is less obviously at odds with Jamaican nation-building efforts.
4. In addition to enhancing immediate benefits, the duality may also

reinforce community residents' vulnerability in that the presence of Wicked Times's private support may negatively impact the benefits received from public sources. The withdrawal of private support might create a situation in which residents are left to fend for themselves under conditions of limited opportunity.
5. *www.plunkett.co.uk/history/historym.htm.*
6. In the time that I participated in Youth Organization meetings, Dads attended on only two occasions. Frustratingly, these two meetings were ones I was unable to attend.
7. JAMAL is the acronym for a state-sponsored literacy program, which many people see as carrying a stigma with it.
8. This is a reference to oral sex designed to challenge, insult, and publicly shame the object of the insult.
9. Homosexual.
10. These are all references to men who engage in oral sex.
11. At times the discourse around "ghetto culture" among residents of Guy Town was so anthropological that it was difficult to discern whether it was a product of the life of the community itself, or a product of social scientists' teachings about their research on "ghetto culture" being assimilated and read back by the area's residents.
12. "No fuck" is a slang insult used by men to suggest that they are not able to get sex from women.
13. It is important to note here that even if he did desire fully bourgeois status, it is unlikely that he would be able to attain it because his lack of formal education and music industry background would be largely unacceptable to his bourgeois peers.

Bibliography

Adams, L. Emilie. 1991. *Understanding Jamaican Patois: An Introduction to Afro-Jamaican Grammar*. Kingston: Kingston Publishers.
Adorno, Theodor. 1982. "On the Fetish Character in Music and the Regression in Listening." In *The Essential Frankfurt School Reader*, edited by Andrew Arato and Eike Gebhardt, 270–99. New York: Urizen Books.
Alexander, Jack. 1977. "The Role of the Male in the Middle-Class Jamaican Family: A Comparative Perspective." *Journal of Comparative Family Studies* 8 (3): 369–89.
Alexander, M. Jacqui. 2005. *Pedagogies of Crossing: Meditations on Feminism, Sexual Politics, Memory, and the Sacred*. Durham, NC: Duke University Press.
Alleyne, Mervyn C. 2002. *The Construction and Representation of Race and Ethnicity in the Caribbean and the World*. Kingston: University of the West Indies Press.
Alonso, Ana Maria. 1994. "The Politics of Space, Time and Substance: State Formation, Nationalism and Ethnicity." *Annual Review of Anthropology* 23: 379–405.
Amit, Vered, ed. 2002. *Realizing Community: Concepts, Social Relationships and Sentiments*. London: Routledge.
Amit, Vered, and Nigel Rapport, eds. 2002. *The Trouble with Community: Anthropological Reflections on Movement, Identity and Collectivity*. London: Pluto Press.
Anderson, Benedict. 1991. *Imagined Communities: Reflections on the Origin and Spread of Nationalism*. New York: Verso.
Anderson, Birgitte, Zeljka Kozul-Wright, and Richard Kozul-Wright. 2000. *Copyrights, Competition and Development: The Case of the Music Industry*. Prepared for United Nations Conference on Trade and Development. No. 145. January.
Anderson, Patricia, and Michael Witter. 1994. "Crisis, Adjustment and Social Change: A Case Study of Jamaica." In *Consequences of Structural*

Adjustment: A Review of the Jamaican Experience, edited by Elise LeFranc, 1–55. Kingston: Canoe Press.

Ang, Ien. 1991. *Desperately Seeking the Audience.* New York: Routledge.

Appadurai, Arjun. 1996. *Modernity at Large: Cultural Dimensions of Globalization.* Minneapolis: University of Minnesota Press.

Ardener, Shirley, and Sandra Burman, eds. 1995. *Money-Go-Rounds: The Importance of Rotating Savings and Credit Associations for Women.* Oxford: Berg.

Austerlitz, Paul. 1997. *Merengue: Dominican Music and Dominican Identity.* Philadelphia: Temple University Press.

Austin, Diane. 1983. "Culture and Ideology in the English-Speaking Caribbean: A View from Jamaica." *American Ethnologist* 10 (2): 223–40.

———. 1984. *Urban Life in Kingston, Jamaica: The Culture and Class Ideology of Two Neighborhoods.* New York: Gordon and Breach.

Austin-Broos, Diane. 1997. *Jamaica Genesis: Religion and the Politics of Moral Orders.* Chicago: University of Chicago Press.

Averill, Gage. 1994. "'Mezanmi, Kouman Nou Ye? My Friends, How Are You?': Musical Constructions of the Haitian Transnation." *Diaspora* 3 (3): 253–71.

———. 1997. *A Day for the Hunter, a Day for the Prey: Popular Music and Power in Haiti.* Chicago: University of Chicago Press.

Baker, Houston A., Jr. 1993. *Black Studies, Rap and the Academy.* Chicago: University of Chicago Press.

Balibar, Etienne, and Immanuel Wallerstein. 1995. *Race, Nation, Class: Ambiguous Identities.* New York: Verso.

Balutansky, Kathleen M., and Marie-Agnes Sourieau, eds. 1998. *Caribbean Creolization: The Dynamics of Language, Literature, and Identity.* Gainesville: University Press of Florida.

Banton, Michael. 1987. *Racial Theories.* New York: Cambridge University Press.

Barrett, James, and David Roediger. 1997. "Inbetween Peoples: Race, Nationality, and the 'New Immigrant' Working Class." *Journal of American Ethnic History* 16: 3–44.

Barrow, Steve, and Peter Dalton. 1997. *Reggae: The Rough Guide.* London: Penguin.

Barth, Fredrik. 1966. *Models of Social Organization.* Royal Anthropological Institute Occasional Paper No. 23. London.

Barthes, Roland. 1957. *Mythologies.* New York: Hill and Wang.

Basch, Linda, Nina Glick-Schiller, and Cristina Szanton Blanc. 1994. *Nations Unbound: Transnational Projects, Post-colonial Predicaments and Deterritorialized Nation-States*. Newark, NJ: Gordon and Breach Publishers.

Bayart, Jean-François. 1999. *The Criminalization of the State in Africa*. London: Villiers Publications.

Beckford, George. 1971. "Plantation Society." *Savacou* 5: 7–22.

———. 1980. *Small Garden . . . Bitter Weed: Struggle and Change in Jamaica*. London: Zed.

Beckles, Hilary. 1990. *The History of Barbados*. London: Cambridge University Press.

Beenie Man. 1995. "Got to Mek a Living." Newark: Peter Pan Industries.

Benjamin, Walter. 1969. *Illuminations*. New York: Schocken Books.

Bennett, Tony, et al. 1986. *Popular Culture and Social Relations*. Milton Keynes, England: Open University Press.

Benton, Lauren. 2005. "Legal Spaces of Empire: Piracy and the Origins of Ocean Regionalism." *Comparative Studies in Society and History* 47 (4): 700–724.

Besson, Jean. 1993. "Reputation and Respectability Reconsidered: A New Perspective on Afro-Caribbean Peasant Women." In *Women and Change in the Caribbean*, edited by J. Momsen, 15–37. Kingston: Ian Randle Publishers.

Booth, William James. 1994. "On the Idea of the Moral Economy." *American Political Science Review* 88 (3): 653–67.

Bounty Killer. 1999. "Look." Mad House Records.

Bourdieu, Pierre. 1984. *Distinction: A Social Critique of the Judgment of Taste*. Cambridge: Harvard University Press.

———. 1990. *The Logic of Practice*. Stanford: Stanford University Press.

Bourne, Compton, and S. M. Allgrove. 1995. *Prospects for Exports of Entertainment Services for the English-Speaking Caribbean: The Case of Music*. Washington D.C.: World Bank.

Boyd, Todd 1997. *Am I Black Enough for You? Popular Culture from the 'Hood and Beyond*. Bloomington: University of Indiana Press.

Brathwaite, Edward. 1971. *The Development of Creole Society in Jamaica, 1770–1820*. Oxford: Clarendon Press.

Bratlinger, Patrick. 1983. *Bread and Circuses: Theories of Mass Culture as Social Decay*. Ithaca, NY: Cornell University Press.

———. 1990. *Crusoe's Footprints: Cultural Studies in Britain and America*. New York: Routledge.

Brereton, Bridget, and Kevin A. Yelvington, eds. 1999. *The Colonial Caribbean in Transition: Essays on Postemancipation Social and Cultural History*. Gainesville: University Press of Florida.

Brown, Karen McCarthy. 1991. *Mama Lola: A Voudou Priestess in Brooklyn.* Berkeley: University of California Press.

Browne, Katherine E. 2004. *Creole Economics: Caribbean Cunning under the French Flag.* Austin: University of Texas Press.

Browne-Gloude, Winnifred. 2011. *Higglers in Kingston: Women's Informal Work in Jamaica.* Nashville: Vanderbilt University Press.

Bryan, Patrick E. 2002. *Philanthropy and Social Welfare in Jamaica: An Historical Survey.* 2nd ed. Kingston: Sir Arthur Lewis Institute of Social and Economic Studies.

Burgess, Earnest, and Donald J. Bogue. 1967. *Urban Sociology.* Chicago: University of Chicago Press.

Bush, Barbara. 1990. *Slave Women in Caribbean Society, 1650–1838.* London: James Curry.

Campbell, Horace. 1987. *Reggae and Resistance: From Marcus Garvey to Walter Rodney.* Trenton: Africa World Press.

Cardoso, Fernando Henrique. 1972. "Dependency and Development in Latin America." *New Left Review* 74 (July/August): 83–95.

Cashmore, Earnest. 1979. *Rastaman: The Rastafarian Movement in England.* London: Unwin Paperbacks.

Cassidy, Frederic G. 1961. *Jamaica Talk: Three Hundred Years of the English Language in Jamaica.* Cambridge: Cambridge University Press.

Cassidy, Frederic, and R. B. Le Page. 1967. *Dictionary of Jamaican English.* Cambridge: Cambridge University Press.

Castells, Manuel. 1976. "Theory and Ideology in Urban Sociology." In *Urban Sociology*, edited by C. G. Pickvance, 60–84. London: Methuen.

Cecile. 2002. "Respect Your Wife." London: Greensleeves.

Chambers, Ian. 1986. *Popular Culture: The Metropolitan Experience.* London: Methuen.

Chang, Kevin O'Brien, and Wayne Chen. 1998. *Reggae Routes: The Story of Jamaican Music.* Philadelphia: Temple University Press.

Chatterjee, Partha. 1993. *The Nation and Its Fragments: Colonial and Post-colonial Histories.* Princeton: Princeton University Press.

Chevannes, Barry. 1992. "The Formation of Garrison Communities." Paper presented at the symposium *Grassroots Development and the State of the Nation.* In Honour of Carl Stone, Faculty of Social Sciences, University of the West Indies, Mona, November 16–17.

———. 1994. *Rastafari: Roots and Ideology.* Syracuse: Syracuse University Press.

———. 1996. *They Cry "Respect": Urban Violence and Poverty in Jamaica.* Kingston: Center for Population, Community and Social Change,

Department of Sociology and Social Work, University of the West Indies, Mona.

———. 1999. "What We Sow and What We Reap: Problems in the Cultivation of Male Identity in Jamaica." Grace Kennedy Foundation Lecture, Kingston, Jamaica (March).

———. 2001. *Learning to Be a Man: Culture, Socialization and Gender Identity in Five Caribbean Communities*. Kingston: University of the West Indies Press.

Citizens Action for Free and Fair Elections. 1998. *The 1997 General Elections in Jamaica: The Establishment of CAFFE and Its Role in the Electoral Process*. Kingston: CAFFE.

Clapham, Christopher. 1982. "Clientelism and the State." In *Private Patronage and Public Power: Political Clientelism in the Modern State*, edited by Christopher Clapham, 162–92. New York: St. Martin's Press.

Clarke, Colin. 1975. *Kingston Jamaica: Urban Growth and Social Change, 1692–1962*. Berkeley: University of California Press.

Clarke, Edith. 1966. *My Mother Who Fathered Me*. London: George Allen and Unwin.

Clifford, James. 1988. *The Predicament of Culture: Twentieth-Century Ethnography, Literature, and Art*. Cambridge: Harvard University Press.

———. 1994. "Diasporas." *Cultural Anthropology* 9 (3): 302–38.

Comaroff, Jean, and John L. Comaroff. 2001. "Millennial Capitalism: First Thoughts on a Second Coming." In *Millennial Capitalism and the Culture of Neoliberalism*, edited by Jean Comaroff and John L. Comaroff, 1–56. Durham, NC: Duke University Press.

———. 2004. "Criminal Justice, Cultural Justice: The Limits of Liberalism and the Pragmatics of Difference in the New South Africa." *American Ethnologist* 31 (2): 188–204.

———. 2006. "Law and Disorder in the Postcolony: An Introduction." In *Law and Disorder in the Postcolony*, edited by Jean Comaroff and John L. Comaroff, 1–56. Chicago: University of Chicago Press.

Comaroff, John L., and Jean Comaroff. 2002. "Occult Economies and the Violence of Abstraction: Notes from the South African Postcolony." In *From the Margins: Historical Anthropology and Its Futures*, edited by Brian Keith Axel, 267–302. Durham, NC: Duke University Press.

Connell, John, and Chris Gibson. 2004. "World Music: Deterritorializing Place and Identity." *Progress in Human Geography* 28 (3): 342–61.

Cooper, Carolyn. 1993. *Noises in the Blood: Orality, Gender and the "Vulgar" Body of Jamaican Popular Culture*. Durham, NC: Duke University Press.

———. 2004. *Sound Clash: Jamaican Dancehall Culture at Large*. New York: Palgrave Macmillan.

Copland, David. 1985. *In Township Tonight! South Africa's Black City Music and Theater*. New York: Longman.

Cornell, Stephen, and Douglas Hartmann. 1998. *Ethnicity and Race: Making Identities in a Changing World*. London: Pine Forge Press.

Coronil, Fernando. 1997. *The Magical State: Nature, Money, and Modernity in Venezuela*. Chicago: University of Chicago Press.

Crahan, Margaret E., and Franklin W. Knight. 1979. *Africa and the Caribbean: The Legacies of a Link*. Baltimore: Johns Hopkins University Press.

Curtin, Philip. 1968. *Two Jamaicas: The Role of Ideas in a Tropical Colony; 1830–1865*. Westport: Greenwood Press.

———. 1969. *The Atlantic Slave Trade: A Census*. Madison: University of Wisconsin Press.

Das, Veena, and Deborah Poole. 2004. "State and Its Margins: Comparative Ethnographies." In *Anthropology in the Margins of the State*, edited by Veena Das and Deborah Poole, 3–33. Santa Fe: School of American Research Press.

Davies, Omar. 2000a. "Economic Policy Options for the 21st Century." In *Contending with Destiny: The Caribbean in the 21st Century*, edited by Kenneth Hall and Denis Benn, 93–96. Kingston: Ian Randle Publishers.

———. 2000b. *Reggae and Our National Identity: The Forgotten Contribution of Peter Tosh*. Bob Marley Lecture 3 prepared for the Institute of Caribbean Studies, Reggae Studies Unit. University of the West Indies, Kingston.

———. 2005. "2005/2006" Jamaica Budget Opening Presentation." April 14. www.mof.gov.jm.

Davies, Wayne K. D., and David T. Herbert. 1993. *Communities within Cities: An Urban Social Geography*. London: Belhaven Press.

Davila, Arlene. 1997. *Sponsored Identities: Cultural Politics in Puerto Rico*. Philadelphia: Temple University Press.

Davis, David Brion. 1966. *The Problem of Slavery in Western Culture*. Ithaca, NY: Cornell University Press.

Davis, Stephen, and Peter Simon. 1982. *Reggae International*. New York: R&B Publishing.

de Certeau, Michel. 1988. *The Practice of Everyday Life*. Berkeley: University of California Press.

Denisoff, R. Serge. 1986. *Tarnished Gold: The Record Industry Revisited*. New Brunswick, NJ: Transaction Books.

Douglas, Mary, and Baron Isherwood. 1979. *The World of Goods*. New York: Basic Books.

Douglass, Lisa. 1992. *The Power of Sentiment: Love, Hierarchy, and the Jamaican Family Elite*. Boulder: Westview Press.

Drake, St. Claire, and Horace T. Cayton. 1962. *Black Metropolis: A Study of Negro Life in a Northern City*. New York: Harcourt, Brace and World.

Du Bois, W. E. B. 1973. *The Souls of Black Folk*. Millwood, NY: Kraus-Thompson Organization.

Dumont, Louis. 1977. *From Mandelville to Marx: The Genesis and Triumph of Economic Ideology*. Chicago: University of Chicago Press.

During, Simon. 1997. "Popular Culture on a Global Scale: A Challenge for Cultural Studies?" *Critical Inquiry* 23 (Summer): 818–33.

Dyson, Michael Eric. 1993. *Reflecting Black: African American Cultural Criticism*. Minneapolis: University of Minnesota Press.

Eagleton, Terry. 1996. *Literary Theory: An Introduction*. Minneapolis: University of Minnesota Press.

Eisenstadt, S. N., and L. Roniger. 1984. *Patrons, Clients and Friends: Interpersonal Relations and the Structure of Trust in Society*. London: Cambridge University Press.

Elephant Man. 2003. "Bad Man." VP Records.

Erlmann, Viet. 1996. *Nightsong: Performance, Power, and Practice in South Africa*. Chicago: University of Chicago Press.

Escobar, Arturo. 1991. "Anthropology and the Development Encounter: The Making and Marketing of Development Anthropology." *American Ethnologist* 18 (4): 658–82.

———. 1995. *Encountering Development: The Making and Unmaking of the Third World*. Princeton: Princeton University Press.

Etzioni, Amitai. 1988. *The Moral Dimension: Toward a New Economics*. New York: Free Press.

Fabian, Johannes. 1986. *Language and Colonial Power*. Berkeley: University of California Press.

———. 1998. *Moments of Freedom: Anthropology and Popular Culture*. Charlottesville: University Press of Virginia.

Fanon, Frantz. 1967. *Black Skin, White Masks*. New York: Grove Press.

Feld, Steve, and Donald Brenneis. 2004. "Doing Anthropology in Sound." *American Ethnologist* 31 (4): 461–74.

Ferguson, James. 1990. *The Anti-Politics Machine: "Development," Depoliticization, and Bureaucratic Power in Lesotho*. Cambridge: Cambridge University Press.

———. 2009. "The Uses of Neoliberalism." *Antipode* 41 (S1): 166–84.

Ferguson, James, and Akhil Gupta. 2002. "Spatializing States: Toward an Ethnography of Neoliberal Governmentality." *American Ethnologist* 29 (4): 981–1002.

Fernandez Olmos, M., and Lizabeth Paravisini-Gebert. 1997. *Sacred Possessions: Voudou, Santeria, Obeah and the Caribbean*. New Brunswick, NJ: Rutgers University Press.

Figueroa, Mark. 1994. "Garrison Communities In Jamaica 1962–1993: Their Growth and Impact on Political Culture." Paper presented to the symposium Democracy and Democratization in Jamaica: Fifty Years of Adult Suffrage. Faculty of Social Sciences, University of the West Indies, Mona, December 6–7.

Firth, Raymond. ed. 1967. *Themes in Economic Anthropology*. London: Tavistock Publications.

Fiske, John. 1989. *Understanding Popular Culture*. London: Unwin Hyman.

Foner, Nancy. 1983. "Jamaican Migrants: A Comparative Analysis of the New York and London Experience." Presented at the Conference on Migration and the New York Labor Market. Sponsored by the New York Research Program in Inter-American Affairs, New York University. May 6.

———. 1987. *New Immigrants in New York*. New York: Columbia University Press.

Ford-Smith, Honor. 1986. *Lionheart Gal: Life Story of Jamaican Women*. London: Women's Press.

Foster, C., and A. Valdman, eds. 1984. *Haiti—Today and Tomorrow: An Interdisciplinary Study*. Lanham, MD: University Press of America.

Foster, Robert. 1991. "Making National Cultures in the Global Ecumene." *Annual Review of Anthropology* 20: 235–60.

Foucault, Michel. 1985. *The History of Sexuality. Vol. 1, An Introduction*. New York: Pantheon.

Francis-Jackson, Chester. 1995. *The Official Dancehall Dictionary: A Guide to Jamaican Dialect and Dancehall Slang*. Kingston: Kingston Publishers.

Freeman, Carla. 2000. *High Tech and High Heels in the Global Economy: Women, Work, and Pink-Collar Identities in the Caribbean*. Durham, NC: Duke University Press.

Frow, John. 1995. *Cultural Studies and Cultural Value*. Oxford: Clarendon Press.

Galvin, Anne M. 2011. "Governing the Margins: Crime Containment and Community Development in Kingston, Jamaica." In *NEAA Bulletin: Borders, Margins, and Passages*, edited by Anne M. Galvin, 91–105. New York: Northeastern Anthropological Association.

———. 2012. "Caribbean Piracies/Social Mobilities: Some Commonalities between Colonial Privateers and Entrepreneurial 'Profiteers' in the 21st Century." *Anthropological Quarterly* 85 (3): 755–84.
Gans, Herbert. 1974. *Popular Culture and High Culture*. New York: Basic Books.
Geertz, Clifford. 1973. *The Interpretation of Cultures: Selected Essays*. New York: Basic Books.
Gellner, Ernest, and John Waterbury, eds. 1977. *Patrons and Clients in Mediterranean Studies*. London: Gerald Duckworth.
Gilroy, Paul. 1992. *"There Ain't No Black in the Union Jack": The Cultural Politics of Race and Nation*. London: Routledge.
———. 1993a. *The Black Atlantic: Modernity and Double Consciousness*. Cambridge: Harvard University Press.
———. 1993b. *Small Acts: Thoughts on the Politics of Black Cultures*. New York: Serpent's Tail Press.
Girvan, Norman. 1971. *Foreign Capital and Economic Underdevelopment in Jamaica*. Surrey: Unwin Brothers.
———. 1993. *Working Together for Development: D.T.M. Girvan on Cooperatives and Community Development 1939–1968*. Kingston: Institute of Jamaica Publications.
———, ed. 1997. *Poverty, Empowerment and Social Development in the Caribbean*. Kingston: Canoe Press.
Glasser, Ruth. 1995. *My Music Is My Flag: Puerto Rican Musicians and Their New York Communities 1917–1940*. Berkeley: University of California Press.
Goldberg, David Theo. 1993. *Racist Culture*. Cambridge: Blackwell.
Gordon, Derek. 1987. *Class, Status and Social Mobility in Jamaica*. Jamaica: Institute of Social and Economic Research, University of the West Indies, Mona.
Gordon, Monica Hyacinth. 1979. *Identification and Adaptation: A Study of Two Groups of Jamaican Immigrants in New York City*. PhD diss., City University of New York.
Graeber, David. 2001. *Toward an Anthropological Theory of Value*. New York: Palgrave.
Gramsci, Antonio. 1997. *Selections from the Prison Notebooks*. New York: International Publishers.
Gray, Obika. 2004. *Demeaned but Empowered: The Social Power of the Urban Poor in Jamaica*. Kingston: University of the West Indies Press.
Gregory, Stephen, and Roger Sanjek. 1994. *Race*. New Brunswick, NJ: Rutgers University Press.

Grossberg, Lawrence, et al. 1992. *Cultural Studies*. London: Routledge.
Gunes-Ayata, Ayse. 1994. "Clientelism: Premodern, Modern, Postmodern." In *Democracy, Clientelism and Civil Society*, edited by Luis Roniger and Ayse Gunes-Ayata. London: Lynne Rienner Publishers.
Gunst, Laurie. 1995. *Born Fi' Dead: A Journey through the Jamaican Posse Underworld*. New York: Henry Holt.
Gupta, Akhil. 1995. "Blurred Boundaries: The Discourse of Corruption, the Culture of Politics, and the Imagined State." *American Ethnologist* 22 (2): 375–402.
Gupta, Akhil, and James Ferguson. 1997. *Culture, Power, Place: Explorations in Critical Anthropology*. Durham, NC: Duke University Press.
Habermas, Jurgen. 1990. *Moral Consciousness and Communicative Action*. Cambridge: MIT Press.
Hall, Stuart. 1980. "Race, Articulation and Social Formations Structured in Dominance." In *Sociological Theories, Race and Colonialism*, edited by UNESCO. Paris: UNESCO.
———. 1990. "Cultural Identity and Diaspora." In *Identity: Community, Culture, Difference*, edited by Jonathan Rutherford, 222–37. London: Lawrence and Wishart.
———. 1992. "Race, Culture, and Communications: Looking Backward and Forward at Cultural Studies." *Rethinking Marxism* 5 (Spring): 10–18.
———. 1996. "What Is This 'Black' in Black Popular Culture?" In *Stuart Hall: Critical Dialogues in Cultural Studies*, edited by David Morely and Kuan-Hsing Chen, 465–75. New York: Routledge.
Hall, Stuart, and Martin Jacques, eds. 1990. *New Times: The Changing Face of Politics in the 1990s*. New York: Verso.
Hall, Stuart, and Paddy Whannel. 1964. *The Popular Arts*. Boston: Beacon.
Handler, Richard. 1994. "Romancing the Low: Anthropology vis-à-vis Cultural Studies vis-à-vis Popular Culture." *PoLAR* 17 (2): 1–6.
Hannerz, Ulf. 1980. *Exploring the City: Inquiries toward an Urban Anthropology*. New York: Columbia University Press.
———. 1996. *Transnational Connections*. New York: Routledge.
Harriott, Anthony. 1994. "Controlling Violence in Jamaica: Developing a Community Based Response." Paper prepared for the Centre for Population, Community and Social Change, Dept. of Sociology and Social Work, University of the West Indies, Mona.
———. 1996. "The Changing Social Organization of Crime and Criminals in Jamaica." *Caribbean Quarterly* 42 (2–3): 61–81.
———. 2000. *Police and Crime Control in Jamaica: Problems of Reforming Ex-colonial Constabularies*. Kingston: University of the West Indies Press.

———. 2001. "The Changing Social Organization of Crime and Criminals in Jamaica." In *Caribbean Sociology: Introductory Readings*, edited by Christine Barrow and Rhoda Reddock, 512–27. Kingston: Ian Randle Publishers.
Harrison, Faye. 1987. "Gangs, Grassroots Politics, and the Crisis of Dependent Capitalism in Jamaica." In *Perspectives in U.S. Marxist Anthropology*, edited by David Hakken and Hanna Lessinger, 186–210. London: Westview Press.
———. 1988. "The Politics of Social Outlawry in Urban Jamaica." *Urban Anthropology* 17 (2–3): 259–77.
———. 1991. "Ethnography as Politics." In *Decolonizing Anthropology: Moving Further Toward an Anthropology for Liberation*, edited by Faye Harrison, 88–109. Washington, DC: American Anthropological Association.
———. 1997. "Gender, Sexuality, and Health in a Turn-of-the-Century "Black Metropolis." *Medical Anthropology Quarterly* 11 (4): 448–53.
Hart, Keith. 2001. *Money in an Unequal World: Keith Hart and His Memory Bank*. New York: Texere.
Harvey, David. 1989. *The Urban Experience*. Baltimore: Johns Hopkins University Press.
———. 1990. *The Condition of Postmodernity*. Cambridge: Blackwell.
———. 1995. "Globalization in Question." *Rethinking Marxism* 8 (4): 1–17.
Hebdige, Dick. 1989. *Hiding in the Light*. New York: Routledge.
———. 1987. *Cut 'n' Mix: Culture, Identity, and Caribbean Music*. New York: Methuen.
———. 1995. *Subculture: The Meaning of Style*. New York: Routledge.
Helg, Aline. 1995. *Our Rightful Share: The Afro-Cuban Struggle for Equality, 1886–1912*. Chapel Hill: University of North Carolina Press.
Herskovitz, Melville. 1941. *The Myth of the Negro Past*. Boston: Beacon Press.
Higman, B. W. 1976. *Slave Population and Economy in Jamaica, 1807–1834*. London: Cambridge University Press.
Holloway, Joseph E. 1991. *Africanisms in American Culture*. Bloomington: Indiana University Press.
Holt, Thomas C. 1992. *The Problem of Freedom*. Baltimore: Johns Hopkins University Press.
Hope, Donna P. 2006a. "Dons and Shottas: Performing Violent Masculinity in Dancehall Culture." *Social and Economic Studies* 55 (½): 115–31
———. 2006b. *Inna di Dancehall: Popular Culture and Politics of Identity in Jamaica*. Kingston: University of the West Indies Press.
———. 2006c. "Passa Passa: Interrogating Cultural Hybridities in Jamaican Dancehall." *Small Axe* 21 (October): 125–39.

———. 2010. *Man Vibes: Masculinities in the Jamaican Dancehall*. Kingston: Ian Randle Publishing.

Horkheimer, Max, and Theodor Adorno. 1972. "The Culture Industry: Enlightenment as Mass Deception." In *The Dialectic of the Enlightenment*, translated by John Cumming, 120–67. New York: Herder and Herder.

Inter-American Development Bank. 2001. *Jamaica: Social Sector Strategy*. Washington, DC: Inter-American Development Bank.

Jahn, Brian, and Tom Weber. 1992. *Reggae Island: Jamaican Music in the Digital Age*. Kingston: Kingston Publishers.

Jamaica Promotions Corporation. *Marketing Plan for Music and Entertainment 1996/1997*. Kingston: Jamaica Film, Music and Entertainment Commission.

James, C. L. R. 1963. *The Black Jacobins: Toussaint L'Ouverture and the San Domingo Revolution*. New York: Vintage.

James, Vanus. 2007. *The Economic Contribution of Copyright-Based Industries in Jamaica: Final Report*. Prepared for the World Intellectual Property Organization.

Jameson, Fredric. 1979. "Reification and Utopia in Mass Culture." *Social Text* 1: 130–48.

———. 1990. *Postmodernism, or the Cultural Logic of Late Capitalism*. Durham, NC: Duke University Press.

Jayawardena, Chandra. 1968. "Ideology and Conflict in Lower Class Communities." *Comparative Studies in Society and History* 10 (4): 413–46.

Junior Kelly. 2000. "Love So Nice." VP/Universal.

Kapferer, Bruce, ed. 1976. *Transaction and Meaning: Directions in the Anthropology of Exchange and Symbolic Behavior*. Philadelphia: Institute for the Study of Human Issues.

Kasinitz, Philip. 1992. *Caribbean New York: Black Immigrants and the Politics of Race*. Ithaca, NY: Cornell University Press.

Keil, Charles, and Steven Feld. 1994. *Music Grooves: Essays and Dialogues*. Chicago: University of Chicago Press.

Kozul-Wright, and Lloyd Stanbury. 1998. "Becoming a Globally Competitive Player: The Case of The Music Industry in Jamaica." Discussion Paper No. 138. United Nations Conference on Trade and Development. October.

Kuper, Adam. 1976. *Changing Jamaica*. Boston: Routledge and Kegan Paul.

Kurtz, Donald V. 1996. "Hegemony and Anthropology: Gramsci, Exegesis, Reinterpretations." *Critique of Anthropology* 16 (2): 103–35.

LaBennett, Oneka. 2011. *She's Mad Real: Popular Culture and West Indian Girls in Brooklyn*. New York: New York University Press.
Lacey, Terry. 1977. *Violence and Politics in Jamaica: 1960–1970*. Manchester: Manchester University Press.
Laclau, Ernesto, and Chantal Mouffe. 1985. *Hegemony and Socialist Strategy*. London: Verso.
LaGuerre, Michel. 1989. *Voodoo and Politics in Haiti*. New York: St. Martin's Press.
Lazarus-Black, Mindie, and S. F. Hirsch, eds. 1994. *Contested States: Law, Hegemony and Resistance*. New York: Routledge.
Levy, Barrington. 1984. "Money Move." Kingston, Jamaica: Power House Records.
Lexxus. 1999. "Halla Halla." Kingston, Jamaica: Mentally Disturbed.
Lipsitz, George. 1994. *Dangerous Crossroads: Popular Music, Postmodernism, and the Poetics of Place*. New York: Verso.
Locke, Alain. 1992. *Race Contacts and Interracial Relations: Lectures on the Theory and Practice of Race*. Washington, DC.: Howard University Press.
Lopez, Jennifer. 2002. "Jenny from the Block." Sony.
Mad Cobra. 1996. "Ever Tight." London: Greensleeves.
———. 2003. "Dem Fi Goweh." Kingston: Builders.
Mahler, Sarah J. 1995. *American Dreaming: Immigrant Life on the Margins*. Princeton: Princeton University Press.
Makie, Erin. 2005. "Welcome the Outlaw: Pirates, Maroons, and Caribbean Countercultures." *Cultural Critique* 59 (Winter): 24–62.
Mandelbaum, Seymour J. 2000. *Open Moral Communities*. Cambridge: MIT Press.
Manuel, Peter, et al. 1995. *Caribbean Currents: Caribbean Music from Rumba to Reggae*. Philadelphia: Temple University Press.
Marcus, George E. 1995. "Ethnography in/of the World System: The Emergence of Multi-sited Ethnography." *Annual Review of Anthropology* 24: 95–117.
Marcuse, Herbert. 1966. *One Dimensional Man: Studies in the Ideology of Advanced Industrial Society*. Boston: Beacon Press.
Margolis, Maxine. 1994. *Little Brazil: An Ethnography of Brazilian Immigrants in New York City*. Princeton: Princeton University Press.
Marsden, Steven. 2002. "Diwali." Greensleeves.
Massey, Douglas. 1998. *Worlds in Motion: Understanding International Migration*. Oxford: Clarendon Press.
Massey, Douglas, et al. 1993. "Theories of International Migration: A Review and Appraisal." *Population and Development Review* 19 (3): 431–66.

Maultsby, Patricia. 1991. "Africanisms in African-American Music." In *Africanisms in American Culture*, edited by Joseph E. Holloway, 326–55. Bloomington: Indiana University Press.

Mauss, Marcel. 1990 [1950]. *The Gift: The Form and Reason for Exchange in Archaic Societies*. New York: W. W. Norton.

McLaren, Peter. 1995. "Gangsta Pedagogy and Ghettocentricity: The Hip-Hop Nation as Counterpublic Sphere." *Socialist Review* 25 (2): 9–55.

McMichael, Philip. 1996. "Globalization: Myths and Realities." *Rural Sociology* 61: 1.

McRobbie, Angela. 1994. *Postmodernism and Popular Culture*. New York: Routledge.

———, ed. 1997. *Back to Reality? Social Experience and Cultural Studies*. Manchester: Manchester University Press.

Meeks, Brian. 1996. *Radical Caribbean: From Black Power to Abu Bakr*. Kingston: University of the West Indies Press.

———. 2000. *Narratives of Resistance: Jamaica, Trinidad, The Caribbean*. Kingston: University of the West Indies Press.

Melamed, Jodi. 2011. *Represent and Destroy: Rationalizing Violence in the New Racial Capitalism*. Minneapolis: University of Minnesota Press.

Mercer, Kobena. 1994. *Welcome to the Jungle: New Positions in Black Cultural Studies*. New York: Routledge.

Miller, Daniel. 1994. *Modernity: An Ethnographic Approach. Dualism and Mass Consumption in Trinidad*. New York: Berg.

Mills, Charles W. 1987. "Race and Class: Conflicting or Reconcilable Paradigms?" *Social and Economic Studies* 36 (2): 69–108.

Mintz, Sidney. 1974. *Caribbean Transformations*. Chicago: Aldine.

———, ed. 1974. *Slavery, Colonialism, and Racism*. New Haven, CT: Yale Publications in Anthropology.

———. 1985. *Sweetness and Power: The Place of Sugar in Modern History*. New York: Viking.

Mintz, Sidney, and Richard Price. 1976. *The Birth of African-American Culture: An Anthropological Perspective*. Boston: Beacon Press.

Mohammed, Patricia, and Catherine Shepherd, eds. 1999. *Gender in Caribbean Development*. Kingston: Canoe Press.

Moore, Brian L., and Michele A. Johnson. 2000. *"Squalid Kingston" 1890–1920: How the Poor Lived, Moved and Had Their Being*. Mona: Social History Project.

Moore, Robin D. 1997. *Nationalizing Blackness: Afrocubanismo and Artistic Revolution in Havana, 1920–1940*. Pittsburgh: University of Pittsburgh Press.

Morley, David, and Kuan-Hsing Chen, eds. 1996. *Stuart Hall: Critical Dialogues in Cultural Studies*. New York: Routledge.
Morris, Meaghan. 1998. *Too Soon Too Late: History in Popular Culture*. Bloomington: Indiana University Press.
Munroe, Trevor. 1972. *The Politics of Constitutional Decolonization: Jamaica 1944–1962*. Kingston: Institute of Social and Economic Research.
———. 1999. *Renewing Democracy into the Millennium: The Jamaican Experience in Perspective*. Kingston: University of the West Indies Press.
Mussche, Steffen Patrick. 2008. *Wi Likkle but Wi Tallawah: Narratives of Nation Branding: Intellectual Property Governance and Identity Politics in Jamaica*. Master's thesis, University of Oslo.
Negus, Keith. 1996. *Popular Music in Theory*. Hanover: Wesleyan University Press.
Nettleford, Rex. 2001. *Mirror, Mirror: Identity, Race and Protest in Jamaica*. Kingston: LMH Publishing.
Norris, Katrin. 1962. *Jamaica: The Search for an Identity*. London: Oxford University Press.
Ohmann, Richard. 1996. *Selling Culture: Magazines, Markets, and Class at the Turn of the Century*. New York: Verso.
Olwig, Karen Fog. 1993. *Global Culture, Island Identity: Continuity and Change in the Afro-Caribbean Community of Nevis*. Philadelphia: Harwood.
———. 1999. "The Burden of Heritage: Claiming a Place for West Indian Culture." *American Ethnologist* 26 (2): 370–88.
Omi, Michael, and Howard Winant. 1994. *Racial Formation in the United States: From the 1960s to the 1990s*. New York: Routledge.
Ong, Aihwa. 1987. *Spirits of Resistance and Capitalist Discipline: Factory Women in Malaysia*. New York: State University of New York Press.
———. 1999. *Flexible Citizenship: The Cultural Logics of Transnationalism*. Durham, NC: Duke University Press.
Ong, Aihwa, and Donald Nonini. 1997. *Ungrounded Empires: The Cultural Politics of Modern Chinese Transnationalism*. New York: Routledge.
Paine, Robert. 1976. "Two Modes of Exchange and Mediation." In *Transaction and Meaning: Directions in the Anthropology of Exchange and Symbolic Behavior*, edited by Bruce Kapferer, 63–86. Philadelphia: Institute for the Study of Human Issues.
Panadeiros, M., and W. Benfield. 2010. "Productive Development Policies in Jamaica." IDB Working Paper Series #IDB-WP-128. Washington, DC: Inter-American Development Bank.
Parry, J., and M. Bloch. 1989. *Money and the Morality of Exchange*. Cambridge: Cambridge University Press.

Parsons, Talcott. 1962. *Toward a General Theory of Social Action*. New York: Harper and Row.
Patterson, Orlando. 1982. *Slavery and Social Death: A Comparative Study*. Cambridge: Harvard University Press.
Patterson, P. J. 2000. "Mobilizing Human Resources in Support of Caribbean Development." In *Contending with Destiny: The Caribbean in the 21st Century*, edited by Kenneth Hall and Denis Benn, 7–11. Kingston: Ian Randle Publishers.
Pavlik, Melissa. 2013. "Mass Media and Rape Culture in America." Blog. *The Triple Helix Online: A Global Forum for Science in Society*, August 27. triplehelixblog.com/2013/08/mass-media-and-rape-culture-in-america.
Perkins, William Eric, ed. 1996. *Droppin' Science: Critical Essays on Rap Music and Hip Hop Culture*. Philadelphia: Temple University Press.
Pessar, Patricia. 1995. *A Visa for a Dream: Dominicans in the United States*. Boston: Allyn and Bacon.
———. 1999. "Engendering Migration Studies: The Case of New Immigrants in the United States." *American Behavioral Scientist* 42 (4) (January): 577–600.
Petras, James, and Henry Veltmeyer. 2001. *Globalization Unmasked: Imperialism in the 21st Century*. New York: Zed Books.
Phillips, Peter. 1988. "Race, Class, Nationalism: A Perspective on Twentieth Century Social Movements in Jamaica." *Social and Economic Studies* 37 (3): 97–123.
Planning Institute of Jamaica. 2000. *Jamaica Human Development Report 2000*. Kingston: Planning Institute of Jamaica.
———. 2002. *Economic and Social Survey: Jamaica 2001*. Kingston: Planning Institute of Jamaica.
Pinnock, Agostinho M. N. 2007. "'A Ghetto Education Is Basic': (Jamaican) Dancehall Masculinities as Counter-Culture." *Journal of Pan African Studies* 1 (9): 47–84.
Poole, Deborah. 2004. "Between Threat and Guarantee: Justice and Community in the Margins of the Peruvian State." In *Anthropology in the Margins of the State*, edited by Veena Das and Deborah Poole. Santa Fe: School of American Research.
Portes, Alejandro. 1997. *The Urban Caribbean: Transition to the New Global Economy*. Baltimore: Johns Hopkins University Press.
Post, Ken. 1978. *Arise Ye Starvelings: The Jamaican Labour Rebellion of 1938 and Its Aftermath*. Boston: Martinus Nijhoff.
Potash, Chris. 1997. *Reggae, Rasta, Revolution: Jamaican Music from Ska to Dub*. New York: Schirmer Books.

Radaway, Janice. 1984. *Reading the Romance: Women, Patriarchy, and Popular Literature*. Chapel Hill: University of North Carolina Press.

Robotham, Don. 1980. "Pluralism as an Ideology." *Social and Economic Studies* 29: 69–89.

———. 1991. "The Development of a Black Ethnicity in Jamaica." In *Garvey: His Work and Impact*, edited by Rupert Lewis and Patrick Bryan, 23–38. Trenton, NJ: Africa World Press.

———. 1998. "Transnationalism in the Caribbean: Formal and Informal." *American Ethnologist* 25 (2): 307–21.

———. 2000. "Blackening the Jamaican Nation: The Travails of Black BOURGEOISIE in a Globalized World." *Identities: Global Studies of Culture and Power* 7 (1): 1–37.

———. 2003. "How Kingston Was Wounded." In *Wounded Cities: Destruction and Reconstruction in a Globalized World*, edited by Jane Schneider and Ida Susser, 111–28. New York: Berg.

———. 2005. *Culture, Society, Economy: Bringing Production Back In*. New York: Sage Publications.

———. 2011. "Anthropology and the Present Moment." *Transforming Anthropology* 19 (2): 154–61.

Rodney, Walter. 1981. *A History of the Guyanese Working People, 1881–1905*. Baltimore: Johns Hopkins University Press.

Roitman, Janet. 2004. "Productivity in the Margins: The Reconstitution of State Power in the Chad Basin." In *Anthropology in the Margins of the State*, edited by Veena Das and Deborah Poole, 191–224. Santa Fe: School of American Research.

———. 2006. "The Ethics of Illegality in the Chad Basin." In *Law and Disorder in the Postcolony*, edited by Jean Comaroff and John L. Comaroff, 247–72. Chicago: University of Chicago Press.

Roniger, Luis. 1994. "The Comparative Study of Clientelism and the Changing Nature of Civil Society in the Contemporary World." In *Democracy, Clientelism and Civil Society*, edited by Luis Roniger and Ayse Gunes-Ayata, 1–19. Boulder, CO: Lynne Rienner Publishers.

Rose, Nikolas. 1999. *Powers of Freedom: Reframing Political Thought*. Cambridge: Cambridge University Press.

Rose, Tricia. 1994. *Black Noise: Rap Music and Black Culture in Contemporary America*. Hanover: Wesleyan University Press.

Rosendahl, Mona. 1997. *Inside the Revolution: Everyday Life in Socialist Cuba*. Ithaca, NY: Cornell University Press.

Ross, Andrew. 1989. *No Respect: Intellectuals and Popular Culture*. New York: Routledge.

Ross, Andrew, and Tricia Rose. 1994. *Microphone Fiends: Youth Music and Youth Culture.* New York: Routledge.
Said, Edward W. 1979. *Orientalism.* New York: Vintage.
———. 1993. *Culture and Imperialism.* New York: Vintage.
Sakolsky, Ron, and Fred Wei-Han Ho, eds. 1995. *Sounding Off! Music as Subversion/Resistance/Revolution.* New York: Autonomedia.
Sandell, Jillian. 1995. "Out of the Ghetto and into the Marketplace: Hoop Dreams and the Commodification of Marginality." *Socialist Review* 25 (2): 57–82.
Sanjek, Roger. 1990, "Urban Anthropology in the 1980s: A World View." *Annual Review of Anthropology* 19: 151–86.
Sargent, Carolyn, and Michael Harris. 1998. "Bad Boys and Good Girls: The Implications of Gender Ideology for Child Health in Jamaica." In *Small Wars: The Cultural Politics of Childhood,* edited by Nancy Scheper-Hughes and Carolyn Sargent, 202–27. Berkeley: University of California Press.
Sassen, Saskia. 1991. *The Global City.* Princeton: Princeton University Press.
Saunders, Patricia J. 2003. "Is Not Everything Good to Eat, Good to Talk: Sexual Economy and Dancehall Music in the Global Marketplace." *Small Axe* 13 (March): 95–115.
Saxton, Alexander. 1990. *The Rise and Fall of the White Republic: Class Politics and Mass Culture in Nineteenth Century America.* New York: Verso.
Sayer, Andrew. 2000. "Moral Economy and Political Economy." *Studies in Political Economy.* 61 (Spring): 79–103.
Schmidt, Steffan W., et al., eds. 1977. *Friends, Followers and Factions: A Reader in Political Clientelism.* Berkeley: University of California Press.
Schneider, Jane, and Peter Schneider. 2002. "The Mafia and al-Qaeda: Violent and Secretive Organizations in Comparative and Historical Perspective." *American Anthropologist* 104 (3): 776–82.
Scott, David. 1999. *Refashioning Futures: Criticism after Postcoloniality.* Princeton: Princeton University Press.
Scott, James. 1976. *The Moral Economy of the Peasant: Rebellion and Subsistence in Southeast Asia.* New Haven, CT: Yale University Press.
———. 1990. *Domination and the Arts of Resistance: Hidden Transcripts.* New Haven, CT: Yale University Press.
———. 1996. "The Aftermaths of Sovereignty: Post-colonial Criticism and the Claims of Political Modernity." *Social Text* 48: 1–26.
———. 1998. *Seeing Like a State: How Certain Schemes to Improve the Human Condition Have Failed.* New Haven, CT: Yale University Press.

Sexton, Adam. 1995. *Rap on Rap: Straight Up Talk on Hip-Hop Culture.* New York: Delta.
Shepherd, Verena, et al. 1995. *Engendering History: Caribbean Women in Historical Perspective.* New York: St. Martin's Press.
Shepherd Verena, and Glen L. Richards, eds. 2002. *Questioning Creole: Creolisation Discourses in Caribbean Culture.* Kingston: Ian Randle Publishers.
Skelton, Tracey. 1995. "'I Sing Dirty Reality, I Am Out There for the Ladies': Lady Saw, Women, and Jamaican Ragga Music, Resisting Patriarchy." *Phoebe: Journal of Feminist Theory, Scholarship and Aesthetics* 7: 86–104
Slobin, Mark. 1993. *Subcultural Sounds: Micromusics of the West.* Middletown, CT: Wesleyan University Press.
———. 1994. "Music in Diaspora: The View from Euro-America." *Diaspora* 3: 3.
Smith, M. G. 1965. *The Plural Society in the British West Indies.* Berkeley: University of California Press.
Smith, Raymond T. 1967. "Social Stratification, Cultural Pluralism and Integration in West Indian Societies." In *Caribbean Integration: Papers on Social, Political and Economic Integration,* edited by S. Lewis and T. G. Matthews, 226–58. Rio Pedras: Institute of Caribbean Studies, University of Puerto Rico.
———. 1996. "Hierarchy and the Dual Marriage System in West Indian Society." In *The Matrifocal Family: Power, Pluralism, and Politics,* edited by Raymond T. Smith, 59–80. New York: Routledge.
Spivak, Gayatri. 1996. *The Spivak Reader: Selected Works of Gayatri Spivak.* New York: Routledge.
Spragga Benz. 1994. "No Funny Guy Thing." VP/Universal.
Stanley Niaah, Sonjah. 2010. *DanceHall: From Slave Ship to Ghetto* (Series: African and Diasporic Cultural Studies). Ottawa: University of Ottawa Press.
Stephen, Cornell, and Douglas Hartmann. 1998. *Ethnicity and Race: Making Identities in a Changing World.* Pine Forge Press.
Stephens, Evelyne Huber, and John D. Stephens. 1986. *Democratic Socialism in Jamaica: The Political Movement and Social Transformation in Dependent Capitalism.* Princeton: Princeton University Press.
Stephens, Tanya. 2004 "Tek Him Back." VP Records.
Stewart, Kingsley. 2002. "'So Wha, Mi Nuh Fi Live To?': Interpreting Violence in Jamaica through the Dancehall Culture." IDEAZ 1 (1): 17–28.
Stoler, Anne Laura. 1995. *Race and the Education of Desire: Foucault's History*

of Sexuality and the Colonial Order of Things. Durham, NC: Duke University Press.

Stolke, Verena. 1974. *Marriage, Class and Colour in Nineteenth Century Cuba: A Study of Racial Attitudes and Sexual Values in a Slave Society*. Oxford: Cambridge University Press.

Stolzoff, Norman C. 1998. "Murderation: The Question of Violence in the Sound System Dance." *Social and Economic Studies* 47 (1): 55–64.

———. 2000. *Wake the Town and Tell the People: Dancehall Culture in Jamaica*. Durham, NC: Duke University Press.

Stone, Carl. 1973. *Class, Race and Political Behavior in Urban Jamaica*. Kingston, Jamaica: Montrose Printery.

———. 1985. *Democracy and Clientelism in Jamaica*. New Brunswick: Transaction Books.

———. 1986. *Class, State and Democracy in Jamaica*. New York: Praeger.

Stone, Carl, and Aggrey Brown, eds. 1977. *Essays on Power and Change in Jamaica*. Kingston: Jamaica Publishing House.

Storey, John. 1998. *An Introduction to Cultural Theory and Popular Culture*. Athens: University of Georgia Press.

Strickon, Arnold, and Sidney M. Greenfield, eds. 1972. *Structure and Process in Latin America: Patronage, Clientage and Power Systems*. Albuquerque: University of New Mexico Press.

Sutton, Constance. 1987. *Caribbean Life in New York City: Sociocultural Dimensions*. New York: Center for Migration Studies of New York.

Takaki, Ronald. 1990. *Iron Cages: Race and Culture in 19th Century America*. New York: Oxford University Press.

Tannenbaum, Frank. 1992. *Slave and Citizen*. Boston: Beacon Press.

Taylor, Timothy Dean. 1993. *The Voracious Muse: Contemporary Cross-Cultural Musical Borrowings, Culture, and Postmodernism*. PhD diss., University of Michigan.

Thomas, Deborah A. 2002. "Democratizing Dance: Institutional Transformation and Hegemonic Re-ordering in Postcolonial Jamaica." *Cultural Anthropology* 17 (4): 512–50.

———. 2004. *Modern Blackness: Nationalism, Globalization, and the Politics of Culture in Jamaica*. Durham, NC: Duke University Press.

———. 2011. *Exceptional Violence: Embodied Citizenship in Transnational Jamaica*. Durham, NC: Duke University Press.

Thompson, Denys, ed. 1973. *Discrimination and Popular Culture*. London: Heineman Educational Books.

Toop, David. 1991. *Rap Attack 2: African Rap to Global Hip-Hop*. New York: Serpent's Tail.

Trouillot, Michel-Rolf. 1990. *Haiti: State against Nation: The Origins and Legacy of Duvalierism*. New York: Monthly Review Press.
———. 1992. "The Caribbean Region: An Open Frontier in Anthropological Theory." *Annual Review of Anthropology* 21: 19–42.
Tsing, Anna. 2000a. "The Global Situation." *Cultural Anthropology* 15 (3): 327–60.
———. 2000b. "Inside the Economy of Appearances." *Public Culture* 12 (1): 115–44.
Ulysse, Gina A. 2007. *Downtown Ladies: Informal Commericial Importers, a Haitian Anthropologist, and Self-Making in Jamaica*. Chicago: University of Chicago Press.
Veal, Michael E. 2000. *Fela: The Life and Times of an African Music Icon*. Philadelphia: Temple University Press.
Vickerman, Milton. 1999. *Crosscurrents: West Indian Immigrants and Race*. New York: Oxford University Press.
Vybz Kartel. 2004. "Pussy Jaw." Greensleeves.
Waldinger, Roger. 1996. *Still the Promised City? African-Americans and New Immigrants in Post-industrial New York*. Cambridge: Harvard University Press.
Walker, Judith-Ann. 2002. *Development Administration in the Caribbean: Independent Jamaica and Trinidad and Tobago*. New York: Palgrave.
Wallace, Michelle, ed. 1992. *Black Popular Culture*. Seattle: Bay Press.
Wallerstein, Immanuel. 1974. *The Modern World-System*. New York: Academic Press.
Wallis, Roger, and Krister Malm. 1984. *Big Sounds from Small Peoples*. London: Constable.
Waterman, Christopher Alan. 1990. *JuJu: A Social History and Ethnography of an African Popular Music*. Chicago: University of Chicago Press.
Waterman, Richard Allen. 1952. "African Influences on the Music of the Americas." In *Acculturation in the Americas*, edited by Sol Tax, 207–18. Chicago: University of Chicago Press.
Waters, Anita. 1989. *Race, Class and Political Symbols: Rastafari and Reggae in Jamaican Politics*. New Brunswick, NJ: Transaction Books.
———. 2006. *Planning the Past: Heritage Tourism and Post-colonial Politics at Port Royal*. Lanham, MD: Lexington Books.
Waters, Mary. 1999. *Black Identities: West Indian Immigrant Dreams and American Realities*. New York: Russell Sage Foundation.
———. 1990. *Ethnic Options: Choosing Identities in America*. Berkeley: University of California Press.

West, Cornel. 1993. *Keeping the Faith: Philosophy and Race in America*. New York: Routledge.
Williams, Brackette F. 1991. *Stains on My Name, War in My Veins: Guyana and the Politics of Cultural Struggle*. Durham, NC: Duke University Press.
Williams, Eric. 1944. *Capitalism and Slavery*. London: Deutsch.
———. 1957. "Race Relations in Caribbean Society." In *Caribbean Studies: A Symposium*, edited by Vera Rubin, 54–60. Kingston: Institute of Social and Economic Relations.
Williams, Raymond. 1975. *The Country and the City*. New York: Oxford University Press.
———. 1977. *Marxism and Literature*. Oxford: Oxford University Press.
———. 1983. *Keywords: A Vocabulary of Culture and Society*. New York: Oxford University Press.
Willis, Paul 1977. *Learning to Labour: How Working Class Kids Get Working Class Jobs*. Farnborough, England: Saxon House.
Wilson, Peter J. 1969. "Reputation and Respectability: A Suggestion for Caribbean Ethnology." *Man* 4 (1): 70–84.
———. 1973. *Crab Antics: The Social Anthropology of English-Speaking Negro Societies of the Caribbean*. New Haven, CT: Yale University Press.
Witter, Michael. 2004. *Music and the Jamaican Economy*. Report prepared for United Nations Conference on Trade and Development/ World Intellectual Property Organization. Geneva, Switzerland: UNCTAD/ WIPO.
Wolf, Eric. 1982. *Europe and the People without a History*. Berkeley: University of California Press.
Yudice, George. 2003. *The Expediency of Culture: Uses of Culture in the Global Era*. Durham, NC: Duke University Press.

Index

African Americans, 118, 165, 187n10
African culture, 81. *See also* Pan-Africanism
African neoliberalism, 3, 5
Afrocentric ideologies, 150, 171
Alexander, M. Jacqui, 72
Anderson, Patricia, 11
area leaders
  difference between dons and, 65–66
  educational levels, 61
  loyalty to, 59
  political patronage, 50–67
  use of violence, 72–73
  See also dons; informal community power structures
arms. *See* weapons
artists. *See* dancehall performers; DJs
Atlantic Records, 136–37
authenticity, 85–86, 131–32, 135, 140, 171–72, 187n7
Averill, Gage, 15

"Bad Man" (Elephant Man), 92–93
badness, 91–95, 98, 184n13
"Basic Income Grant" (South Africa), 169
"batty" men, 43, 94. *See also* homosexuality
Better Communities model, 150, 173

Bhangra (South Asian dance music), 124
"big ups," 105, 109
black history, 90, 146, 156
Black Nationalism, 7, 12, 155
blackness
  cultural assertions of, 4, 81
  modern, 13, 187n9
blacks
  elites, 81
  empowerment of, 22, 25–26, 165
  family structures, 14–15, 170
  middle class, 12, 26–27, 69, 70
  working class, 76–84, 99–101, 133, 165
Bogle, John, 79
"Boom Bye Bye" (Buju Banton), 94
Bounty Killer, 91–92, 132–33, 187n7
Bourdieu, Pierre, 10
"bowing" (oral sex), 93–94
Brand Jamaica, 113–14, 131, 141
Brazil, 173
Brigadier Jerry, 78
Buju Banton, 94, 135

Canada, 129–32
capitalism, 7, 11–12, 136, 148
  and individualism, 30–31, 150
Capleton, 90

Caribbean
  and global economy, 147–48
  influence of North America on, 118
  societal stratification, 8–9
  as zone of legal demystification, 10, 172, 182n11
Cecile, 98, 102
Chevannes, Barry, 88, 178n2, 184n11
childcare, 31, 160
children
  educational attainment, 59, 73–74, 156
  fathering of, 22, 41, 76, 88, 97, 144, 178n10
  gender roles, 100
  sexual behavior, 71–73
  at street dances, 108–9
  summer camp program, 162–64
Christianity, 26–27, 90, 94
  reputation and, 44–45
citizenship, 6, 22, 84, 143–45, 164–65, 173–74
  community, 22, 143–45, 155, 174
  global, 12–13, 15, 59, 80, 127, 143–45, 172
  national, 22, 143–45, 173–74, 187n9
Clarke, Colin, 29
class
  black middle class, 12, 26–27, 69, 70
  elites, 7, 12, 67, 70, 77, 80–82, 104, 171
  middle class, 35, 99–102, 127, 178n1, 183n2
  skin tone and, 185n16
  working class, black and urban, 76–84, 99–101, 133, 165
  See also poverty
closed exchanges, 30–31

Cold War, 25
colonialism, 5, 7–8, 10–12, 14–15, 112, 144, 182n11
  anticolonialism, 47, 150
  postcolonial nations, 4, 8, 77, 79, 81, 89, 168, 172, 174
Comaroff, Jean and John L., 5
Common Entrance Exam, 74
communism, 26. *See also* democratic socialist policy
community citizenship, 22, 143–45, 155, 174
community development programs, 2, 5–8, 13–14, 16, 22–23, 143–44, 164–65, 171
  better communities model, 150–51
  dancehall industry sponsorship, 7, 148–50, 165, 167, 171
  local power structures and, 173–75
  principles of, 155
  problems with, 162–64, 173–75
  public image of, 145, 160–61
  skills center, 145–48, 152
  See also youth organization programs
community justice system. *See* justice
"concubines," 98
conflict resolution, 158–59, 164, 171
Congress of South African Trade Unions, 169
"conscious" music, 90
Cooper, Carolyn, 77, 184n7
corners, 70, 73, 84–85
  security corner, 104–5, 107, 167, 182n15
  as social space, 34–35
corruption, 7, 50, 65–67, 83, 89
"cow horn," 93–94, 185n15

Crab Antics (Wilson), 9, 180n19
creole nationalist project, 6, 12–13, 80
creolization, 8
  musical, 112
crime
  in ghetto communities, 83, 87–89, 91–92, 143–44, 171, 173
  robbery, 68, 70–71, 146
  security and, 52, 103–4, 117–18, 182n15
  See also violence
crossover success, 132–33, 135–39, 187n10
Cuba, 26
culture style music, 77, 88, 89, 105

dancehall
  characteristics of, 76–79
  as coconstitutive with ghetto communities, 77–78, 110
  creative wordplay in, 123
  culture style, 77, 88, 89, 105
  dancing and dance steps, 79, 102–3, 106–8
  in debates over Jamaican culture, 7, 16, 76–78, 80–81, 113, 171
  genre designations, 139
  "juggling" sessions, 78, 183n5
  lyrics, 21, 76–78, 81–84, 89–97, 123–24
  modeling, 102
  normative values in, 77–78, 89–95
  public consumption of, 21, 103–10
  rhythms, building of, 124–25
  rhythm styles, 78
  roots and culture music, 77
  "rub-a-dub" sessions, 78
  as sexually explicit and violent, 89–95

  "slackness," 77, 89–90, 99–103
  "sound clashes," 78, 183n5
dancehall music industry
  distribution, 78, 112, 114, 128, 137–39
  in downtown Kingston, 115
  employees, 126–27
  family atmosphere of, 119–23
  ghetto roots of, 126
  male dominance in, 96–98, 101–2, 121–23, 164
  marketing, international, 22, 111–12, 131–32, 136–39, 171–72
  multinational record companies and, 111, 133, 138–39, 141
  origins of, 115–17
  owned and managed by performers, 115–16, 125–26
  production companies, 115–19
  professionalism, 21–22, 111–12, 126, 127–41, 172
  public relations, 127
  relationship between artistry and career-building strategies, 112, 129–40
  renting out studio time, 125
  studio politics of recording songs, 123–27
  vibes, 112, 127–41
  violence in, 187n5
  working relationships with North American and European music industry, 127–29, 133–40, 172
dancehall performers
  authenticity, 85–86, 131–32, 135, 140, 171–72, 187n7
  crossover success, 132–33, 135–39, 187n10
  exit clauses, 140

dancehall performers (*continued*)
  local and international success, 132–40
  marginality and ghetto backgrounds of, 16, 85–89
  stereotypes of, 76
  superstar status, 86–87, 116–17
  women as, 97–103
  younger, 187n4
Dancehall Queen contests, 102–3
dancing and dance steps, 79, 102–3, 106–8
Das, Veena, 10, 110
Davies, Omar, 142
debt servicing, 27, 168
"Dem Fi Goweh" (Mad Cobra), 92
democratic socialist policy, 4, 25–26, 47–48, 165, 169, 170
digital music, downloadable, 186n2
"dis/place," 16
dispute resolution. *See* conflict resolution
distribution, 78, 112, 114, 128, 137–39
  genre designations and, 139
Diwali, 125
DJs, 77–79, 91, 94, 96–99, 102, 115, 135, 146
  career paths, 85–87
  at street dances, 105–8
  studio work, 119–20, 123–25
  See also dancehall performers
dons
  criminality of, 83–84
  difference between area leaders and, 65–66
  independence facilitated by drugs and weapons trade, 60–63, 88
  murder of, 2, 67–68
  political patronage, 50–67
  use of title, 179n9
  See also area leaders; informal community power structures
downtown ghetto communities, 7
  dancehall music in, 84–95
drug trade, 51, 60–63, 88

Economic and Social Survey of Jamaica (Planning Institute of Jamaica), 88
economic exchanges. *See* giving, moral economies of
economy, Jamaican national
  dancehall and, 129, 141
  import restrictions, 13
  limited growth of, 6, 27, 168, 174–75
  modernization of, 114
  privatization of government-owned industries, 13
  regulation of, 11
  safety and stability, importance of, 59
  transition from industrial to service, 141, 147–48
education
  area leaders, level of, 61
  children, 59, 73–74, 156
  men as priority in programs, 159–60, 164
  program goals, 145
  women, rates of, 185n18
  See also remedial education classes
egalitarianism, 26, 31, 170, 187n4
elections, 51–55
  area leaders and MPs, 60
  violence, 51–53
  voter manipulation, 50
Elephant Man, 79, 92–93

elites, 7, 12, 67, 70, 77, 80–82, 104, 171
employment
  discrimination in, 87
  formal, 1, 5, 30
  and giving, 35–37
  limited access to, 27, 166, 168–70, 173–75
  in music industry, 87, 113
  through community development projects, 152
  unemployment, 5, 6, 36, 45, 88
  women, 38, 160
English language. *See* Standard English
Entertainment Advisory Board, 113
entrepreneurs, 16, 155
  loyalty and protection in community, 48–49
  See also patronage
Escobar, Arturo, 143–44
Espeut, Peter, 82–83
Europe
  economy of, 7
  value systems, 9, 15, 25, 27, 95
European Union, 113, 147
"Ever Tight" (Mad Cobra), 95–96
exit clauses, 140

family
  fathering of children, 22, 41, 76, 88, 97, 144, 178n10
  recording studios as, 119–23
  structures, 14–15, 170
Feld, Steven, 90, 186n1
Ferguson, James, 3–4, 5, 15, 169
Ferguson, Roderick, 14
Food Stamp Program, 28
foreign investment, 59, 111, 144, 171–73

Freeman, Carla, 123
Free Trade Zone, 36

"gal," as controversial term for women, 81–84
gambling, 179n8
gangster persona, 76, 92
gang wars, 62, 68. *See also* tribal war
ganja (marijuana), 76, 106, 119, 129
garrisons, 6
  defined, 178n8
  development of, 51
  votes, tampering with, 52
  See also ghetto communities
gender
  inequality, 96–97
  sexual violence and, 72
  social class and, 9
  See also masculinity; men; patriarchy; womanhood; women
gender norms, 16, 161, 169
  in dancehall, 89–95
generosity, 25, 29–33, 45. *See also* giving, moral economies of
genre designations for dancehall, 139
ghetto communities
  black working class, 76–81
  characteristics of, 25
  and dancehall music, 21, 126
  downtown, 1–3, 28–29, 178n3
  overcrowding in, 28–29, 34–36
  political populations in, 110
  social life, 34–36
Girvan, D. T. M., 150
giving, moral economies of, 20, 45, 74, 168–69, 171
  breakdown of system, 31
  on corners, 35
  everyday forms of exchange, 29–34

giving, moral economies of, (*continued*)
  gender roles and, 37–42
  "haves" and "have-nots," 1, 35–37
  as informal taxation on the poor, 169, 173
  in middle class, 178n1
  reputation and respectibility, 25–27, 29–37, 120–21
  See also patronage
global citizenship, 12–13, 15, 59, 80, 127, 143–45, 172
global economy and globalization, 7, 11, 111, 142
  competetiveness, 9, 113, 168
  See also neoliberal globalization
Golding, Bruce, 66–67
gossip, 42–44, 95, 106, 164, 179n6
  importance of, 33
  rules around appropriateness, 182n15
  shaming through, 179n6
Gray, Obika, 3
greediness, 31
GSAT examination, 156
guns. *See* weapons

"Halla Halla" (Lexxus), 96
Harriott, Anthony, 88
Harrison, Faye, 185n22
hip-hop, 106, 118, 135, 139, 165
HIV/AIDS, 185n19
homework programs, 156
homosexuality
  "batty" men, 43, 94
  derogatory terms for, 79, 180n21
  taboo on, 89, 94–95, 187n7
Hope, Donna, 15–16
Horace Plunkett Foundation, 150
housing, as tool in political patronage, 50, 68

Human Development Report (Planning Institute of Jamaica), 88
Hype, John, 79

identity
  gender normativities and, 89, 187n9
  Jamaican national, 110, 131–32, 168
  subculture, 135
illegal activities, 10, 22, 65, 68–69, 144, 172, 182n11
illegal arms. *See* weapons
illiteracy, 155–56, 160
income-generating projects, 155
individualism, capitalistic, 30–31
informal community power structures
  development initiatives, 173–75
  governance, 144–45, 164–66, 169, 171
  promotion of stability and security, 59, 67–68, 75, 144–45, 173–74
  state power structures, relationship to, 47, 50–69, 173–74
  See also justice
information and communication technologies (ICTs), 114, 147–48
Inter-American Development Bank, 27
International Monetary Fund (IMF), 13, 17

Jamaica
  funding for social safety net services, 13, 25, 27, 143, 168–70
  GDP, 113
  globalization, role of nation-state in, 10–11
  neoliberalism and, 3, 174–75

state's relationship to informal
community justice systems, 47,
50–69, 174
See also economy, Jamaican
national; music industry,
Jamaican
Jamaica (Norris), 178n5
Jamaica Labour Party (JLP), 25,
50–55, 62, 167
Jamaican Music Network, 113
Jamaica Social Investment Fund, 8,
14, 22, 146, 168
Jamaica Welfare, 150
JAMAL (literacy program), 156,
188n7
JLP. *See* Jamaica Labour Party
"juggling" sessions, 78, 183n5
Junior Kelly, 161
justice
informal community systems,
56–58, 63–69, 165–66
relationship of state and informal
community system, 47, 50–69,
174
state system, 57–58, 61–62, 65,
171, 174

Keil, Charles, 90
Kingston
class differences in, 111
dancehall as product of black
working class, 76–81
downtown, 1–6, 28–29, 178n3
Halfway Tree (boundary between
uptown and downtown), 111,
115
overcrowding in, 28–29, 34–36
uptown, 178n3
See also garrisons; ghetto
communities

Labba Labba, 79
LaBennett, Oneka, 186n28
Lady Saw, 102, 132
legal demystification, 10, 172,
182n11
Levy, Barrington, 25
Lexxus, 96
liberal multiculturalism, 4, 11–12
literacy, 155–56, 160
local power structures. *See* informal
community power structures
"Look" (Bounty Killer), 91–92
"Love So Nice" (Junior Kelly), 161
lyrics, dancehall, 21, 76–78, 81–84,
89–97, 123–24

Mad Cobra, 92, 95–96
male gaze, 108
Manley, Michael, 4, 25, 47
Manley, Norman, 150
marginalized groups
as constitutive spaces, 10, 21
dancehall performers, 16, 85–89
discourses on deserving and
undeserving poor, 172
political and electoral involvement,
26
marijuana (ganja), 76, 106, 119, 129
marketing, international, 22, 111–12,
131–32, 136–39, 171–72
masculinity, 22, 26
alternative markers of, 88–90
crisis of, 173
dancing and, 186n27
ghetto-based, 89–95
normative, 22, 44–45, 72, 88–90,
98–99, 144
provider role as norm, 88, 170,
173
reputation and respectability, 84

masculinity (*continued*)
  socialization in, 161
  violence and, 158–59
"matie war," 97–99
McMichael, Philip, 11
"meanness" (stinginess), 29–31
Melamed, Jodi, 11
member of Parliament (MP)
  activities during election periods, 53–55
  relationship to area leaders, 56, 63–64
  request for organized community voice, 149–50
  role in intercommunity conflicts, 61, 64
  role in maintaining order, 63–67
men
  dominance in dancehall music industry, 96–98, 101–2, 121–23, 164
  fathering of children, 22, 41, 76, 88, 97, 144, 178n10
  as financial providers for women, 37–42
  pathologized for being "reproductive" not "productive," 14–15, 170
  in relationships with multiple women, 97–98, 185n19
  reputation and respectability, 39
  role models for, 157
meritocracy, 126
Mico College, 168
middle class, 12, 26–27, 35, 69, 70, 99–102, 127, 178n1, 183n2
Middle East, as references to badness, 184n13
Ministry of Tourism and Sports, 113
modeling, 102

"Money Move" (Levy), 25
moral economies of giving. *See* giving, moral economies of
moral values, 27, 91–92
Mr. G, 185n19
murder
  of dons, 2, 67–68
  rates during election periods, 51
music industry, international
  business culture of, 129–30
  imperialism in, 112
  monopolization by United States and Japan, 114
  multinational record companies, 111, 133, 138–39, 141
music industry, Jamaican
  breaking into, 99–101
  business culture of, 127–40
  influence in downtown Kingston communities, 87
  international working relationships, 127–29, 133–40, 172
  linkages with development programs, 2, 6
  market value of, 113
  modernization of, 114
  and national economy, 111–15

national citizenship, 22, 143–45, 173–74, 187n9
national development, 142–43, 147–48, 168–75
  community center model, 150
  critiques of, 144
  privatization, 166
  See also community development programs
national identity, 9, 15, 77, 81–84. *See also* identity

National Industrial Policy, 112
nation building, 6–8, 13–14, 16–17,
   143–44, 156, 168, 171, 187n3.
   See under People's National Party
   (PNP)
neoliberal globalization, 9–13, 93, 168
   anti-racisms, 11–12
   definition of, 3
neoliberal governance, 3, 143, 174–75
   contradictions within Jamaican
      society, 2–5, 22–23, 174–75
   impacts of, 170, 172
   redistribution of resources, 28
neoliberal multiculturalism, 11–13,
   15, 79, 96, 143
nicknames, 42, 180n19
No Doubt, 132–33, 187n7
"No Funny Guy Thing" (Spragga
   Benz), 94
Non-Aligned Movement, 26
Norris, Katrin, 178n5
North America
   economy, 7, 39
   gender relations, 39
   influence on Caribbean culture,
      118

open-ended exchanges, 30–31
organized crime, 3, 88
   governance and, 5–6
   political patronage and, 50, 65–68
   used as extension of state power,
      174
ownership, 115–16, 125–26

Pan-Africanism, 22, 143, 171
party politics
   distribution of work to
      constituents, 53
   influence on voting patterns, 75
   infrastructure improvements by, 53
   loyalty and alienation, 53–54,
      166, 170–71, 174
   and population armament, 3
   relationship with area leaders or
      "dons," 59–63
   support of, 47–48
   and urban black working class
      constituency, 81–84
   See also Jamaica Labour Party
      (JLP); People's National Party
      (PNP); political patronage
patois, 84, 89
   in dancehall, 132–33
patriarchy, 89, 95–96, 122,
   182nn16–17
patronage, 4, 26, 45–46, 74–75
   dancehall music industry, 6–8, 14,
      69–70, 73–74
   drug and gun trade, role in, 60–63
   by entrepreneurs, 48–49
   overview of, 47–48
   private, 20–21, 169, 171
   stability provided by, 67–69
   types of power, 34
   and violence, 72
   See also political patronage
Patterson, P. J., 13–14, 110, 142, 147
   use of "gal" in speech, 81–84
People's National Party (PNP), 4,
   150, 166, 170–71
   development programs, 6, 7, 13,
      142–43
   empowerment of blacks, 22,
      25–26, 165
   leadership of, 12, 81
   nation building, 143–44, 156–57
   political patronage, 47, 50–55, 62
performers. *See* dancehall performers;
   DJs

personal responsibility, 4, 16, 162
Peterkin, Patrick, 181n1
Petras, James, 11
piracy, tolerance of, 182n11
Planning Institute of Jamaica, 141
plantation society, 8, 80, 170
pluralism, 8
PNP. *See* People's National Party
police, 58, 64–67, 70–71. *See also* justice
policing of gender norms. *See* gender norms
political loyalty and alienation, 53–54, 166, 170–71, 174
political parties. *See* party politics
political patronage, 47–48, 60, 68, 173
   dons or area leaders, 50–67
   and organized crime, 65–68
   overview of, 50–51
political violence, 50–53
Poole, Deborah, 10, 110
pop music, 132–39
popular culture, 15, 77–78, 84, 135, 183n3
postcolonialism. *See under* colonialism
poverty
   approaches to, 168–75
   dancehall and, 118–21
   economic and social stratification within, 177n4
   in Kingston, 28–29
   and lack of social services, 27–28
   redistribution of resources within, 30
   See also giving, moral economies of
power structures. *See* informal community power structures
prisons, 57

Private Sector Development Program, 113
privatization, 13, 16
production, 14–15, 93, 114–15
   modernization of, 144
   skills, 147
professionalism, 21–22, 111–12, 126, 127–41, 172
promiscuity, 76, 81–84, 98, 185n19
prostitution, 41–42, 97
public-private partnerships, 7, 13–14, 143
public spaces, dancehall performance and expression in, 80, 104. *See also* corners; street dances
"Pussy Jaw" (Vybz Kartel), 93–94

R&B music, 99, 105, 138–39, 187n10
race, 9, 11–13, 76, 80
   classifications of, 95–96, 178n7, 185n16
   cultural assertions of blackness, 4, 81
   global racial hierarchies, 12
   inequalities, 172–73
   modern blackness, 13, 187n9
rape, 57, 71–72, 122, 182n16
Rastafarianism, 90, 129
"rate" and "ratings," 34
Recording Industry of Jamaica, 113
recording studios
   politics of, 123–27
   rental of, 125
   See also dancehall music industry
"Red Plate," 185n19
reggae music, 101, 105, 129–33, 137–41, 184n6, 184n8
   as distinct from pop music, 138–39

as Jamaican cultural tradition, 113–14, 130–31, 141
remedial education classes
　incentives to attend, 160
　for men and at-risk youth, 143, 146, 155–60, 174
　for women, 17, 153, 159–60
reputation and respectability, 144–45, 169, 172
　Christianity as source of, 44–45
　in ghetto culture, 90, 115–16
　giving and generosity, 25–27, 29–42, 120, 179n7
　interpersonal violence and, 42–45
　loyalty and, 49
　maintenance of community ties for ghetto authenticity, 85–86
　protection resulting from, 70
　saving face, 158–59
　theorizations of, 8–9
research methodology, 17–20
resource redistribution. *See* giving, moral economies of
respect, 45, 70
　for dance hosts, 49
　social significance of, 33–34
　use of word, 34
　See also reputation and respectability
rhythms, building of, 124–25
rhythm styles, 78
Robotham, Don, 12, 29, 81, 178n1
rock music, 132, 135, 139
roots and culture music, 77
Rose, Nikolas, 11
"rotating credit associations," 179n8
"rub-a-dub" sessions, 78
"running a battery" (sexual assault), 72
"running a boat" (communal cooking), 35

rural areas, 29, 61, 144, 150–51
rural development model, 173
rural poverty, 184n8

safety net. *See* social safety net
Saunders, Patricia J., 93, 135
Scott, David, 15
Scott, James, 9–10
Sean Paul, 136–37
security, 35, 52, 67, 103–4, 117–18, 164, 171, 174, 182n15
security corner, 104–5, 107, 167, 182n15
selectors, 78–79, 104–5, 107–8, 115. *See also* dancehall performers; DJs
self-reliance, 4, 16, 45, 92, 155
service economies, 141, 147–48
Seventh Day Adventists, 44–45
sexuality, 71–72, 93–97
　attitudes toward oral sex, 93–94
　in dancehall lyrics, 89–95
　in dancing, 107–8
　in music industry, 101–2, 122
　promiscuity, 76, 81–84, 98, 185n19
　prostitution, 41–42, 97
　See also homosexuality
sexually transmitted infections, 185n19
sexual violence, 57, 71–72, 122, 182n16
Shaggy, 132–33
shaming, 42, 44
　through gossip, 179n6
sharing
　of blessings, 37, 70
　importance in ghetto culture, 178n2
　See also giving, moral economies of

"short up short up," 53, 181n6
Sizzla, 90
"skettel" (prostitutes), 41–42, 97
skills center, 145–48, 152
skin bleaching, 95–96
"slackness," 77, 89–90, 99–103
slavery, 8, 15, 79–80, 112, 144, 170
social capital, 26, 126
   lack of, 43
social intimacy, 35
social mobility, 26, 127, 165
social safety net, 13, 25, 27, 143, 168–70
Social Sector Strategy Report on Jamaica (Inter-American Development Bank), 27
social status, 26
   sharing of resources and, 29–34
Social Welfare Commission, 150
"sound clashes," 78, 183n5
sound systems, 74, 84–85, 103–9, 115–16
South Africa, redistributive practices in, 169, 173
Spragga Benz, 94
Standard English, 84, 134, 148
   adoption by dancehall performers, 132–33
Stanley Niaah, Sonjah, 15, 79–80, 186nn26–27
status hierarchies, 104, 109
Stephens, Tanya, 97–99, 102
Stewart, Kingsley, 183n1
Stone, Carl, 51
street dances, 80, 103–9
   children at, 108–9
   and community power structures, 104, 109
   DJs at, 105–8
   hosts, prestige of, 49, 103, 109

summer camp program, 162–64
superstar status, 86–87, 116–17

"tall up tall up," 53, 181n6
taxation on working poor, informal, 169, 172
teaching. *See* education; remedial education classes
technology as resource, 11. *See also* information and communication technologies (ICTs)
"Tek Him Back," 98–99
Thomas, Deborah, 12–13, 187n9
"throwing partners," 179n8
Tivoli Gardens, 66–67
tourism, 22, 59, 113–14, 144, 178n7
"tracing," 95
training, skills, 74
transnationalism, 10, 13
tribal war, 52, 61–62, 181n4

unemployment. *See* employment
United Nations, "felt needs" approach, 150–52
United States
   migration to, 36, 44
   music industry, 105–6, 118, 132–39
   performers, 132–33
   popular culture, 135
University of the West Indies, 22, 126–27, 145–46, 155, 160
uptown/downtown, 7
urban areas
   overcrowding in, 28–29, 34–36
   visibility of poor in, 76, 80–81
   See also ghetto communities
urban improvisers, 5–6, 115, 172
urbanization, 144
U-Roy, 78

values
  community, 108–9
  in Jamaican society, 183n1
  moral, 27, 91–92
  normative, 77–78, 89–95
Veltmeyer, Henry, 11
vibes, 112, 127–41
violence, 2–3, 20, 59
  by at-risk youth, 143, 174
  in dancehall industry, 187n5
  in dancehall lyrics, 89–95
  gang wars, 62, 68
  "matie wars," 97–99, 186n25
  political, 50–53
  relationship to reputation and respectibility, 34, 42–45
  in response to insults, 158–59
  sexual, 57, 71–72, 122, 182n16
  tribal war, 52, 61–62, 181n4
  See also crime
voting. *See* elections
VP Records, 128, 136–38
Vybz Kartel, 93–94

Wales, Josey, 78
Waterman, Christopher, 104
wealth, power of, 34
wealth redistribution. *See* giving, moral economies of
weapons
  ghetto youth and, 53, 160–61, 167, 174
  supplied to communities by government officials, 50–51, 61
  trade, 3, 50–51, 60–63, 67, 88
Weber, Max, 10
white elites, 81
Wilson, Peter J., 8–9, 26, 179nn6–7, 179n13, 180n19
Witter, Michael, 11, 113

womanhood
  in dancehall music and lyrics, 76–78, 81–84, 95–97, 186n26
  as polluting to men, 93, 95–96, 181n7
  working-class ideal of, 122–23
women
  access to, as status marker for masculinity, 82–83
  as dancehall artists and employees, 97–103, 122–23
  dependence on men, 39–41
  domesticity, 99–100
  education, rates of, 185n18
  employment, 38, 160
  financial relationships with men, 37–42
  income, 38
  as "maties" (sharing men), 97–99
  middle class, 99–102
  regulation and policing of, 16
  relationships with men, 96–99
  sexuality of, 77, 95–97, 101–3, 107–8
  as "skettel" (prostitutes), 41–42, 97
  working class, 99–101
World Bank, 17, 113
world music, 139, 186n1

Yellow Man, 78
youth organization programs, 146–64
  dancehall industry sponsorship, 148–50, 154–57
  executive board members, 162–64
  fees for participation, 153–54
  felt needs, 151–52
  leadership of, 162–64
  as means of political representation, 148–49

youth organization programs (*cont.*)
   men's involvement in, 154
   misuse of funds, 163–64, 168
   origins of, 148–49
   participation, barriers to, 152
   women's involvement in, 153–54
   See also community development programs

www.ingramcontent.com/pod-product-compliance
Lightning Source LLC
Chambersburg PA
CBHW070801230426
43665CB00017B/2449